TruTH

TruTH

24 FRAMES PER SECOND

Edited by Gavin Delahunty with Kelly Filreis

Essays by Anna Katherine Brodbeck and Gavin Delahunty

Dallas Museum of Art
Distributed by
Yale University Press, New Haven and London

CONTENTS

DIRECTOR'S FOREWORD

Truth: 24 frames per second is the first major group exhibition and catalogue at the Dallas Museum of Art devoted to time-based media. Using strategies of documentary, montage, and appropriation, the artists featured in the exhibition address topics most pressing in our current era, including racial identity, sexuality, violence, protest, globalism, and ethics. They, in turn, grapple with the slippery definition of "truth"—whether that means using film and video to engage with social and political issues, or exploring the seeming objectivity of documentary film itself. Each work in *Truth: 24 frames per second* confronts and transforms the reality from which it developed, a task that is both rigorous and rich with possibilities.

The roster of works in this exhibition demonstrates the rich holdings in film and video that the DMA has amassed over two decades; nine of the twenty-four works exhibited are from the Museum's permanent collection. The DMA began collecting film and video in 1998 and has continued to build a collection of groundbreaking and thought-provoking works, a reflection of the growing prominence of moving images in contemporary art practice.

The exhibition and catalogue were conceived by Gavin Delahunty, the Hoffman Family Senior Curator of Contemporary Art; Anna Katherine Brodbeck, the Nancy and Tim Hanley Assistant Curator of Contemporary Art; Kelly Filreis, Temporary Projects Coordinator for Contemporary Art and formerly the McDermott Graduate Intern for Contemporary Art; and Chelsea Pierce, Curatorial Administrative Assistant for Contemporary Art, who collaboratively developed the checklist and selected the artist interviews and other short texts accompanying each section of the catalogue. Eric Zeidler, Publications Manager, shepherded the catalogue through all stages of production.

We are much indebted to the artists, curators, and scholars whose texts are featured in the publication: Dara Birnbaum and Hans Ulrich Obrist; Mark Bradford and Anita Hill; Anna Katherine Brodbeck; Phil Collins and Suzanne Weaver; Bruce Conner and the 1968 Flaherty Seminar; Gavin Delahunty; Ben Eastham; Omer Fast; Jean Fisher; Morgan Fisher; Coco Fusco, Guillermo Gómez-Peña, and Anna Johnson; Tatiana Gaviola and Kelly Filreis; Catherine Gund and Sarah Schulman; Arthur Jafa and Antwaun Sargent; Caoimhín Mac Giolla Léith; Zoe Leonard and Sarah Schulman; Steve McQueen and Adrian Searle; Patricia Mellencamp; Shirin Neshat and Gerald Matt; Pratibha Parmar; Ben Rivers; Rachel Rose and Aily Nash; Anri Sala, Massimiliano Gioni, and Michele Robecchi; Chick Strand; Jean-Marie Straub and Danièle Huillet with Sally Shafto; Ulrike Groos; and Charles Wylie.

We also wish to acknowledge with gratitude the ACT UP Oral History Project; *BOMB* magazine; the Estate of Jean Fisher; the Film Society of Lincoln Center; *Flash Art*; *Frieze* magazine; the Hammer Museum; Hauser & Wirth Collection; Hollybush Gardens; *Interview* magazine; the *Journal of Film and Video*; Kunsthalle Wien; the Laurenz Foundation, Schaulager; Serpentine Galleries; Tate Publishing; and the University of Illinois Press.

We thank Miko McGinty, Rebecca Sylvers, and Claire Bidwell of Miko McGinty Inc. for the book's provocatively modern design and feel, Catherine Comeau for her meticulous editing, and Patricia Fidler and Roland Coffey at Yale University Press, our distributor.

An exhibition of this scale and complexity required the expertise of a great number of people. At the DMA, we thank Tamara Wootton Forsyth, Associate Director of Collections, Exhibitions, and Facilities Management; Joni Wilson-Bigornia, Exhibitions Manager; and Rachel

Spradley, Exhibitions Assistant, for their important contributions to this undertaking throughout the planning and installation stages. Jessica Harden, Director of Exhibition and Museum Design, and Skye Malish Olson, Exhibition Designer, were responsible for the appealing design of the exhibition space. We further acknowledge Fran Baas, Associate Conservator, Conservation; Jill Bernstein, Director of Communications and Public Affairs; Kim Bryan, Associate Director of Development; Cynthia Calabrese, Director of Development; Giselle Castro-Brightenburg, Imaging Manager; Katie Cooper, Assistant Registrar for the Permanent Collection; Kimberly Daniell, Senior Manager of Communications, Public Affairs, and Social Media Strategy; Aubrey DeZego, Director of Institutional Giving; Carol Griffin, Registrar for Acquisitions and Deaccessions; Ingrid van Haastrecht, Director of Membership Operations and Analysis; Mike Hill, Senior Preparator, Special Exhibitions; John Lendvay, Head Preparator; Melissa Hartley Omholt, Associate Registrar for Exhibitions; Emily Schiller, Digital Collections Content Coordinator, Education; Isabel Stauffer, Director of Collections Management; and Elena Torok, Assistant Conservator of Objects. We thank Amanda Blake, Head of Family, Access, and School Experiences; and Stacey Lizotte, Head of Adult Programming and Multimedia Services, for organizing the engaging public programming related to the exhibition. For her guidance, we are indebted to Amber Bemak, Assistant Professor of Film and Media Arts at Southern Methodist University. Lance Lander, Manager of Gallery Technology and Innovation, deserves a special acknowledgment for his expertise in the installation and running of these films and videos, for his many valuable suggestions, and for his assiduous and indispensable assistance throughout the project.

We are deeply grateful to the lenders of the works that round out the exhibition checklist: Alexander Gray Associates; the Art Institute of Chicago; Aubin Pictures; Bortolami, New York; Canyon Cinema; the Conner Family Trust; Pilar Corrias; Gavin Brown's enterprise; Tatiana Gaviola; Hauser & Wirth; Hollybush Gardens; Kali Films; Kate MacGarry Gallery; Kohn Gallery; Marian Goodman Gallery; Miguel Abreu Gallery; The Rachofsky Collection; Simon Preston Gallery; Thomas Dane Gallery; and Video Data Bank. We also thank the following galleries for their assistance: Galerie Chantal Crousel; Gladstone

Gallery; James Cohan Gallery; Kerlin Gallery; Sprüth Magers; and Tanya Bonakdar Gallery.

We are indebted to Marguerite Hoffman, Marian Goodman, and TWO x TWO for AIDS and Art Fund. Their belief in the curatorial vision has enabled a complete project to be realized. Marguerite Hoffman is a leader and influencer whose unbending altruism toward the DMA is exemplary. Four of the works in the exhibition carry her name, either in contributed support or as outright gifts. We are enormously grateful to her and to Thomas Lentz for their steadfast support. Marian Goodman's foresight with regard to the pivotal role of the moving image within contemporary art was transformative for her eponymous gallery and for the artists with whom she has tirelessly advocated, a number of them presented here for the first time. TWO x TWO for AIDS and Art is an annual fundraising event that jointly benefits amfAR, The Foundation for AIDS Research, and the Dallas Museum of Art. The fund ensures we are able to deliver meaningful and ambitious contemporary programming at the DMA. We offer special thanks to Christine Sisk and Culture Ireland for their support of the Irish artists in the exhibition and thereby for promoting the very best of Irish arts worldwide. We also acknowledge our partner American Airlines for their assistance with artists' travel.

Finally, we would like to extend our appreciation to the artists for their uncompromising exploration of reality and truth through film and video. It is our hope that this catalogue and the accompanying exhibition will bring renewed attention and scholarly inquiry to the issues raised in these twenty-four works of time-based media.

Agustín Arteaga
The Eugene McDermott Director

REaLITY WITHIN A FRAME

by Gavin Delahunty

> To know and not to know, to be conscious of complete truthfulness while telling carefully constructed lies, to hold simultaneously two opinions which cancelled out, knowing them to be contradictory and believing in both of them, to use logic against logic, to repudiate morality while laying claim to it. . . .[1]
>
> —George Orwell, *1984*

In 2016 the Oxford Dictionaries' Word of the Year was *post-truth*, an adjective defined as "relating to or denoting circumstances in which objective facts are less influential in shaping public opinion than appeals to emotion and personal belief."[2] Although the term has been in use since the early 1990s, events on both sides of the Atlantic saw a spike in its frequency in 2016—making it so familiar that it could be used without further clarification in news headlines and political commentary. The era of post-truth politics poses particular questions for the medium of film, which, since its inception in the late nineteenth century, has been claimed to surpass all other forms of representation in duplicating reality.[3] French film director Jean-Luc Godard's well-known statement "cinema shows truth at the rate of 24 frames per second"[4] posits that the moving image is particularly well placed to ethically and creatively capture "reality" on screen. Godard is not suggesting that filmic representations are unequivocally true, but that they can frame what remains of reality and as such effectively participate in a meaningful construction of it. But what is the role of moving image art now, in the age of scripted reality television, fake documentaries, and actual events that seem like hoaxes? Inspired by the Dallas Museum of Art's important collection of artists' films, *Truth: 24 frames per second* presents work by twenty-four artists from the 1960s to the present day. In the age of "alternative facts," these artists can draw our attention to marginalized or excluded societal positions and challenge the powers that may be keeping them hidden or silenced. The exhibition asks how one might most effectively and ethically triangulate reality, meaning, and form—and, of course, what the vexed position of art might be in relation to them.[5] The show is designed around three filmic techniques—appropriation, documentary, and montage—that have been selected to confront the viewer with actual pieces of reality within a particular frame. These approaches have been chosen to create rich combinations, not as the neutral picturing of reality, but as a way of coming to terms with it.

The authenticity and truthfulness of lens-based media have long been open to contestation and debate. In 1878 Eadweard Muybridge successfully captured the stride of a galloping horse. The results were widely publicized, and he spent the ensuing years improving his technique, photographing men and women performing everyday chores. Muybridge's intention was to faithfully capture human locomotion. However, critics were quick to point out that his images—though real—were somehow untrustworthy. The photographs documented something the human eye was unable to see. The question then arose, which is truer, the image depicting things as they are, or the way we believe them to happen? The artists selected for this exhibition put this hypothesis to work. Their understanding, and use of, our innate distrust of imagery awakens a certain questioning in us of what is real and what is unreal, what is true and what is false.[6]

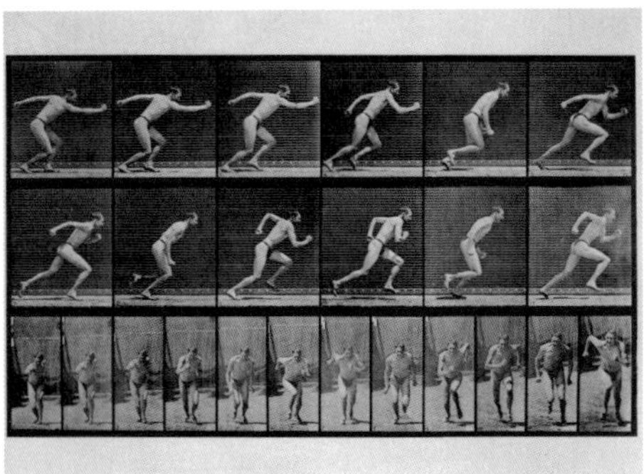

Eadweard Muybridge, *Animal Locomotion*, c. 1887. Courtesy of the Library of Congress

The exhibition begins almost a century after Muybridge, with Bruce Conner's REPORT (1963–1967). Shocked by the assassination of John F. Kennedy in Dallas and the media coverage of the event, Conner appropriated segments of news narration and repetition of stock footage in order to forensically dissect the shooting. Conner's

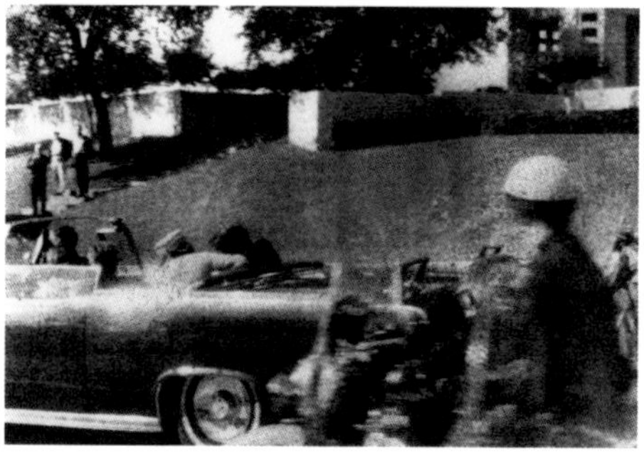

President John F. Kennedy slumps into the arms of his wife, Jacqueline, immediately after he was shot as his motorcade made its way through Dealey Plaza in Dallas, November 22, 1963. Courtesy of UPI/Newscom

collaged imagery and famed editing expertly mourns Kennedy's loss by replicating, through the medium of film, the emotional experience of the event as it recurs in memory. Using this technique, Conner transformed the footage into a dynamic element that comments upon the uncertainty and panic that surrounded the events that day and the mainstream media's chaotic handling and reporting of them. In the hands of the artist, the same repertoire of imagery that was beamed into millions of homes worldwide is transformed and extended into a potent message that raises questions about the event, the accuracy of the reporting, and the reality it projected. The Kennedy assassination spurred a plethora of conspiracy theories in the years that followed, including accusations of the involvement of the CIA, the Mafia, Lyndon B. Johnson, Fidel Castro, or the KGB. A poll taken in the early 2000s indicated that the majority of Americans still believe in some form of conspiracy surrounding this seismic event.[7] At a moment when conspiracy theorists are receiving unprecedented attention in the mainstream media, Conner's REPORT is striking in its contemporary relevance.

Roughly contemporaneous with Conner's REPORT is Morgan Fisher's *Documentary Footage* (1968), which presents a young nude woman sitting on a chair recording herself asking a series of scripted questions: "What is your hair like?" "What color are your eyes?" "What is your skin like?" The list of questions focuses purely on the physical appearance of the actor (skin color, body shape, etc.). The recording is then played back and the questions answered by the same actor in a nuanced and captivatingly natural way, as if they were being heard for the first time. It is a master class in hypophora, a technique in which the speaker poses a question and then answers in a manner that makes the statement authentically his or her own. This device is sometimes used in public speaking to ensure that questions are always answered correctly and with believable authority. In *Documentary Footage* Fisher interrogates the nature of truth and the claim of documentary film to represent it.

During the 1980s the media response to the AIDS pandemic on both sides of the Atlantic was as chaotic as the response to the assassination of JFK. Many commentators characterized this response as a kind of "moral panic," in which "rumor . . . substitutes for news when institutional channels fail."[8] Throughout the 1980s rumors and misinformation regarding HIV and AIDS spread unabated, shamelessly perpetuated by the mainstream media. This "moral panic" played out, in the words of sociologist Jeffrey Weeks, in "a spiraling escalation of the perceived threat, leading to a taking up of absolutist positions and the manning of moral barricades; the emergence of an imaginary solution—in tougher laws, moral isolation, a symbolic court action; followed by the subsidence of the anxiety, with its victims left to endure the new proscription, social climate and legal penalties."[9] Catherine Gund and Zoe Leonard's *Keep Your Laws off My Body* (1990) encapsulates and responds to this bleak climate, juxtaposing intimate images of a lesbian couple with protests against the inadequacy of New York's AIDS policy in 1989 and texts that outline legislative values that discriminated against members of the lesbian, gay, bisexual, and transgender (LGBT) communities at that time.

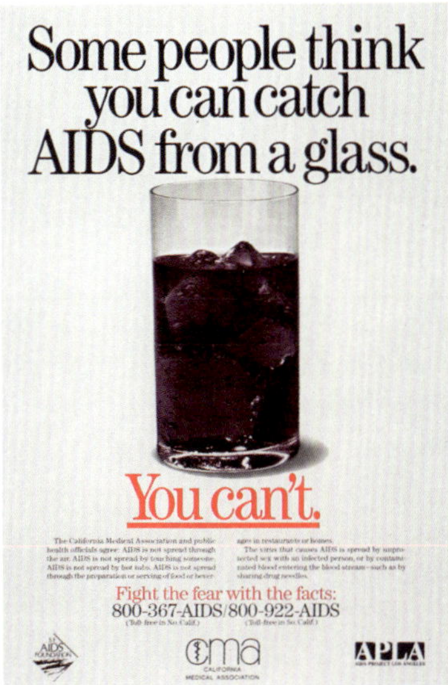

"Fight the Fear with Facts" poster, c. 1985. Courtesy of the California Medical Association and the San Francisco AIDS Foundation

Another film made in 1990, Dara Birnbaum's *Tiananmen Square: Break-In Transmission*, concentrates on the television broadcasting of the 1989 student and worker uprising in China, culminating in the killing of several hundred protesters and the arrest of thousands more. Birnbaum presents documentation of the revolt and its broadcast on an open network of LCD screens. With viewers free to move, unrestricted, between the monitors in order to piece together snippets of information, the work reveals the fragmentary way in which the events were disseminated at the time and the potential for the control,

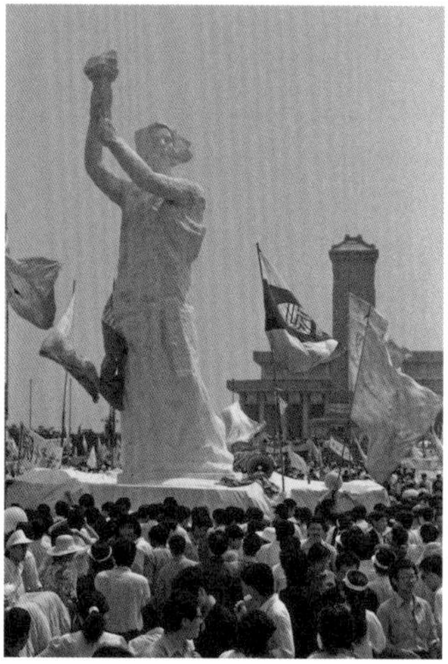

Tiananmen Square student protests, 1989. IUPUI University Library; photo by Edgar Huang

editing, and censorship of these images. One of the video channels concentrates on the moment the Chinese government cut off the satellite transmissions of foreign broadcasters, including CBS and CNN. Another channel concentrates on the methods used by the protesters to disseminate information following this break in transmission, including images sent by fax machine. A hidden surveillance switcher reassembles the images on a large-screen monitor, highlighting the cuts and edits made to news footage. Birnbaum asks, "When your eyes are focused on what is being presented by a television network, on the news item they've selected and edited for viewing, what are you missing or *not* seeing?"[10]

Rosemarie Trockel's 1996 video *Zum Beispiel Balthasar, 6 Jahre* (For example, Balthasar, age 6) (1996) was the first work to enter the DMA's collection when the museum began collecting "new media" in 1998. Trockel's video opens with a boy and girl walking in the countryside carrying a suitcase and a backpack. This sequence is contrasted with imagery of them at play. The abrupt editing of the film suggests that their young, carefree life is somehow under threat. What they are fleeing remains unclear: war, ethnic and religious conflict, corruption and crime, or the devastating consequences of climate change. Clues in the film, however, make clear that we are witnessing their flight to safety. Balthasar's laughter contrasts with the image of exodus along a country road. Willie Doherty's *Ghost Story* (2007) shares this central image of a pathway whose travelers are haunted by images from the past. Filmed in Derry, Northern Ireland, the video intersperses footage of the city with close-ups of eyes, creating a sense of paranoia and anxiety. The voice-over recounts memories of murder and violence that permeate the landscape like specters, causing the narrator to see "shadowlike figures" lurking in the trees. *Ghost Story* expertly surveys the complexities of place, identity, and memory, the fraught relations between experience and representation, between reality and illusion.[11]

James Coleman's video installation *Untitled* (2011–2015) is distinct from many other works in the exhibition in that it does not respond to a particular historical event. Yet in its depiction of a fairground carousel, the film references a carousel of another kind, the slide projector that has remained central to Coleman's practice despite—or perhaps because of—its technological obsolescence. Rosalind Krauss has described slide projection in terms of a "paradoxical collision between stillness and movement that the static slide provokes right at the interstice of its changes."[12] Situated between still photography and the moving image, the slide show involves projecting light through analogue images that are themselves the product of light imprinted on a photosensitive surface. The work therefore engages with analogue photography's claim to truth—its status as an indexical trace that declares "that has been."[13] Digital photography no longer stands in this indexical relationship with the world, calling this truth claim into question. By producing *Untitled* as a digital video, Coleman pivots between the analogue and the digital, still and moving images, photography's claims to veracity and its potential for manipulation.

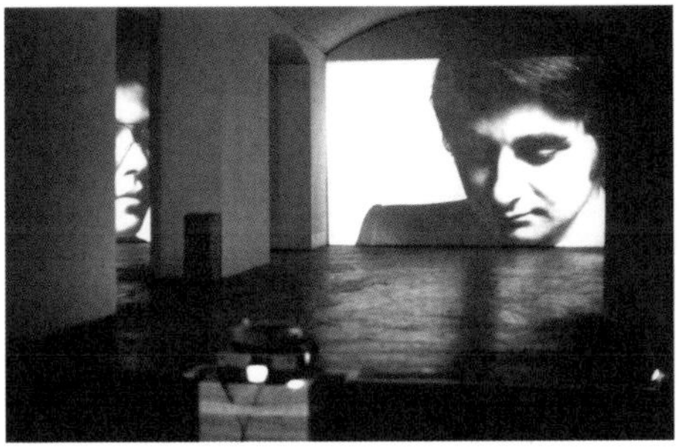

James Coleman, *Clara and Dario,* 1975. Projected images with synchronized audio narration. Installation at Studio Marconi, Milan, 1975. Courtesy of the artist and Marian Goodman Gallery

Whereas Coleman has mined the potential of near-obsolescent technologies like the slide projector, John Gerrard makes use of the most sophisticated gaming technology to demonstrate the impact our new digital existence is having on our construction of meaning. *Western Flag (Spindletop, Texas)* (2017) has an integrity of its own in that it is a live simulation of a flag of black smoke flying in a virtual replica of Spindletop, Texas, the birthplace of the modern oil industry. Once the site of the most productive oil field in the world, Spindletop is now a desolate and depopulated landscape. Gerrard's simulation of this vast, desertificated area unfolds in real time, so that the site in Spindletop corresponds with the actual time of day set as Central Standard Time. Used to lend a sense of veracity to film or computer graphics, real time is utilized by Gerrard to construct a world so convincing that we believe

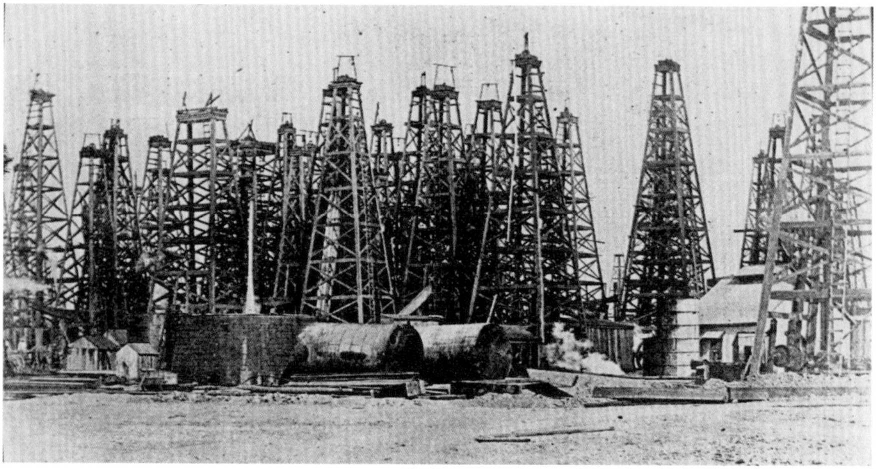

Spindletop oil field, 1903. Courtesy of the Texas Energy Museum, Beaumont, Texas

his flag of smoke is really flying, right now, in Spindletop. *Western Flag* extends beyond our understanding of the indexical relationship between photograph and photographed and styles of documentary filmmaking such as direct cinema to probe their historic contradictions as ever having had a reliable integrity. It is a perceptually realistic image and even though, on one level, we understand it to be illusory, Gerrard, who used a drone to complete a comprehensive survey of the real site, taking ten to fifteen thousand pictures over a ten-thousand-square-meter area, provides us with enough information to convince us of its reality. He sets up a correspondence between our basic understandings of virtual simulation (how was this made?) and its connection to reality (how can this be?). Perhaps Gerrard's invented form that references carbon dioxide emissions and fossil fuels depletion as a natural resource drives home more effectively the debates surrounding the reality of climate change better than the experts, charities, the media, and government's confusing and often contradictory messaging.

Also included in *Truth: 24 frames per second* is Arthur Jafa's *Love Is the Message, The Message Is Death* (2016), a film that is vastly ambitious in its scope and method of historiographical montage. It is a multilayered and deeply personal tracing of black American identity and its representation in the mass media, all sonically triggered by Kanye West's gospel hip-hop track "Ultralight Beam." Sources include Hollywood films, news and sports coverage, home movies, police dash-cam footage, and videos downloaded from YouTube. In its use of appropriation and montage, *Love Is the Message* echoes Conner's REPORT and his earlier film A MOVIE (1958), in which he collaged together found footage taken from newsreels, short films, B movies, and stag films. However, Jafa's film departs from Conner's work in several significant ways. Moments occur whereby fragments are linked and molded together by black expressivity. A dynamic interrelation of human form between each frame operates on a level that connects gesture, movement, and the contour of the body. In a 2017 recording Jafa explains: "One of my concepts is black visual intonation . . . a technical means by which to make frames behave like black vocal intonation. It's essentially a series of micro slow motions so footage is manipulated to place emphasis on certain things in the movement."[14] One reading of this is perhaps Jafa making reference to Giorgio Agamben's somewhat cryptic dictum that "the element of cinema is gesture and not image."[15] He is certainly commenting on what distinguishes the African American gesture, suggesting that it is not simply performative but made up of intense self-reflexive conversions of oppression into beauty. "An expressive modality [African Americans] carry around in [their] nervous system . . . they beat us and we turn that shit into art."[16] It is a technique used by Jafa to allow viewers to see and feel the reality of each scene while commenting on the lack of integration or rationalization of the black body in society. This attention to the black body challenges mainstream media claims to represent it and, perhaps worse, their success in denying it. The force and challenge of Jafa's work is its confrontation of conventional media and its attempt to free imagery from totalizing cultural relativism. *Love Is the Message* is a crucible of emotion, a powerful manifesto on human relations that raises the questions: Whose history is being recorded? Whose history is being saved?

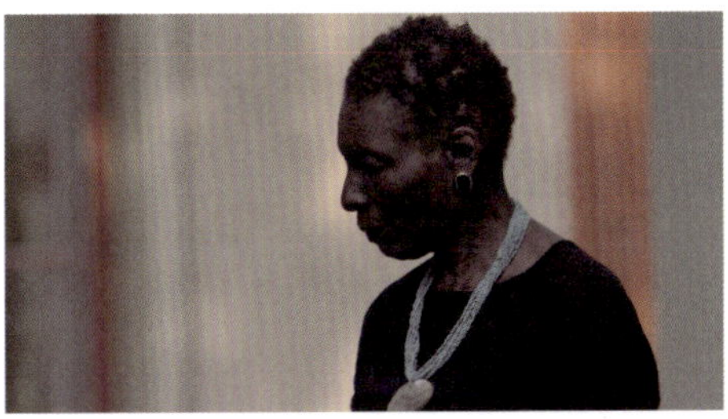

Film still (Hortense Spillers), *Love Is the Message, The Message Is Death*, 2016. Spillers, a critic and scholar, was first featured in Arthur Jafa's 2013 documentary *Dreams Are Colder than Death*, a film that examines the epistemological roots of being black in America. Courtesy of the artist and Gavin Brown's enterprise, New York/Rome

Jafa's film and several others in *Truth: 24 frames per second* draw our attention to something that is, or has been, endured by an individual or a group. The exhibition, in other words, has an ethical dimension. While this aspect is certainly present, there is no predetermined message or goal. These are subjects for exploration and interpretation in a heightened audiovisual setting. The exhibition should create awareness but only in the way that an unexpected transformative experience can interrupt a daily routine. In the same way, if we understand the exhibition as a form of communication, it does not simply comment on actualities in our society such as widespread discrimination, bias, or deliberate misinformation, but rather it presents a complex view of the real, with no single dominant view, a reality formed by a vibrant and brilliant multitude of perspectives.

Notes

This essay is dedicated to the memory of Jean Fisher (October 17, 1942–December 12, 2016) and her early championing of several artists in this exhibition.

1 George Orwell, *1984*. (New York: Signet Classics/New American Library, 1961), 35.

2 "Oxford Dictionaries Word of the Year 2016 Is . . . ," https://en.oxforddictionaries.com/word-of-the-year/word-of-the-year-2016.

3 This claim was formulated most famously by French film theorist André Bazin in a series of essays written between 1944 and 1958, anthologized in Bazin, *What Is Cinema?* vols. I and II (Oakland: University of California Press, 1967).

4 Jean-Luc Godard, *Le petit soldat* (The little soldier), directed by Godard (1963; Paris: Les Productions Georges de Beauregard).

5 This point is made in the excellent volume dedicated to documentary *Documentary Across Disciplines*, Erika Balsom and Hila Peleg, ed. (Cambridge, MA: MIT Press, 2016).

6 In his essay "Notes on Gesture," in *Means Without End* (Minneapolis: University of Minnesota Press, 2000), Agamben extends seminal tropes in film philosophy such as Muybridge's motion studies and draws comparison between their initial reception and their distrust as imagery.

7 Art Swift, "Majority in US Still Believe JFK Killed in a Conspiracy," posted by Gallup, November 15, 2013, http://www.gallup.com/poll/165893/majority-believe-jfk-killed-conspiracy.aspx.

8 Stanley Cohen, *Folk Devils and Moral Panics: The Creation of the Mods and Rockers* (New York; London: Routledge, 2011), 175.

9 Jeffrey Weeks, *Sexuality and Its Discontents: Meanings, Myths, and Modern Sexualities*, 1985, quoted in Simon Watney, *Policing Desire: Pornography, AIDS, and the Media* (Minneapolis: University of Minnesota Press, 2000), 40.

10 Barbara Schröder and Karen Kelley, "Art: Interview: Dara Birnbaum," *BOMB* magazine, 104, Summer 2008.

11 For a detailed exploration of *Ghost Story* see Declan Long's superb "Invisible Matter: On Willie Doherty's *Ghost Story* (2007)" posted in *Declan Long: essays and reviews*, May 23, 2017, https://declanlongtexts.wordpress.com/2013/05/23/invisible-matter-on-willie-dohertys-ghost-story-2007/.

12 Rosalind E. Krauss, "Reinventing the Medium," *Critical Inquiry* 25, no. 2, "Angelus Novus": Perspectives on Walter Benjamin (Winter 1999), 297.

13 Roland Barthes, *Camera Lucida: Reflections on Photography*, trans. Richard Howard (New York: Farrar, Straus, and Giroux, 1981).

14 *Arthur Jafa and Greg Tate in Conversation: Love Is the Message, The Message Is Death,* https://vimeo.com/209649169.

15 Giorgio Agamben, "Notes on Gesture," *Means Without End: Notes on Politics,* trans. Vincenzo Binetti and Cesare Casarino (Minneapolis: University of Minnesota Press, 2000), 54–55.

16 *Arthur Jafa and Greg Tate in Conversation: Love Is the Message, The Message Is Death.*

THE WORLD WON'T LISTEN

The Ambiguity of Language and Tone in Time-Based Media

by Anna Katherine Brodbeck

In the opening scene of *Intervista* (1999), Anri Sala discovers a 16 mm film containing an interview his mother, Valdet Sala, gave on Albanian state television during the 1970s as a leader of the Communist Youth party. The film is silent, and as Valdet has no memory of giving the interview, Anri hires lip readers from a school for the deaf to "transcribe" the mute film. In the scenes that follow, Anri reinterviews his mother, who is incredulous when confronted with the forgotten words of her youth: "I don't believe this. It's absurd . . . it's just spouting words." *Intervista* presents a collision of two realities that are now incompatible, Enver Hoxha's dictatorship and present-day Albania, and the possibility that the new political regime has eviscerated what came before. In his essay on the film, Søren Grammel asks, "Is it possible to say that the breakdown of the political systems of the so-called Eastern bloc also indicates a breakdown of language?"[1]

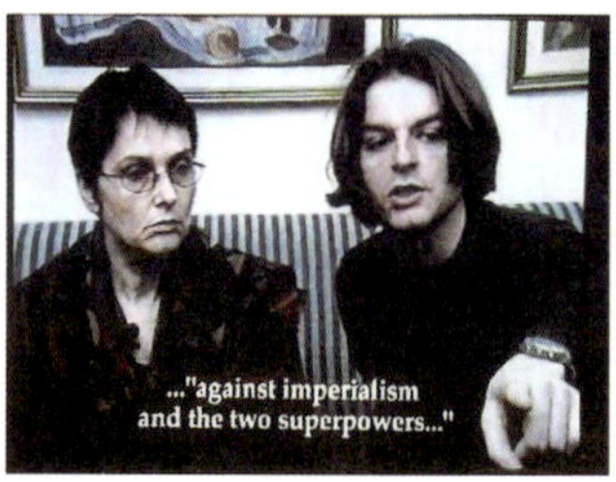

Anri Sala, *Intervista*, 1998. Video, color, sound. © 2017 Artists Rights Society (ARS), New York/VG Bild-Kunst, Bonn

Morgan Fisher's *Documentary Footage* (1968), a historic touchstone for the development of time-based media art, also critically examines the interview format. In this film a nude, seated woman records herself on tape, asking a series of questions aimed at assessing one's defining physical characteristics. She then stands up, plays back her questions, and, assuming a distinct voice, answers them. The dual roles played by the actor, who controls both the queries and the responses, calls the veracity of the interview as an objective document into question.

The ambiguity of language has important implications for time-based media, which often employ linguistic or narrative devices. Like

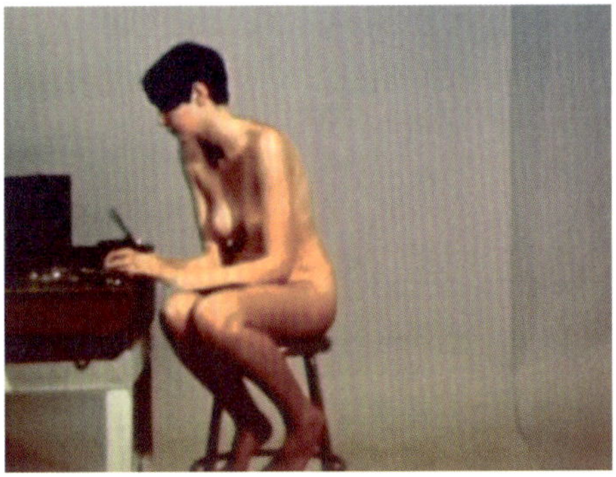

Morgan Fisher, *Documentary Footage*, 1968. 16 mm film, color, sound. © Morgan Fisher. Courtesy of the artist and Bortolami, New York

Intervista, many works in *Truth: 24 frames per second* utilize found footage in order to flirt with the documentary while in fact complicating the neutrality we associate with the genre. As Michael Zyrd observes of documentary films in his interpretation of Craig Baldwin's cult favorite *Tribulation 99: Alien Anomalies Under America* (1991): "The evidential, indexical quality of the photographic image does not signify as evidence until it has been rhetorically framed as such. . . . Rarely does an image speak for itself."[2] But in some instances, language doesn't "speak for itself" either. In the works explored in this short essay, language, like imagery, is framed. It is de- or re-contextualized so that its meaning becomes unstable. The resulting instability of the relationship of language to imagery upends the viewers' faith in narration with jarring effect.

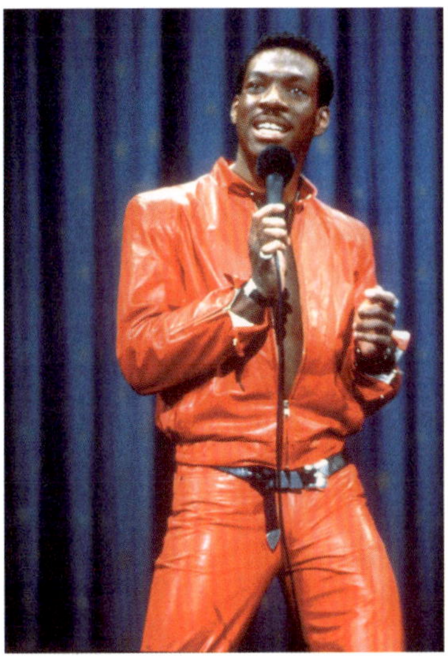

Still from Eddie Murphy, *Delirious*, 1983. Photofest, Inc.

At one extreme, in *Spiderman* (2015) Mark Bradford divorces voice from image altogether. A soundtrack of the artist delivering a stand-up comedy routine is heard, but all viewers see is a closed-caption transcription on a black screen. Of the inspiration for the work, Bradford stated: "I sometimes find some stand-up comedians harsh toward women and Otherness. . . . I remember seeing the Eddie Murphy [stand-up performance] *Delirious* . . . I remember sitting in the audience and thinking: Oh. Gay-bashing has entered into the public domain as being acceptable. . . . Those things do fascinate me because there's no protection for those bodies once they're accepted in the public as being okay for abuse."[3] What is clearly lacking in

Bradford's video is a contextualizing body. While jokes are often brushed off, when homophobia cannot hide behind gesture or be justified in the context of the cultural conventions of stand-up, the written record is all the more damning.

The body is also conspicuously absent from Willie Doherty's *Ghost Story* (2007). A narrator speaks of witnessing a horrific massacre, presumably a part of Northern Ireland's Troubles, and the subsequent haunting of the landscape, evocatively describing the liquid that now oozes from the ground. But the scene that unfolds on the screen is abstracted. The camera travels down a road flanked by trees, the street of a residential village, and a parking lot, but the landscape is devoid of the destruction described in detail by the omniscient voice—the story itself becomes the ghost, lacking any visual manifestation in the landscape.

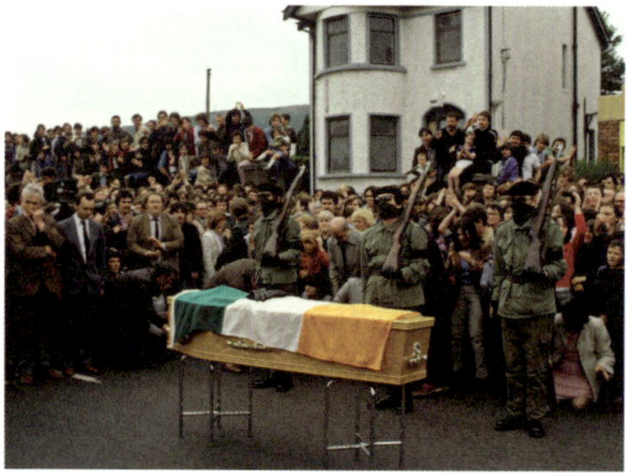

Irish Republican Army funeral, Belfast, Northern Ireland, United Kingdom, 1981. IRA soldiers act as honor guard and fire their rifles over the coffin. © Homer Sykes/Getty Images

Likewise, in Omer Fast's *5,000 Feet Is the Best* (2011), words and images are subtly at odds. This looped video interlaces an interview between Fast and a former Predator drone pilot discussing his experiences on the job with a fictional interview between two actors in which these experiences are only alluded to via meandering fables. One such fable involves a man obsessed with trains who poses as a conductor for a day without incident, only to be arrested upon trying to break into his own apartment—he lost his keys in the day's escapades. Another sets the stage for what appears to be a typical American saga: a nuclear family, tucked safely into a hatchback, takes off on the open road, belongings in tow. They are stopped at a checkpoint run by foreign entities, only to be struck and killed by a missile.

However, the narration and the video's imagery often don't match up. In this way Fast both visualizes inner thoughts not expressed through speech and even suggests the inability of speech to conjure up the correct imagery. In the first instance, the train-obsessed man is imaged erroneously as African American, the race assumed by the

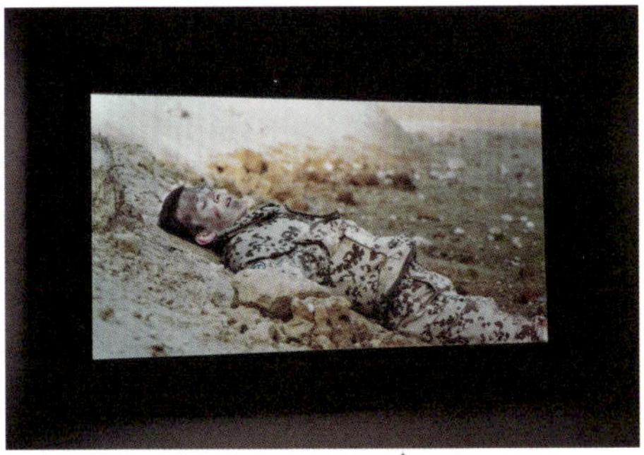

Omer Fast, *5,000 Feet Is the Best*, 2011. High-definition video, color, sound. © Omer Fast

interviewer; when he is corrected, a white actor substitutes for him in the vignette. In the second case, the slain family, blood dripping down their faces, emerges from the car and continues walking down the road as if they were zombies, a grisly possibility that is not alluded to in the interview.

When the fictional drone pilot tells the story of the train-obsessed man, the interviewer asks if the man was in his unit in the armed forces, to which he replies curtly: "No. It's a metaphor." The search for the literal truth is often the enemy of imagination, which is a precondition for empathy. This is illustrated by Fast's treatment of the drone footage that accompanies the narration of the real-life pilot. The footage is not from Pakistan, which he surveyed for the military, but from a bucolic New England village as well as from Nevada, where he now lives and works as a casino security guard—settings that allow viewers who have not been living under these terrifying conditions to consider the victims of drone warfare as their friends and neighbors. Only through imagining ourselves as others are we able to empathize.

The jarring appearance of a familiar character in an unexpected setting also characterizes *Media Burn* (1975), a televised publicity stunt undertaken by the collective Ant Farm. Taped on July 4, 1975, a John F. Kennedy impersonator reflects on a decade the president did not live to see, openly criticizing the current realities of "militarism, monopoly, and the mass media." Not only does he condemn the nation's addiction to television, whose network control reinforces autocratic political systems, but also the very war in Vietnam that the president escalated through increased military spending. The event concludes when the artists crash a Phantom Dream Car outfitted with a closed-circuit camera into a stack of television sets, a fantastical but futile attack on the endless flow of mass media, which, like the war in Vietnam, could not be controlled once unleashed.

At the beginning of this essay, I alluded to Craig Baldwin's *Tribulation 99*, which borrows from the language of conspiracy theories and B movies to tell the true story of US intervention in Latin America.

In Michael Zyrd's analysis, he coined the term *ironic decontextualization* to describe Baldwin's juxtaposition of voice, text, and image to signal ironic intent. Coco Fusco and Paula Heredia's *Couple in the Cage: A Guatinaui Odyssey* (1993) attempts such an ironic decontextualization. The video shows Fusco and Guillermo Gómez-Peña performing as a pair indigenous to the fictitious, recently "discovered" island of Guatinaui in the Gulf of Mexico, caged and on public display in plazas and natural history museums across three continents. Fusco dances in a grass skirt and leopard-print bikini, while Gómez-Peña wears a Mexican wrestling mask and rattles off nonsensical phrases mixed with Nahuatl. Docents provide visitors with incorrect information, and to the surprise of the performers, the seemingly ridiculous situation is taken by many as fact. The resulting video juxtaposes footage from these performances with text and images describing historical incidences in which Amerindians were paraded as attractions in circuses and world's fairs. But the reactions of those who saw Fusco and Gómez-Peña's performance make it clear that Western society has yet to move beyond this shameful legacy of its colonial past.

Indeed, it turns out irony is not always so easily discerned. The recent spread of fake news suggests many have difficulty distinguishing tone, and cases proliferate on social media of users citing satirical sources as if they were earnest, a practice that extends all the way up to the politicians in power.[4] This points to the phenomenon of confirmation bias—an intense desire to be affirmed in one's preexisting beliefs.

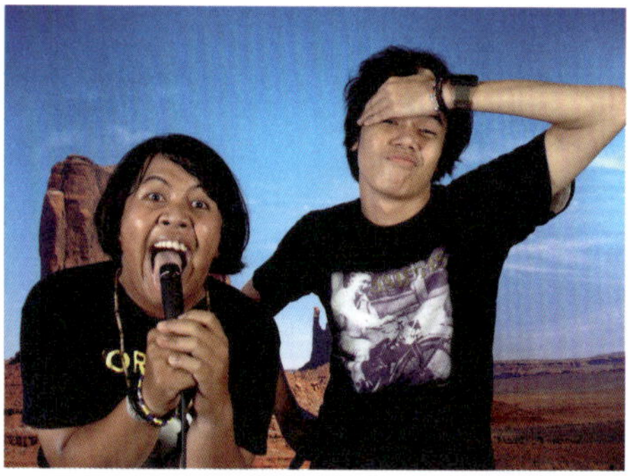

Phil Collins, *the world won't listen*, 2004–2007. Synchronized three-channel video installation, color, sound. © Shady Lane Productions, Berlin

Empathy presents one way out of this bind, a possibility suggested by Phil Collins's *the world won't listen* (2004–2007). A series shot in Colombia, Turkey, and Indonesia, three videos feature karaoke performances of the compilation album of the same name by the Smiths, released by the band due to their frustration that they were not getting airtime from mainstream radio. Although the title points to the inability to connect, the gambit was ultimately successful, and the album became a fan favorite. Collins's three-screen installation synchronizes the performances of participants from these disparate countries, which are all currently involved in violent political crises. This has a poetic resonance when so often a barrage of information deafens the international community to pleas for assistance or cooperation.

While karaoke could be dismissed as frivolous entertainment, it is ultimately an empathic form of impersonation that allows participants to assume the personae of others. Indeed, the role of the global circulation of pop music in uniting diverse peoples under transnational subcultures has been much heralded, a lesson that the world should heed.

Notes

1 Søren Grammel, Charles Esche, and Silke Otto-Knapp, "Finding the Words," *Afterall*, no. 5 (2002), 69.

2 Michael Zryd, "Found Footage Film as Discursive Metahistory: Craig Baldwin's Tribulation 99," *The Moving Image*, vol. 3, no. 2 (Fall 2003), 47.

3 Mark Bradford and Anita Hill, "Conversation: Mark Bradford and Anita Hill," Hammer Museum, Los Angeles, August 2, 2015. Transcribed by Eric Zeidler and Kelly Filreis. hammer.ucla.edu/programs-events/2015/08/mark-bradford-anita-hill/.

4 Alexandra Petri, "How the White House Made Me Real News," *Washington Post*, March 17, 1017, https://www.washingtonpost.com/blogs/compost/wp/2017/03/17/how-the-white-house-made-me-real-news/?utm_term=.727458acd5b9.

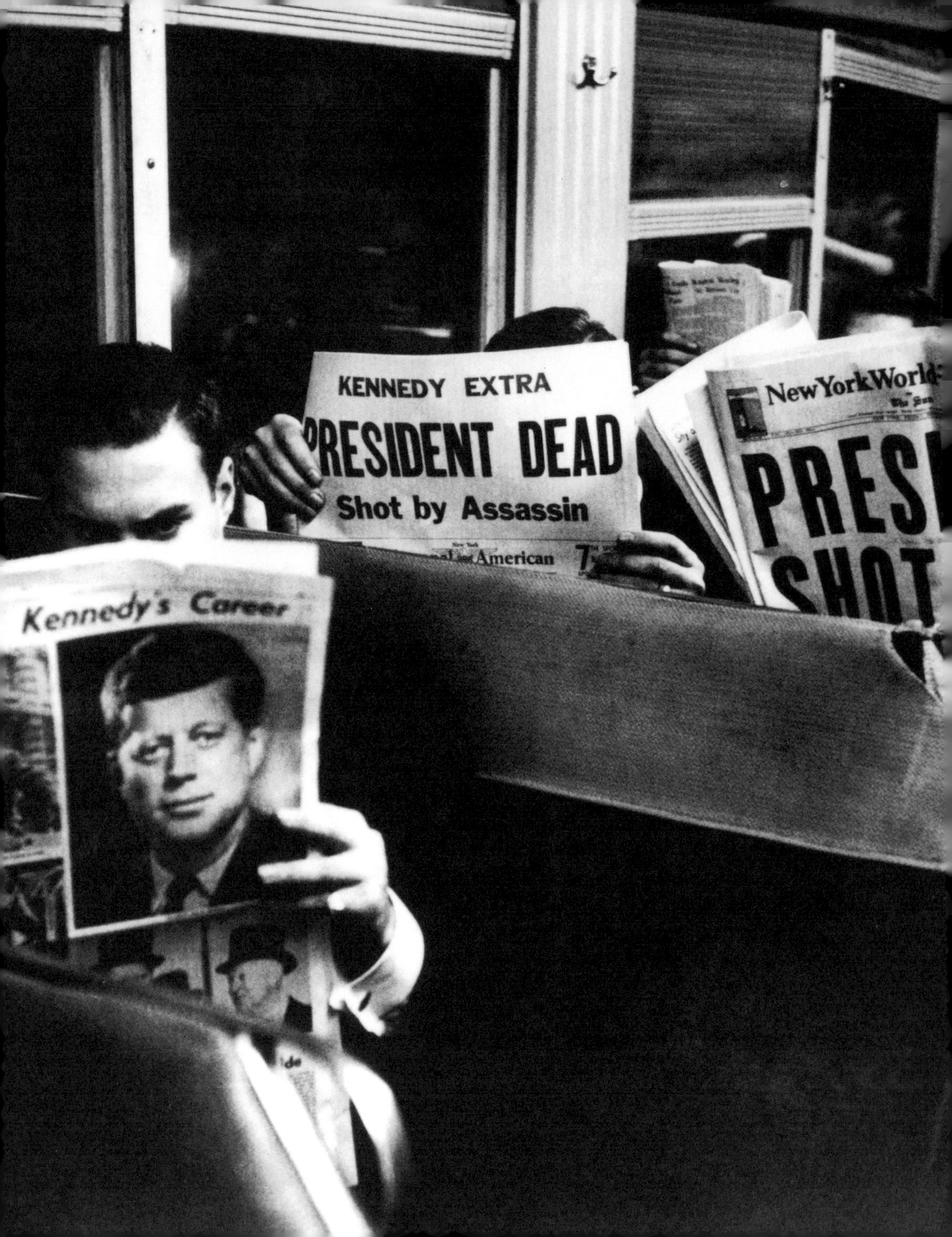
KENNEDY EXTRA
PRESIDENT DEAD
Shot by Assassin
American
New York World
PRES
SHOT
Kennedy's Career

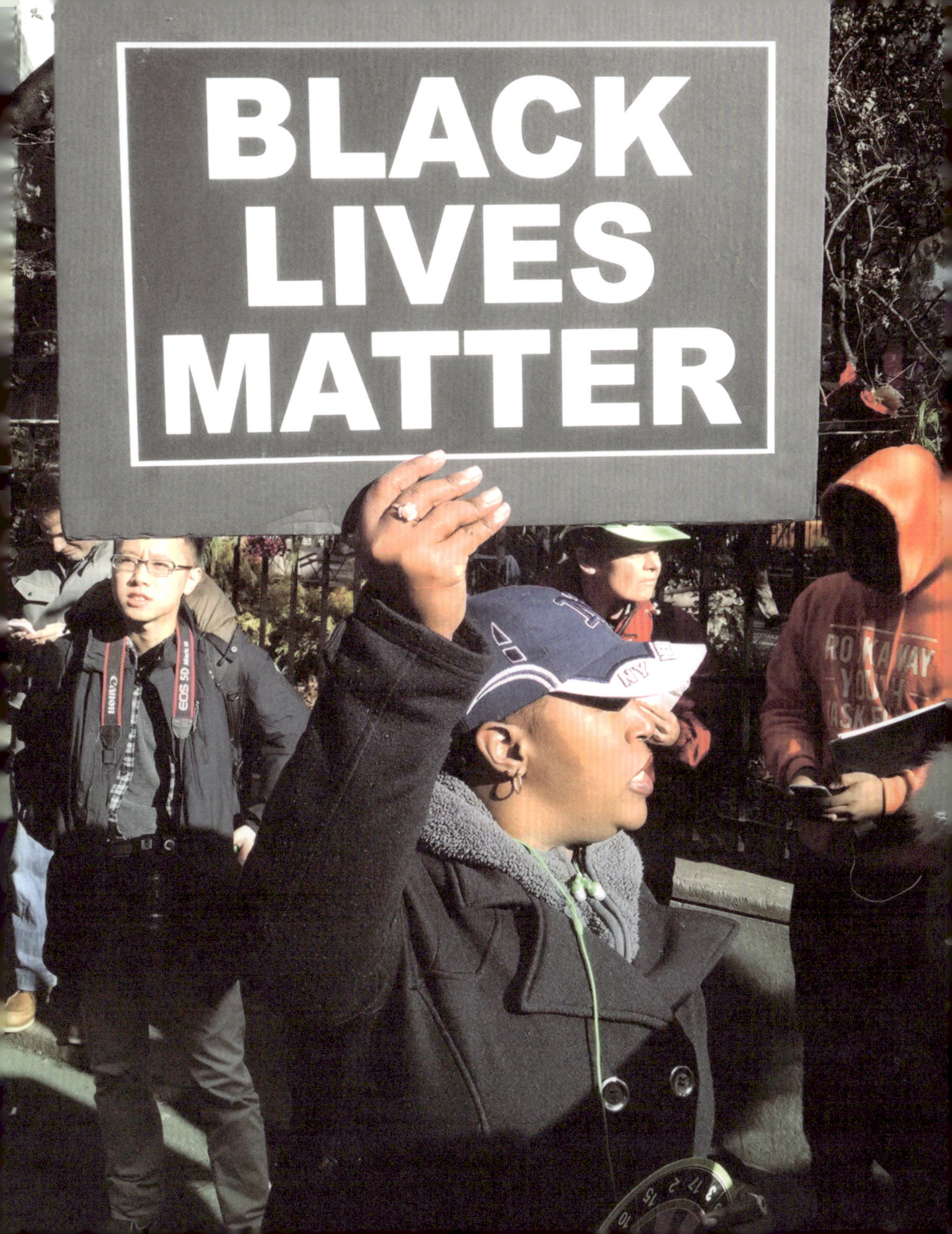
BLACK
LIVES
MATTER

Bruce Conner

REPORT, 1963–1967
16 mm film transferred to digital video and restored, black and white, sound
Running time: 13 minutes
Courtesy of the Conner Family Trust and Kohn Gallery, Los Angeles

Bruce Conner (American, 1933–2008) was born in McPherson, Kansas. He earned his BFA in 1956 from Nebraska University and also attended the Brooklyn Museum Art School and the University of Colorado. He was a pioneer in new media and experimental art forms, and his work has been the subject of numerous monographs and exhibitions around the globe. The Walker Art Center, Minneapolis, organized a major retrospective, *2000 B.C.: The Bruce Conner Story Part II* (1999–2000), which traveled to the Modern Art Museum of Fort Worth; the M. H. de Young Memorial Museum, San Francisco; and the Museum of Contemporary Art, Los Angeles. Most recently the San Francisco Museum of Modern Art organized a retrospective, *BRUCE CONNER: IT'S ALL TRUE* (2016), which traveled to the Museum of Modern Art, New York. His work is in the collections of the Dallas Museum of Art; the Museum of Modern Art, New York; the Whitney Museum of American Art, New York; the Art Institute of Chicago; Museum Moderner Kunst, Vienna; Centre Georges Pompidou, Paris; Hirshhorn Museum and Sculpture Garden, Washington, DC; and the Berkeley Art Museum, California.

1968 FLAHERTY SEMINAR QUESTION AND ANSWER WITH BRUCE CONNER

AUDIENCE MEMBER: How have audiences reacted to [REPORT]?

BRUCE CONNER: They never applaud at the end. They laugh nervously at two points. One is: "Children trying to get across the fence," and maybe a couple of titters during the Frankenstein scene. Sometimes they get very upset—violent.

AM: They wanted to kill you, as I recall, when they saw the version you showed in Boston.

BC: Yeah, I showed it to Al's class.[1] I think that was one of the first times it was shown.

AM: Why did Al's class want to kill you?

BC: Well, the most violent reaction I have gotten from REPORT was from one of the people who was there, and he said it was sacrilegious, immoral, and quite a few other things. And he said, "I didn't vote for the man, but I think what you've done is terrible." The people who were most upset about this were people who said they never voted for the man: "I never really agreed with his politics. I never really agreed with him as a living being." When he died, that made some sort of thing change there. It altered their relationship to him. And that's what the film is about. The first part of REPORT—there's no real film there—it's the sound of the man dying. The second part of REPORT is after the man has died: the exploitation of his death, all the grotesque and sacrilegious and immoral things that were done. And the excuse was that it was respect for the dead and his memory and stuff: Jack Kennedy banks and all sorts of memorabilia and nonsense documentaries and gooey posters.

AM: There's a postcard that's on sale in Love Field in Dallas which has a picture of the [Texas] School Book Depository on it.

AM: What do you mean by "nonsense documentaries"?

BC: Well . . . first thing is—it was repeated when Bobby Kennedy was killed. I was watching television when it happened, and the information you were getting was as confused as the information that was coming out at the end of REPORT. It continued that way, except it became formalized into the form of the media. They tried as hard as they could to control what was coming across. The announcer in the ballroom was still trying to maintain a stance in front of the camera even though the lights were going off. The quality of the color image decayed, it became black and white, and the only color that was coming in were the flesh colors, which were green, pulsating on and off. They interviewed a witness who was in another studio, and they tried to do that split-screen thing, and it wasn't synchronized. And then they started the repeats—the replay of the most popular scene—until finally there was practically only one image you related to. And even more obvious, the offensiveness of the media—the men who were there to record what was happening. Ethel Kennedy saying: "Go away. Get out of the way. He has to be helped." And they stand there with their eyes like this.

They don't move. They stick the microphone in the dying man's mouth. You know, this sort of thing.

I don't know if that answers any question anybody asked.

AM: There's another one from me, in any case. If you felt this strongly about all this, was it your intention in your film to parody this or to put the material together in another way so it will have an effect on people, or what? Or do you know what?

BC: Yes, I know what I was doing. I was obsessed. I was living in Brookline, Massachusetts, which was the birthplace of President Kennedy. He had reserved a plot in the graveyard in Brookline to be buried. His children were already buried there. He was assassinated. I lived seven blocks from where he was born. I decided then that I would dedicate myself to recording what had happened and what would happen in Brookline because he was going to be buried there, and I would live there for the next two or three years to work on that film and make a pilgrimage to the grave every day with my camera and show what had happened. Well, then they took him away from me. I then decided that since I'd gotten a Ford Foundation grant, I could make a film with stock footage. When I started, the big problem was that I had to show what had happened: *the exploitation of the man's death.* That's what I had to show. That's what I wanted to show, and I had to show it because nobody else was. There was tons of other information coming through the media, but this exploitation was the most obvious thing to me.

On his birthday, which was about five months after his assassination, at the hour and minute he was born, I went to the house where he was born. I stood in front of the house. On the way there. I was listening to the radio: "Today we are putting out commemorative stamps of Kennedy." Everybody knew that it was his birthday. Hundreds of people went to the grave. Hundreds of people appeared in Dallas, and I was the only person standing in front of the house in Brookline, Massachusetts, at that moment. That impressed on me that I had some responsibility there. It appeared that I was the only person who would relate to President Kennedy in this way.

The problem in making the film was that in order for me to do the film, I would also have to go through the same processes that those people were using to exploit Kennedy. If the film was completed, then he was as dead as they had made him, and so it took me two and a half years to finish the film. That has something to do with why it changed. Part of the reason why it changed was I didn't want to stop the changes. . . . Life is change, and when REPORT was finished, then he was dead, so it took two and a half years for me to acknowledge that he was dead.

This text was excerpted from a discussion with Bruce Conner at the 1968 Flaherty Seminar, first transcribed and published in *Film Comment*, vol. 5, no. 4 (Winter 1969), 18. Reprinted with permission from *Film Comment* magazine and the Film Society of Lincoln Center.

Note

1 Despite every effort to find out more about the reference to Al's class, we were unsuccessful.

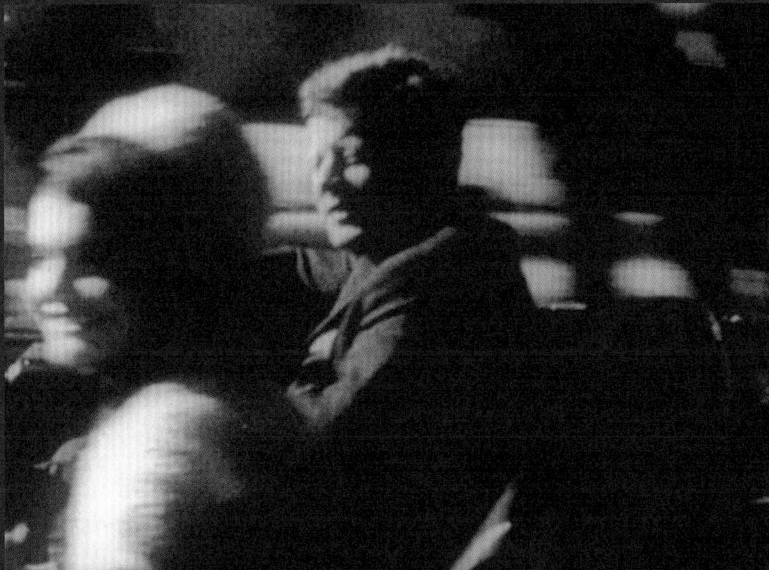

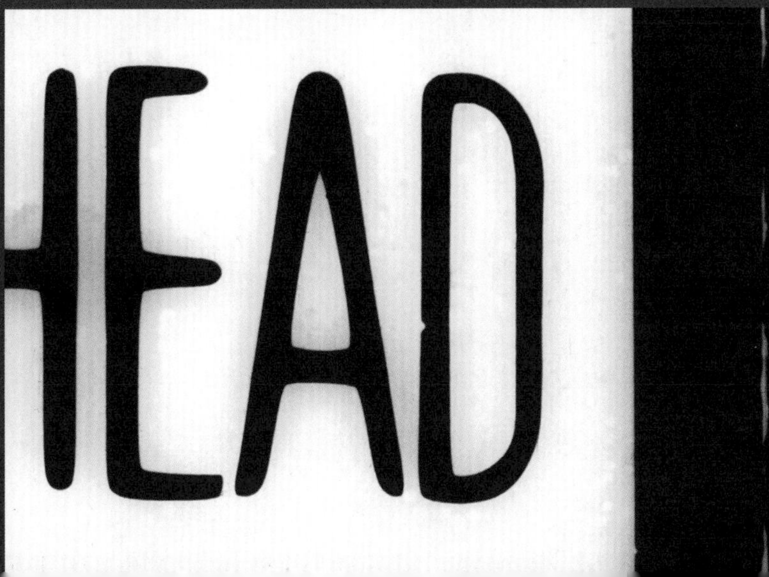
HEAD

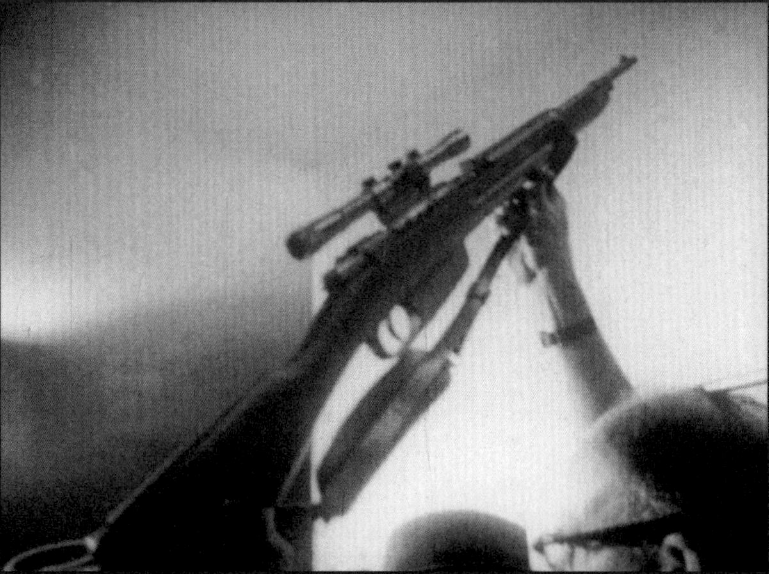

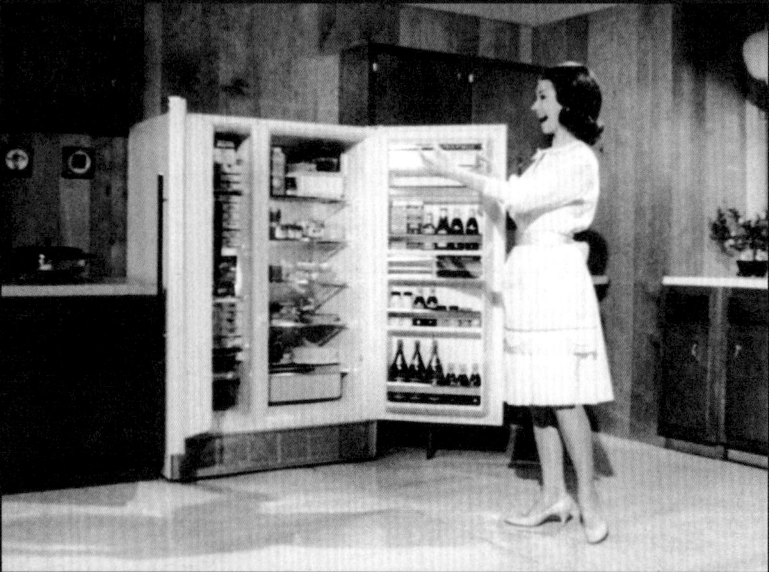

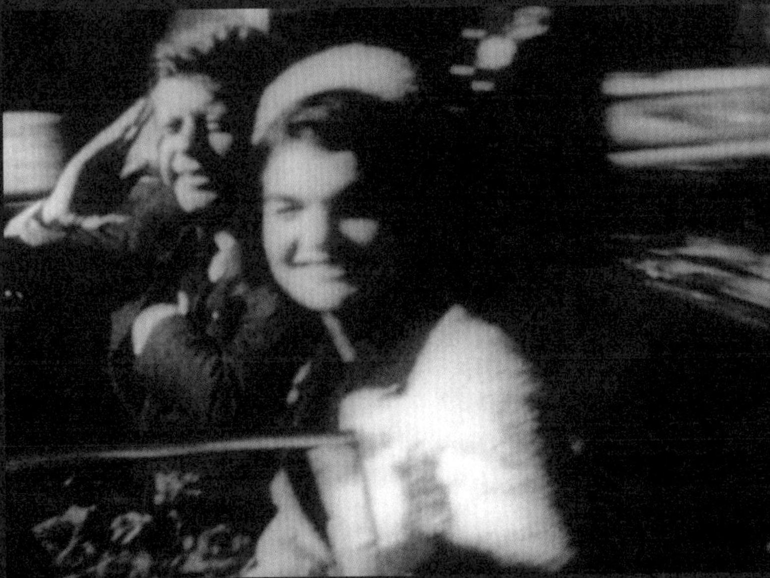

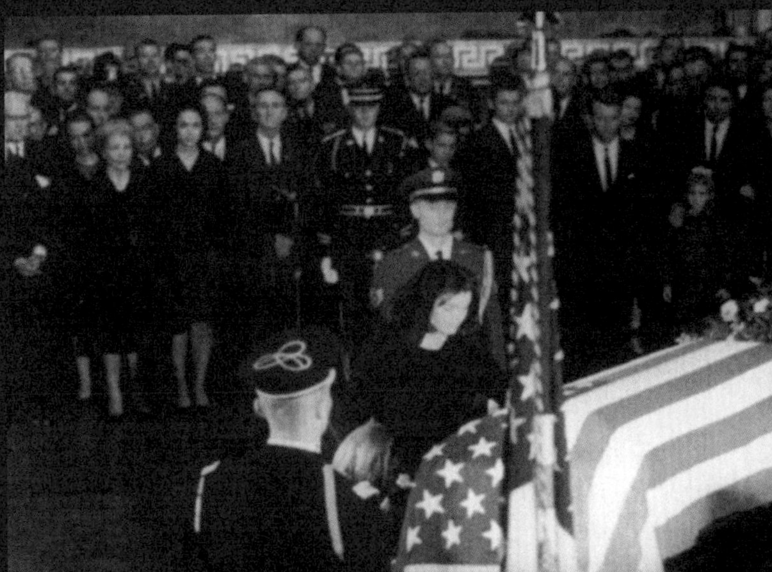

Morgan Fisher

Documentary Footage, 1968
16 mm film, color, sound
Running time: 11 minutes
Courtesy of the artist and Bortolami, New York

Morgan Fisher (American, b. 1942), an artist and filmmaker, was born in Washington, DC. He received an AB in art history from Harvard University, then studied film production in Los Angeles. His early work was predominantly in film. His films have been shown at international film festivals (Berlin, Rotterdam, and London, among others) and in solo screenings or exhibitions at, among other places, Tate Modern, London; the Museum of Modern Art, New York; the Whitney Museum of American Art, New York; and the Museum of Contemporary Art, Los Angeles. In the early 1990s he started making works on paper, then paintings and sculptures. Solo exhibitions that included examples of such work were at Portikus, Frankfurt am Main; Raven Row, London; Museum Abteiberg, Mönchengladbach, Germany; Generali Foundation, Vienna; and the Aspen Art Museum. More recently, he has exhibited photographs. He has been in three Whitney Biennials (1985, 2004, and 2014). A collection of his writings was published by Walther König (2012). He has been a visiting teacher at Brown University; California Institute of the Arts; and the University of California, Los Angeles. He lives and works in Los Angeles.

DOCUMENTARY FOOTAGE

by Morgan Fisher

The idea for *Documentary Footage* came all at once, as it has for several of the other films. A woman, nude, asks questions about physical appearance at regular intervals into a tape recorder. She rewinds the tape, the tape recorder plays the questions back, and she answers them. The idea is graspable in an instant: record, then respond to playback.

I realized after I made the film that it was a translation of a music composition by a friend named Malcolm Brodwick. I had met Malcolm through Thom Andersen. I heard Malcolm's composition in a recital at UCLA in 1965 or 1966. My memory of the piece is that the performer played a solo on the flute that he recorded on a tape recorder that was on the floor next to him on the stage. Then he rewound the tape and played it back and played a second line that together with the part he had just recorded amounted to a duet. I recently asked Malcolm about the piece. He said the title was *Autoformat for Solo Flute and Two Tape Recorders.* As the title alone suggests, my memory of the piece had simplified it. In any case, Malcolm's piece made a strong impression on me. What I carried over into *Documentary Footage* was the diagram of recording a performance, then playing it back to interact with it. There the similarity ends.

The relation between the first performance and the second performance that accompanies the first can be more complicated if the performances use words instead of music. In my memory of Malcolm's piece, the second half seemed like a duet, but this is not the case in *Documentary Footage.* Because it's in the form of questions and answers, it proceeds by turns. But maybe that is a duet of a kind.

I don't know whether Malcolm composed both parts of his piece in advance or composed only the first part and improvised the second, or improvised both parts. The woman in *Documentary Footage* knew that the questions, which I wrote, would be about physical appearance, but she did not see them until just before the shot began. She improvised her answer to each question.

The questions come at regular intervals, but the performer's answers are improvised, so her answers do not always fit neatly into the intervals after the questions. Sometimes her answers are short, and there is a silence before the next question. Sometimes the next question interrupts her answer, and she has to break off the one answer to begin another.

Even though the voice that asks her the questions is her own voice, she answers as if she were responding to a stranger, or as if she had never heard the questions before, when in fact she had recited them a few minutes before. There is a play between her enormous poise, on the one hand, and on the other hand, her seeming alienated from herself.

A musical performance is performed for an audience; that is, it is directed at the audience. In the first half of *Documentary Footage,* when the woman reads the questions, she seems to be performing for no one in particular, perhaps just the tape recorder. In the second half, she directs her answers by turns to several different places: sometimes to the voice coming from the tape recorder, as if the source of the voice could also listen; sometimes to the camera; sometimes to the audience that is not present but that she knows will ultimately see the film.

These several complexities are a large part of what people find pleasurable in the film. I did not foresee that the diagram that is the foundation of the film would make them possible.

I justified choosing a woman because women, I supposed, were far more self-scrutinizing than men about their appearance and their bodies. They would know the answers to the questions without having to pause to examine themselves, or pause as they tried to remember if they knew the answer. A woman would already know. The cause of such self-scrutiny is something the film does not directly address. I hope that the film, in relying on it, brings it out and so is a critique, if only implied, of the forces that produce it.

For a number of years, I felt sheepish that I made the film with a woman. I thought about making a corresponding film with a man. Together they would form a pendant pair, like the portraits of husband and wife in the seventeenth century that were each a separate painting but were intended to hang next to each other.

Documentary Footage is the only film I have ever cast. The people in my other films are workers helping to make the film. Their being willing to help and their having the necessary technical skills are why they are in the films. But for *Documentary Footage* I had to find someone to perform. I didn't know exactly what I was looking for, but when this woman came to the interview, I knew I had found the right person. What so struck me, and what turned out to be so perfect for the film, was her enormous self-confidence and self-love. She was utterly without self-consciousness. Between me and her there could not have been a greater contrast.

Documentary Footage is full of what François Truffaut called "privileged moments,"[1] a concept I will paraphrase as moments that move us in some way that is not deliberate. When we see privileged moments in a commercial film, we sense that the script did not call for them, that the director did not imagine and then succeed in creating them, that they are not the clever inventions of the actor. Instead of being created deliberately, by will, privileged moments are moments that shine forth as moments of grace.

In *Documentary Footage* there is no editing. The moments of grace occur here and there as they will (to echo the second title for Robert Bresson's *A Man Escaped*), within one continuous shot.[2] All the moments of grace in *Documentary Footage* are spontaneous acts of the performer. She puts together certain words, she gestures in a certain way, shifts her weight in a certain way, raises her shoulders in a certain way, sways in a certain way, a certain expression lights up her face, her voice for a moment has a certain tone or shifts in an unforgettable way from one tone to another. I foresaw none of these things. It would have been beyond my power to imagine them. Or if I could have imagined them, it would have been beyond imagining that it was possible to elicit them by directing a performance and so get them on film.

Directing in the usual sense of the word, shaping and controlling a performance, rehearsing until it's the way the director wants it, is a model of filmmaking that *Documentary Footage* absolutely rejects.

Andy Warhol defended his film *Camp* by saying that the technical aspects of the film were deficient but that the people in it were, in his word, fantastic.[3] The technical side of *Documentary Footage* is competent enough, but what Warhol said of his cast I will say of mine. This extraordinary woman and her extraordinary self-possession and self-love and poise make the film what it is.

The film was an act of faith in the power of the performer's personality, and my faith was repaid. As I say, there was no editing. And the film you see was the first take. There was a technical rehearsal, but no rehearsal of her answers. I did a second take, to have something to fall back on in case the first was damaged in the lab, but she had given everything to the first take. In the second, she was trying to remember her answers from the first, and the effort showed.

In *Notes on the Cinematographer,* Bresson says that the foundation of the cinema is improvisation.[4] What I did in making *Documentary Footage* was to create a framework.

The performer improvised in response to the framework, and her improvisations make the film.

I never considered another title for the film. I don't know even now what else I could have called it. The subject of a documentary is usually something that is already in the world that the filmmaker decides to make a film about. What *Documentary Footage* depicts did not exist before I made the film; I created a situation in order to film it. *Documentary Footage* is not a documentary of the usual kind. Instead, it is a documentary of a situation that created fleeting moments, things that occur once and then are gone forever, moments you could never create, and never re-create, no matter how hard you tried.

Calling the film *footage* suggests a casual attitude toward both the original production and how the material was handled afterward. But the term is a form of modesty. I think the word is appropriate because, in not making a larger claim for the film, it shifts emphasis away from me as its maker. This, in turn, makes it possible for the emphasis to fall on the performer, and in the narrow technical sense, it is correct to call it *footage*. The finished film is the film that came from the camera.

Written c. 2005; first published with revisions in *Morgan Fisher: Writings*, edited by Sabine Folie for Generali Foundation, Vienna, and Susanne Titz for Museum Abteiberg, Mönchengladbach (Cologne: Verlag der Buchhandlung Walther König, 2012); revised 2017.

Notes

1 Cf. François Truffaut, "Journal of *Fahrenheit 451*," in *Cahiers du Cinéma in English*, no. 5 (November 1966), 10–22; no. 6 (December 1966), 10–23; no. 7 (January 1967), 8–19.

2 *A Man Escaped or: The Wind Bloweth Where It Listeth* (1956), directed by Robert Bresson. The second part of the title comes from the King James Bible, John 3:8, *Listeth* is an archaic word that means "wishes" or "pleases."

3 Andy Warhol, *Camp* (1965).

4 Note by the author: This is the title in English of Robert Bresson's book that in French has

the title *Notes sur le cinématographe* (Paris: Éditions Gallimard, 1975). *Cinématographe* was the name that Auguste and Louis Lumière gave to their movie camera, patented in 1895, which could also be used to project the film that it took. It is clear that by beginning this word in the title of his book with a lowercase letter, Bresson did not mean this early camera/projector but instead the institution—cinema—of which the *Cinématographe* was one of the principal beginnings and to which it gave a shortened form of its name. Perhaps Bresson chose this word to emphasize the crucial nature of the moment of production. In any event, it's clear he was referring to the cinema, or cinema, and not to the camera. Why the translator chose to translate *cinématographe* as cinematographer, the term for the technical operative who controls a movie camera, I have never understood.

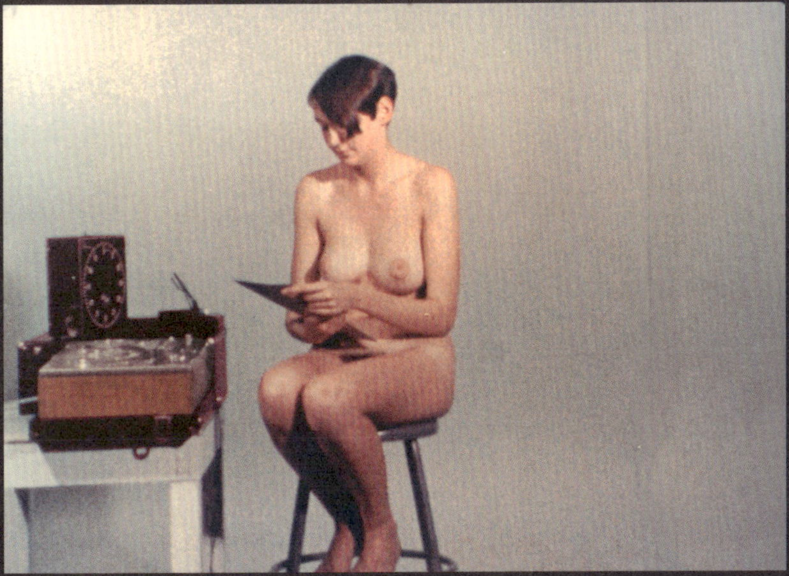

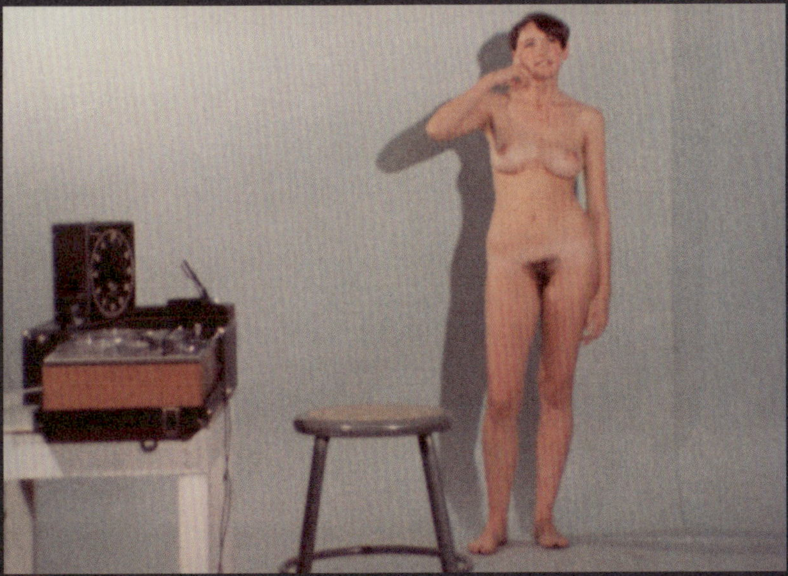

Ant Farm

Media Burn, 1975
Video, color, sound
Running time: 23:02 minutes
Dallas Museum of Art, Laura and Walter Elcock Contemporary Art Fund, 2005.96.2

Ant Farm was an artist group founded in 1968 by architects Chip Lord (American, b. 1944) and Doug Michels (American, 1943–2003) and later joined by Curtis Schreier (American, b. 1944). First exploring dynamic ways to apply their radical architectural practice outside established conventions, the group went on to use film and performance as a countercultural approach to critique mainstream media, culture, and society. Notable projects include *Inflatables*, portable air-filled vinyl structures used for gatherings (1969–1972); *House of the Century* (1972); and performances such as *Citizen's Time Capsule* (1975) and *Cadillac Ranch* (Lord, Marquez, Michels, 1974), an installation of ten half-buried cars in Amarillo, Texas. The Berkeley Art Museum and Pacific Film Archive organized the first retrospective survey of the collective's ten years of work (2004). Other notable exhibitions include the Frac Centre, Orléans, France (2007); and the Gallery of the Graduate School of Architecture, Planning, and Preservation, Columbia University, New York (2008). Ant Farm is included in the collections of the Dallas Museum of Art; the San Francisco Museum of Modern Art; the Museum of Modern Art, New York; and the Art Institute of Chicago. Archival collections are held in the Berkeley Art Museum and Pacific Film Archive and the Avery Library of Architecture and Fine Art at Columbia University.

ANT FARM REDUX: PYROTECHNICS AND EMERGENCE

by Patricia Mellencamp

Have you ever noticed that history records comedy and laughter later than sorrow and tears? Think of Buster Keaton's films. And that history accords a place to individuals more readily than to anonymous groups with zany names? To make entrance into history even tougher, art history prefers tangible, salable objects that can increase in value, not conceptual, performative, video art. Ant Farm is being included in Art History tonight, at last.

I first saw the video work of Ant Farm almost thirty years ago, in the mid- to late 1970s, on a small, dull television under a dark, musty stairwell with a few scattered bent folding chairs in the basement of a fairly large and famous museum. Video didn't used to get much respect from museum culture. Now one wonders if contemporary shows could exist without video installations.

During *Eternal Frame*, Ant Farm and T. R. Uthco's wild and crazy re-creation of the Zapruder film that has become our memory of the [John F.] Kennedy assassination, I had an intense art experience. You know what I mean? It was one of those heightened moments when you know you have witnessed and experienced something truly exceptional. Here was a work that in twenty-four minutes explored the very nature of representation. The intermediated play between still and moving images, between film and video, between performed and live action, between performer and spectator, between tourism and history, between sound and image—the Zapruder film is very short and silent, a single shot, which we often forget because it has borne trillions of words and alternative narratives—between the real and its simulation, between creation and re-creation, between spectacle and tribute, is almost a Socratic dialogue. And it is audacious, fearless, moving, perhaps a bit reckless, and even dangerous.

This tape triggered a realm of response that was deeply unsettling and highly intellectual. It was very different from most video art then, whether West or East Coast video as a plaything of simultaneity and a personal recording mechanism for artists from many fields. Much of it was unedited, rough, often involving a certain tedium. As the video artist Bill Viola once said, "Life without editing is not that interesting." The art critic Rosalind Krauss saw an inherent and deeply boring narcissism in the way artists used the medium, if not in the medium itself. And to be honest, Ant Farm initially used video this way, recording everyday hippie domesticity, historically interesting now but narcissistic and goofily indulgent then.

But Ant Farm's events, re-created as video art, were another story. The tapes are a condensation and preservation of ambitious collective projects that make up a sophisticated critique of television, along with anticipating so many of the concerns of Internet-digital culture. Ant Farm dissected the way television both created and fed upon events and the way these events then made history. Like an ant colony, and the current notions of emergent, or swarm, logic, Ant Farm was a way of working without a central leader, without hierarchy, able to zigzag easily among media, to expand and contract as a group by joining with other artistic groups like TVTV (remember the still powerful and poignant document of the GOP convention, *Four More Years*?) and T. R. Uthco, learning from each other, from feedback, from experience, in projects that were interactive, nomadic, rhizomatic, exemplary of a bottom-up logic that believed that anything was possible and that change was the optimum state.

They also staged the ultimate Platonic question—the relation between reality and representation, between the real and its simulation or in the art world, the questions of the original and its copy, or forgery, which are close to mimicry. The answers to these dilemmas are left up to us, the audience. In *Media Burn* and *Eternal Frame*, Ant Farm not only created what I consider a sophisticated critique of television, but it addressed in just a few minutes the sprawling theoretical debate during the 1980s and early 1990s on postmodernism, simulation, history, and memory; it enacted the complex theories of Gilles Deleuze; and it gave us a way of analyzing Internet culture and digital thought in the present; it is contemporary theory that is focusing on ways of thinking and acting.

Patricia Mellencamp, opening remarks on the occasion of Ant Farm's 2004 retrospective at the Berkeley Art Museum and Pacific Film Archive, first published in "Ant Farm Redux: Pyrotechnics and Emergence," *Journal of Film and Video*, vol. 57, no. 1/2 (Spring/Summer 2005), 46–47. Used with permission of the University of Illinois Press.

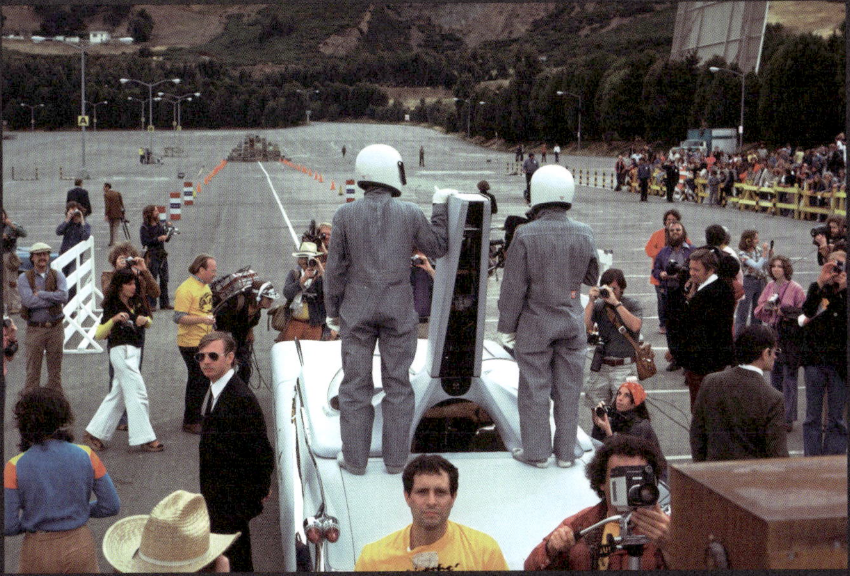

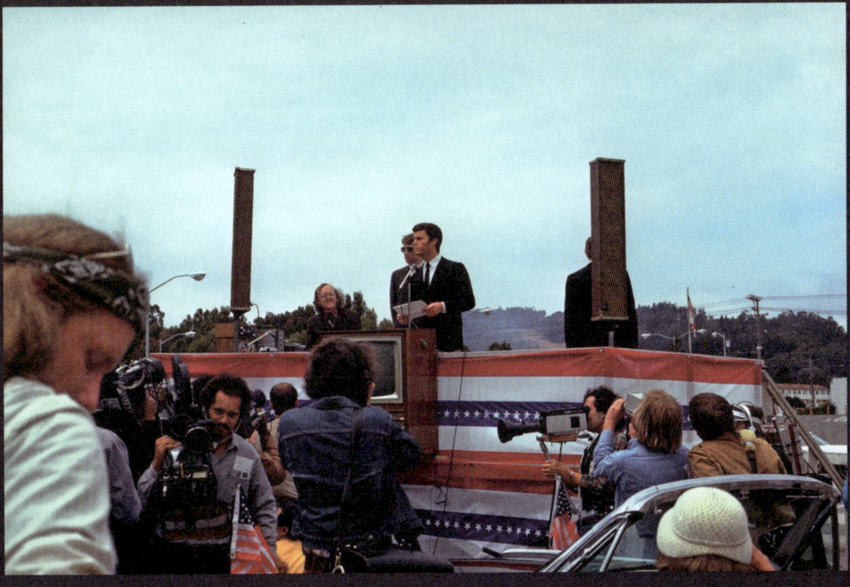

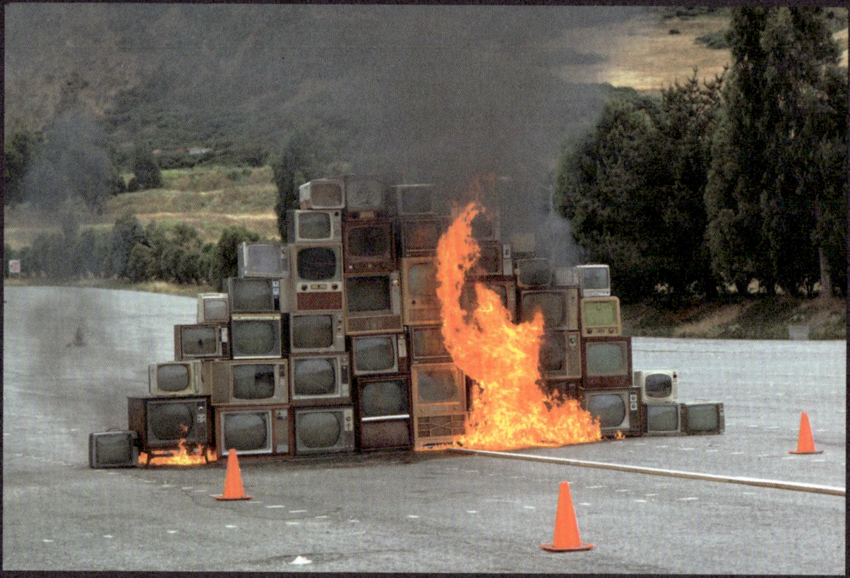

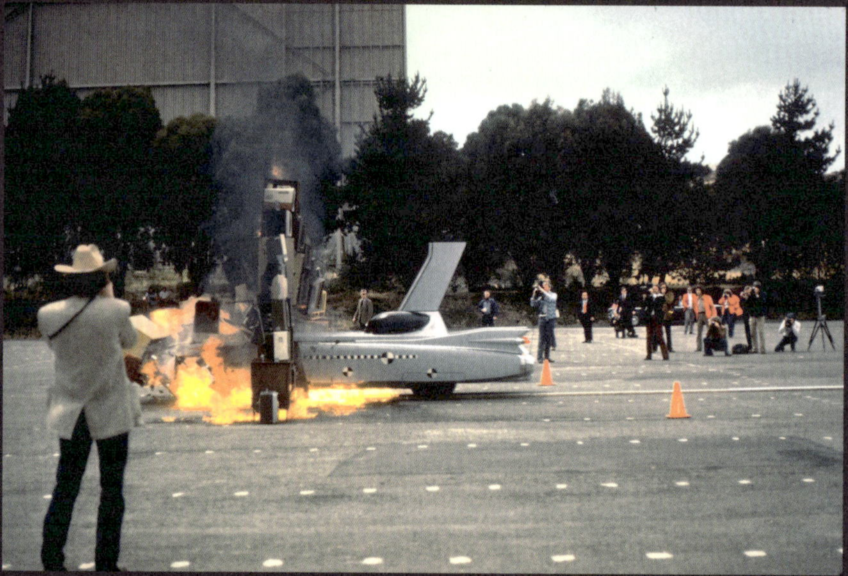

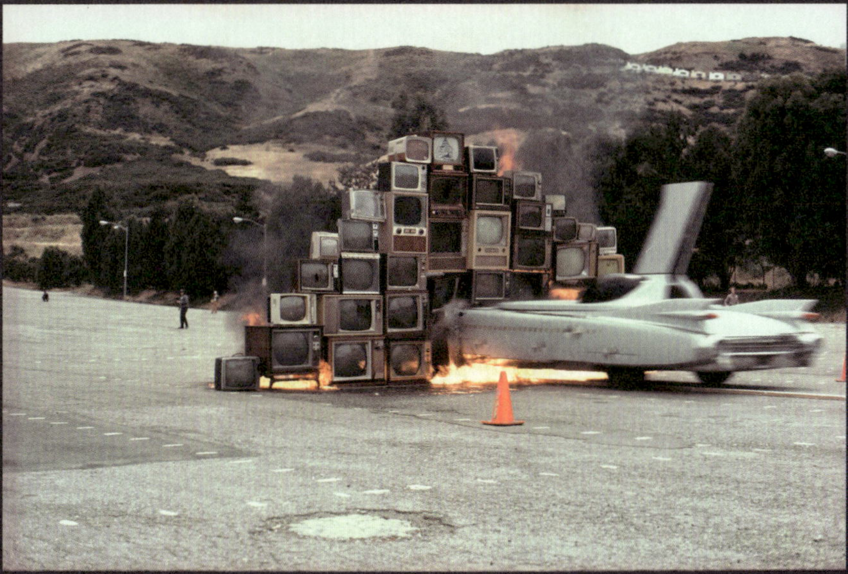

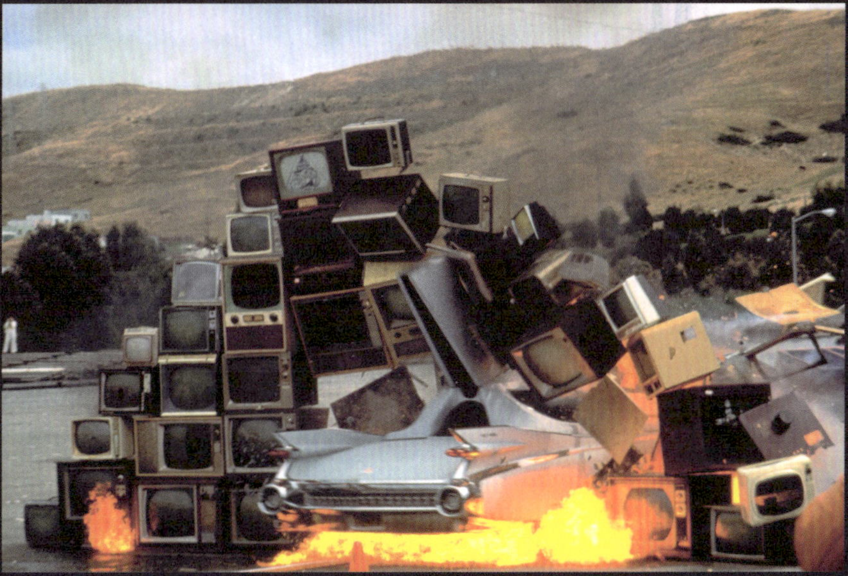

Chick Strand

Cosas de mi vida (Things of my life), 1976
16 mm film, color, sound
Running time: 25 minutes
Courtesy of Canyon Cinema Foundation

Chick Strand (American, 1931–2009) was born in Northern California, studied anthropology at Berkeley in the 1960s, and graduated from the University of California, Los Angeles's ethnography program in 1971. Alongside her career in filmography (she referred to her body of work as "ethnographies of women"), Strand also taught film at Occidental College, Los Angeles, and was a cofounder of the film cooperative Canyon Cinema. In 2016 the Harvard Film Archive presented a retrospective film program that included a near-complete catalogue of the filmmaker's work. Strand is frequently included in film series and screenings at organizations worldwide such as Tate Modern, London (2015), and REDCAT, the Roy and Edna Disney/CalArts Theater in Los Angeles (2006).

WOMAN AS ETHNOGRAPHIC FILMMAKER

by Chick Strand

I have never really thought of myself as a "woman in film," . . . as opposite from "men in film. . . ." I am a filmmaker (although there certainly seem to be many more men in film than women). I am not so stupid as not to see that there are differences in approach, perceptions, values, motivations, and that these differences stem from the way our culture defines men and women and from the way that we are taught to see ourselves and as men see us. The questions and ways to find answers as to what is womanness underneath all the cultural definitions are far too complicated and interrelated to have any overt meaning during the act of creativity (at least for me). I do it . . . I make the film . . . and of course, all the things involved in our concepts of woman and reactions to being a woman come into play in what I do, but I don't stop to analyze my motivations. Neither am I careful to present my films or the women in them in any special light, or with any social significance, or in any special manner . . . except that it's all special in that it comes from me, a woman. I do it as I feel it. I am well aware that my own perceptions and the presentations of them contain many ambiguities that coincide with the difficulties of understanding what has gone on and is going on between men and women (I am talking about the new awareness) in our society. I am simply not an analytical person and have no real interest in sorting things out for the world at large through my films. But there are women who are good at it and should make coherent statements, define the general problems, and suggest solutions through their work.

There is a type of filmmaking in which I think women have an *obligation* to try and present women in a more straightforward manner, and this is in the area of ethnographic film. Information gathering and methodology have already been established in anthropology, and these methods can at least be partially fitted into ethnographic filmmaking. Most anthropologists are male, and they consistently manage to make films about males, overemphasizing the male roles and leaving the women as *secondary* role players. Only rarely have women been the "stars" of ethnographic films. I think that this is not only because men don't think about making films about the women, but also that men believe that women *do* have a secondary place (after all, what is more important, killing each other off or socializing the children?) and because males have a great problem in relating well to women of the culture. Too often fieldwork about women is left to the anthropologist's wife (who is playing a secondary role to her husband's fieldwork) or to female graduate students. Times are changing. Many gifted women anthropologists are working in the field, writing ethnographies, publishing them, and concentrating on the women in the cultures, but too few of them are making good films or allowing women filmmakers to come with them to make films.

The first people I make friends with in another culture are the women because I am a woman and because I have had similar experiences. Even working with very remote cultures, women only have to look at each other and nod, or make a small gesture, while admiring a newborn child or talking about work or men, to know, without words, about the experience. We feel sisterhood, a feeling of shared experience, shared knowledge, and shared intuition (you cannot use that word in male-oriented anthropology) that males can never feel between themselves. No man can make a film about women in another culture if he wants to make a credible film, simply because the communication that he can never know is beyond methodology and beyond a "scientific" approach. What women anthropologists and filmmakers can do is to present the women of the new culture by using the established ways of information gathering and presentation plus a translation of this shared sisterhood.

I made a film about two women of different cultures in an acculturation situation. I knew that no matter how careful I was, there was no way for me to keep myself out of it. If I set up the camera and merely pushed the trigger until I ran out of film, it was still subjective. When, during twenty-four hours, or a week, or a year, should one push the trigger? All is arbitrary, all is random, all is culturally defined. So one can be left with very little to go on. There is no way at all for ethnographic films to be objective. There merely are degrees of subjectivity. So I feel that it makes sense for women to offer their special communication in the form of the ethnographic film. There is no way that an ethnographic film can replace or substitute for the written ethnography. The film should be a complement to the written work. It is a means to get into other perspectives of the culture, to meet them, and to identify with them as fellow human beings.

Chick Strand, "Woman as Ethnographic Filmmaker," *Journal of the University Film Association*, vol. 26, no. 1/2, Women in Film (1974), 16.

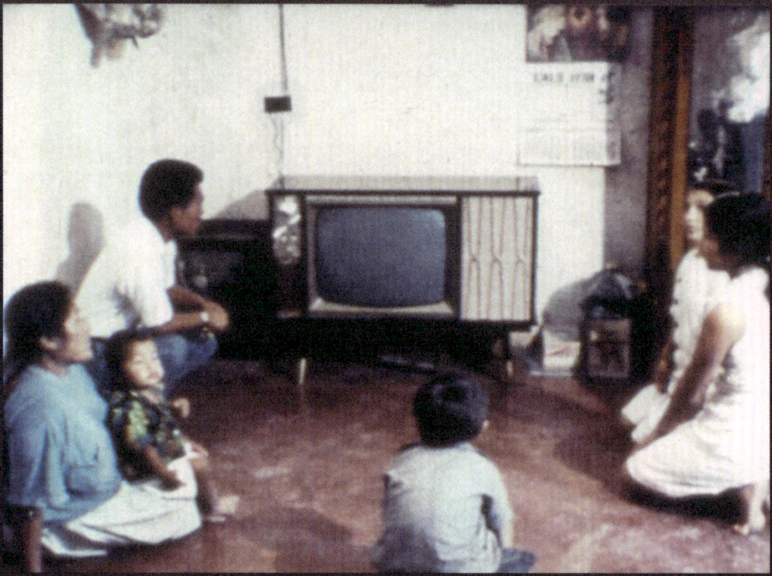

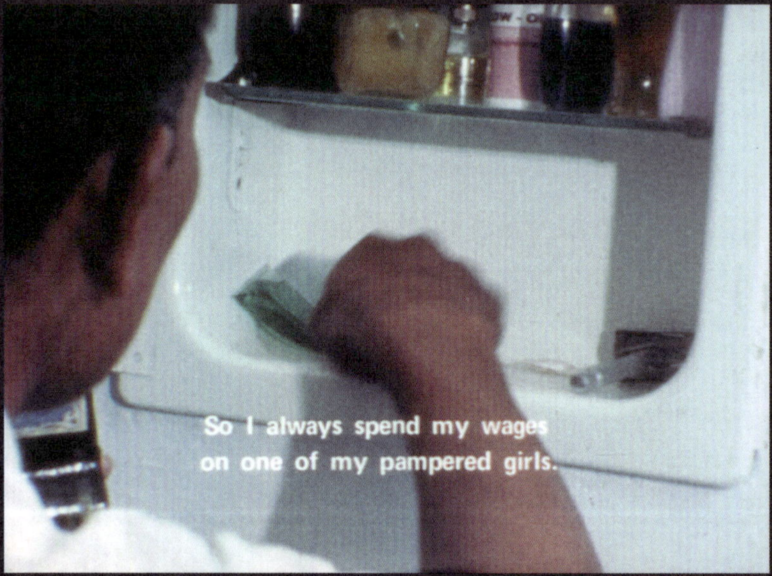
So I always spend my wages
on one of my pampered girls.

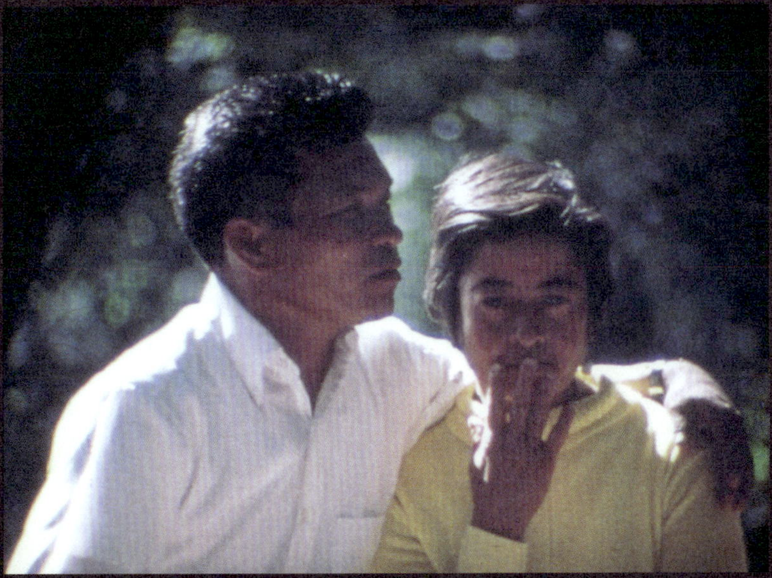

Jean-Marie Straub and Danièle Huillet

En rachâchant, 1982
35 mm film transferred to digital video, black and white, sound
Running time: 7 minutes
Courtesy of Miguel Abreu Gallery, New York

Jean-Marie Straub (French, b. 1933) and Danièle Huillet (French, 1936–2006) collaboratively made films in France, Germany, and Italy over the span of five decades. Ranging from documentaries to interpretations of poetry, painting, and literature, their films—influenced by Marxism and workers' movements—often responded to the urgent social and political issues of their time. Notable works include *The Chronicle of Anna Magdalena Bach* (1968); *Othon* (1970); *From the Clouds to the Resistance* (1979); *Too Early/Too Late* (1982); *Class Relations* (1984); *Sicily!* (1999); and *These Encounters of Theirs* (2006). A husband-and-wife duo, Straub and Huillet were also writers and film critics, and many of their texts were published in a collected volume in 2016. Their work has been screened and exhibited worldwide at venues including the National Gallery of Art, Washington, DC; the Museum of Modern Art, New York; Los Angeles Filmforum; Berkeley Art Museum and Pacific Film Archive; the Venice Film Festival; and the Cannes Film Festival. In 2017 Straub received the Pardo d'onore Manor lifetime achievement award from the Locarno Film Festival.

CINEMA MUST SET FIRE TO LIFE

by Jean-Marie Straub and Danièle Huillet, transcribed, translated, and edited by Sally Shafto

Jean-Marie Straub's Earliest Film Memories

I began to watch films very late because my middle-class family—first off, it was during the war; we were occupied by the Germans. We were considered as belonging to the Third Reich in Metz, and consequently, there were Nazi films, so we didn't go to the cinema. It was a form of political protest. And my mother used to say: we shouldn't go because it smelled like the saddle soap that was used to wax boots—high boots—because the German Army spent its time in the cinemas. And then we didn't want to watch Nazi films. Plus, back then, I didn't know a word of German. So, I saw films for the first time very late; I was no longer very young. It was after the war.

I think that the first film I saw was *Snow White and the Seven Dwarfs* [1937], which didn't interest me and of which I have no memory. Except that the witch obviously frightened me.

On Being Cultivated

I once saw a cultivated man. He's a farmer in Liguria. He knows [Dante Alighieri's] the *Divine Comedy* by heart. He's seventy years old. He's a political activist. He took part in the armed struggle in the Resistance. He is a political militant in his village, in his work. He knows the *Divine Comedy* completely by heart. That man is cultivated. The middle class who has read Karl Marx in French or Italian, [Fyodor] Dostoevsky in English, etc., and [Pierre] Corneille in Esperanto isn't cultivated. It's better to have read one text in your mother tongue and to know it completely. Then you can discover other things. And there, you have an in-depth culture instead of having read everything, seen everything, like [Jean de la] Bruyère's Arrias. . . . "Arrias has read and seen everything, at least he would lead you to think so; he is a man of universal knowledge, or pretends to be."[1] That's the middle class; it's not culture.

On Subject Matter

The experiences that we have in concrete terms in the society in which we live, that interests me, but not my personal biography as such. Just as I'm even less interested in the little ideas that I might have. That's finished. Perhaps that interested me when I was a teenager, like everyone. I don't believe at all in my little ideas. This is what sets me, that sets our first films, apart from [Jean-Luc] Godard's middle period. His films were full of very important—but that didn't interest me to do because, first, he had done it—full of little ideas and personal reflections. What interests me is when I encounter a strong text that resists me and with which I have difficulty, to struggle with this text and to communicate afterward in the form of a film, the result of my work of reflection on this text, because if I think that this text was strong and important for us, it should also be interesting and important for other people. In addition, there is a tactic that [Jacques] Rivette, after seeing *Othon*, called "Leninist" that exists in relation to bourgeois culture—that is, a tactic of expropriation and of proposition for people who never had the chance to encounter a text by Corneille, to expose them to a text by Corneille. Or for people who never go to the opera, to expose them to a musical text of [Arnold Schoenberg's unfinished opera] *Moses and Aaron*, for example.

What Is Cinema?

I've reached a point where I consider that it [cinema] doesn't exist; it isn't interesting. Cinema doesn't exist in itself; it's not a language. Cinema is an instrument, an instrument of analysis, that's all. It shouldn't become an end in itself. Not even under the pretext of *écriture* [style]. It must be an instrument of analysis or interpretation or of an analysis of a situation. . . .

A film doesn't exist in thin air; it's not something ethereal; a sound take is something precise. And the screening of a film, if the screening is worthless, the film doesn't exist. People don't see a film; they see the reflection of a film. It's the same for music. Someone like [Johann Sebastian] Bach, who was a technician, not only a musician technician, he imagined scores for—there's a way of striking notes on a harpsichord that is not at all the string. In one case, it is plucked; in the other, it is struck. It's not at all the same. You can't ignore this; similarly, a Romantic-era organ is meaningless for playing Bach.

What Is Cinema's Role?

Films should help people become conscious a little more than they are, when they are already, or to become conscious when they're not very conscious. And to become conscious, we must learn to use our eyes and ears—that's where it begins because the soul and consciousness don't exist in thin air. It involves the senses. And I don't believe in a political consciousness for the deaf and dumb, or for the deaf and blind. This is not against the deaf and dumb, because they, too, communicate with their senses, but in another way, so it consists in learning and in seeing, and learning and seeing and listening, and in establishing a relationship between what we see and what we hear. And to do it, to reach this result, that consists of making films that are the opposite of the noise of the cultural industry or of the society in which we live that makes people deaf and blind. That's all. And to help them, in contrast, to sharpen their eyes and their ears and to establish relationships between what they hear and what they see. And as a natural extension, to establish relationships between their experiences, experiences that overlap or differ from the subject of the film that is offered to them—either from the time period in which they live, or from a moment from the past. . . .

Cinema must set fire to life because, well, I think it should be left like that because it's good—it's striking. But I can also explain it and repeat it afterward. That way there's a movement back and forth. The Italians say, for the focal point to put a film, to check the focus on a film, the focus is the *fuoco*, fire, because that's where it burns. As children we all had fun making paper burn with a magnifying glass. So the cinema consists of setting life on fire, that is, to learn and to see and to discover life and society and history.

This text was transcribed, translated, and excerpted from Jean-Claude Philippe's interview with Jean-Marie Straub and Danièle Huillet, "Le cinéma n'existe pas en soi, il n'est pas un langage." It was originally broadcast on March 14, 1976, on Philippe's weekly radio program on France Culture, *Le Cinéma des cinéastes.* Courtesy of France Culture, Jean-Marie Straub, and Barbara Ulrich.

Note

1 Note by the translator: Reference to the French philosopher and moralist Jean de la Bruyère. In 1684 he became the tutor to the Duke of Bourbon. Four years later he published *Les Caractères, De la société et de la conversation* (1688), wherein he drew satirical portraits of "characters" at the court of Louis XIV; the book became an immediate success. Straub specifically cites here the character of Arrias, a smooth talker who *"a tout lu, a tout vu, il veut le persuader ainsi; c'est un homme universel, et il se donne pour tel."* ("Arrias has read and seen everything, at least he would lead you to think so; he is a man of universal knowledge, or pretends to be.") From *The "Characters" of Jean de la Bruyère*. Translated by Henri Van Laun. London: John C. Nimmo, 1885.

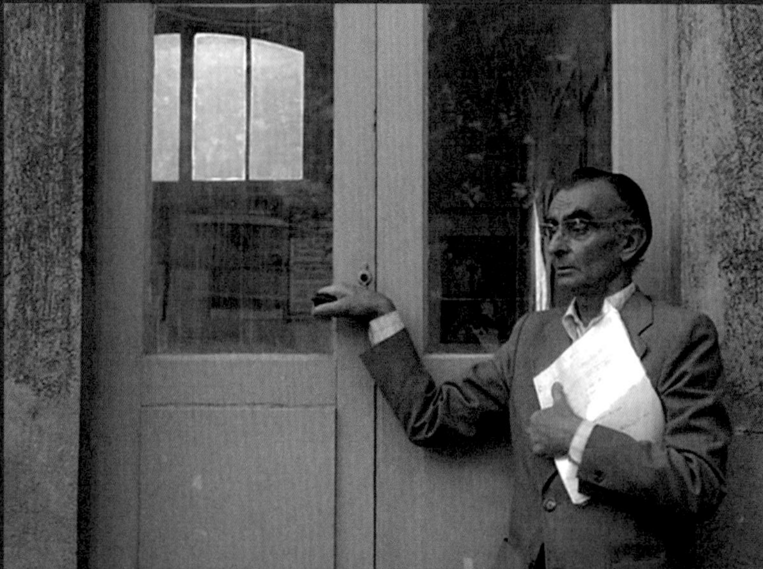

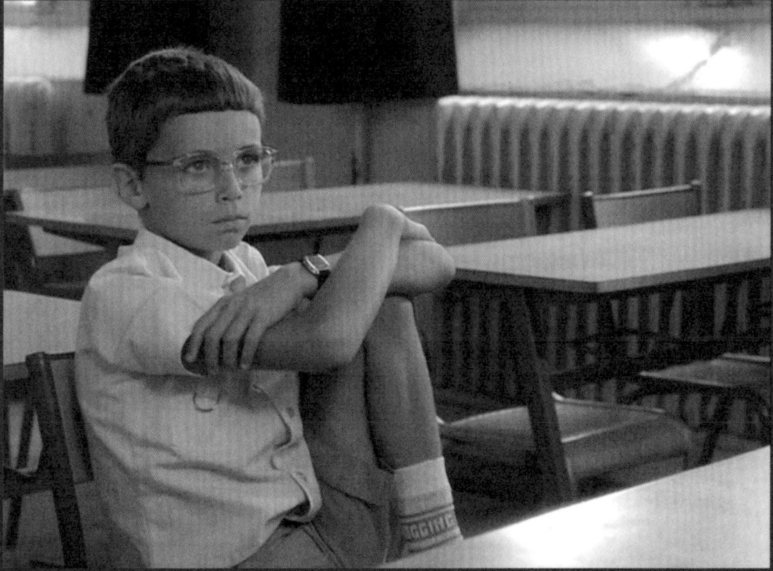

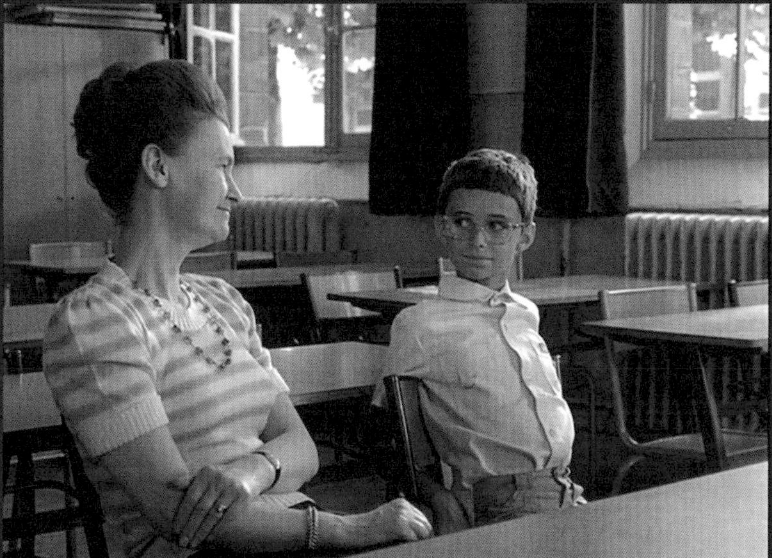

Tatiana Gaviola

No me olvides (Don't forget me), 1988
Video, color, sound
Running time: 13 minutes
Courtesy of the artist

Tatiana Gaviola (Chilean, b. 1956) is an award-winning filmmaker. Born in Santiago, she studied at the School of Communication Arts at the Catholic University of Chile. Her documentaries and feature films have explored the political transformations in Chile since the 1980s. Her first fictional film, *Ángeles* (Angels) made its debut in the film program *Internal Exile: New Films from Chile* at the Museum of Modern Art, New York (1990). Other notable works include *Tiempo para un líder* (Time for a leader) (1982); *Yo no le tengo miedo a nada* (I am not afraid of anything) (1984); *No me olvides* (Don't forget me) (1988); *Mi último hombre* (My last man) (1996); and *Teresa* (2009). In addition to her film work, she served as a member of Chile's Advisory Committee for Cultural Affairs under President Eduardo Frei Ruiz-Tagle and designed the structure and curriculum for the film school of the Vicente Pérez Rosales Technical University, which she directed from 2003 to 2005. From 2007 to 2011 she served as the audiovisual director of the Image of Chile Foundation. Gaviola is currently working on a feature film inspired by Rodrigo Rojas, the young photographer who was burned alive during the dictatorship.

INTERVIEW WITH TATIANA GAVIOLA
by Kelly Filreis

KELLY FILREIS: How did you first become involved with filmmaking?

TATIANA GAVIOLA: I emerged as a filmmaker through a documentary testimonial about women from a camp in Ochagavía who told their complicated yet beautiful stories.

I emerged during the fear of the dictatorship and being a woman in a man's world.

I emerged between an absence of production and an irremediable audacity, the urgency to both survive and to create.

I emerged after an experimental short titled *Yo no le tengo miedo a nada* (I am not afraid of anything), in which my fears skulked amidst the shadows and broken glass. I named each of these fears and I confronted them through heartbreak.

KF: *No me olvides* (Don't forget me) was commissioned in 1988 by the activist group Mujeres por la Vida (Women for Life) to document a major demonstration against [former Chilean President Augusto] Pinochet's violent regime that had been responsible for the disappearance of thousands of Chilean citizens. The demonstration occurred less than two months before the 1988 referendum that would ultimately lead to Pinochet's removal from office. The camera's close proximity to the demonstrators clearly emphasizes the urgency of confronting the reality of life in Chile. Can you further describe the context from which this video developed?

TG: I was involved in meetings organized by Mujeres por la Vida, and it was there that I conceived the documentary as an action that was simultaneously political, superimposed on the map of downtown Santiago.

The one thousand women who carried the one thousand figures bearing the names of the victims of the dictatorship embodied the emotion and pain of exile, murder, disappearance, prison.

Thus, we see in the documentary that the repression during the demonstration attacks the silhouettes just as it did the victims. The figures are consequently burned, torn apart, slit at the throat, and detained.

Through the captured image, we see a metaphor, as the text relates about "each one of the forms of torture represented here."

KF: Your 1982 documentary, *Tiempo para un líder* (Time for a leader), which is about the death of former President Eduardo Frei Montalva, was initially forbidden by the government from public screening. With that in mind, did you feel that there were any risks in making *No me olvides*?

TG: During the dictatorship, I faced many perilous situations.

[While making] a documentary, we were banned from several towns and detained with our equipment. I created a fictional film about the repression, and we filmed in the street without having permits to do so.

There was both exposure and risk in what we were doing. Yet it was the only way of working in this profession while having a political stance that was opposed to the dictatorship.

KF: Where were your videos shown during Pinochet's rule? How did audiences respond to your work?

TG: There were alternative networks that existed among the general populace and students during the military dictatorship. At times and for brief periods, there were projections in theaters, but never in the mass media.

KF: You have shifted from making documentaries throughout the 1980s to feature films such as *Teresa*. How has this impacted your approach to your subject matter?

TG: Every full-length, short, documentary, or fictional film opens up new territory.

In my fictional films such as *Ángeles* (Angels), *Mi último hombre* (My last man), or *Teresa*, there is an interconnecting thread informed by my interest in historical memory, politics, and the insurrectionary presence of women.

This interview is taken from an e-mail correspondence between Tatiana Gaviola and Kelly Filreis in June 2017. Translation from the Spanish by Eriksen Translations Inc.

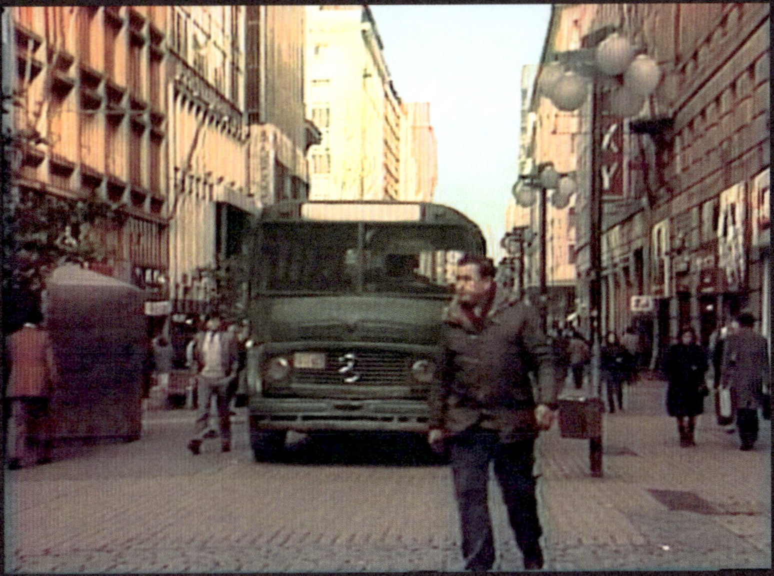

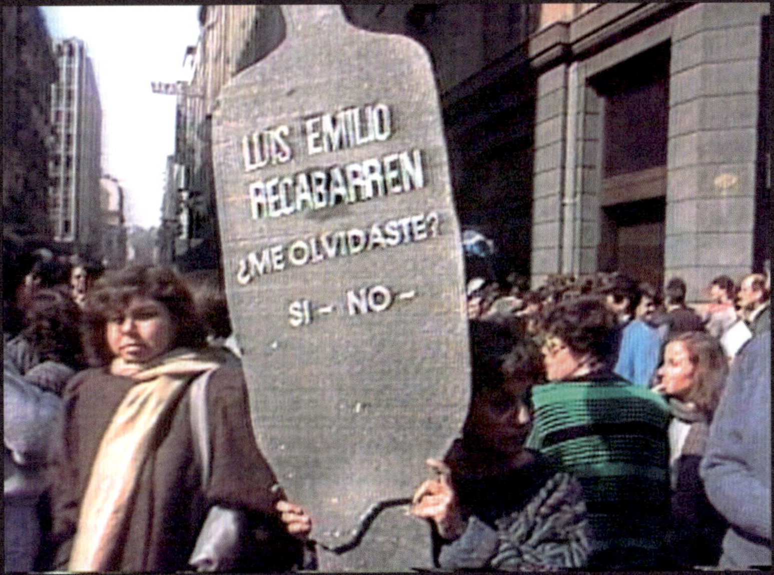
LUIS EMILIO
RECABARREN
¿ME OLVIDASTE?
SI – NO –

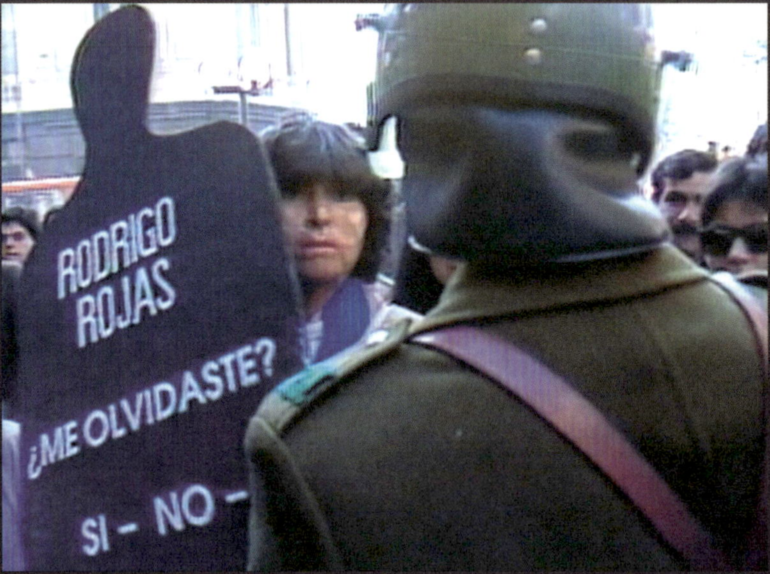
RODRIGO
ROJAS
¿ME OLVIDASTE?
SI - NO -

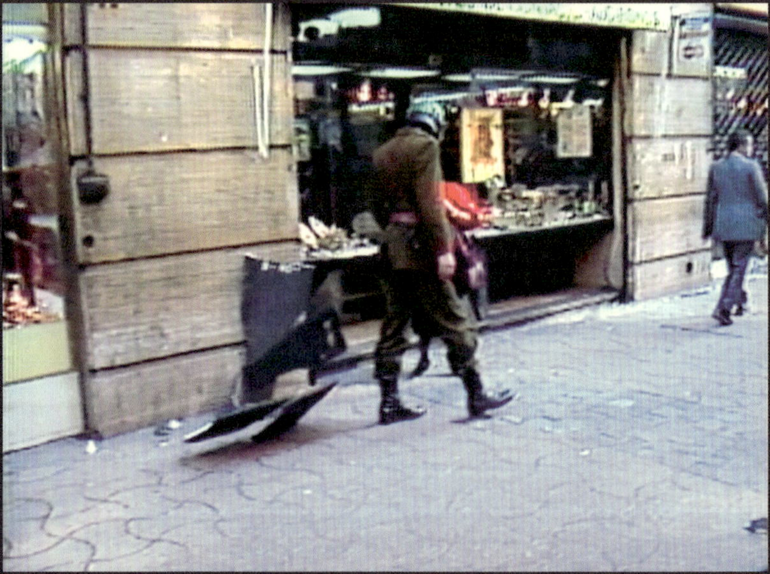

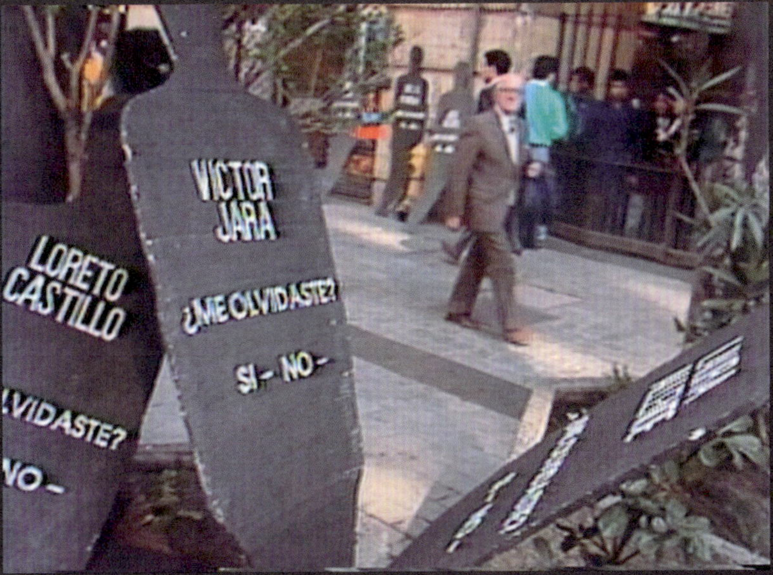
VICTOR
JARA
¿ME OLVIDASTE?
SI - NO -
LORETO
CASTILLO

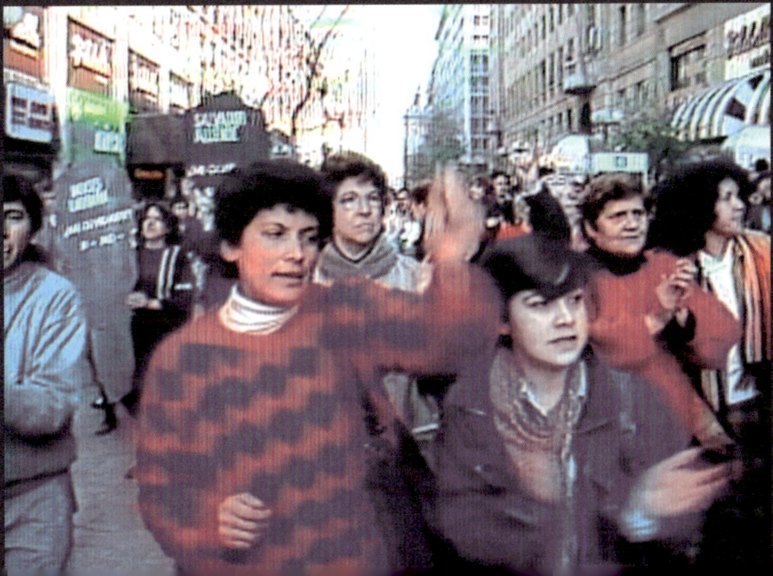

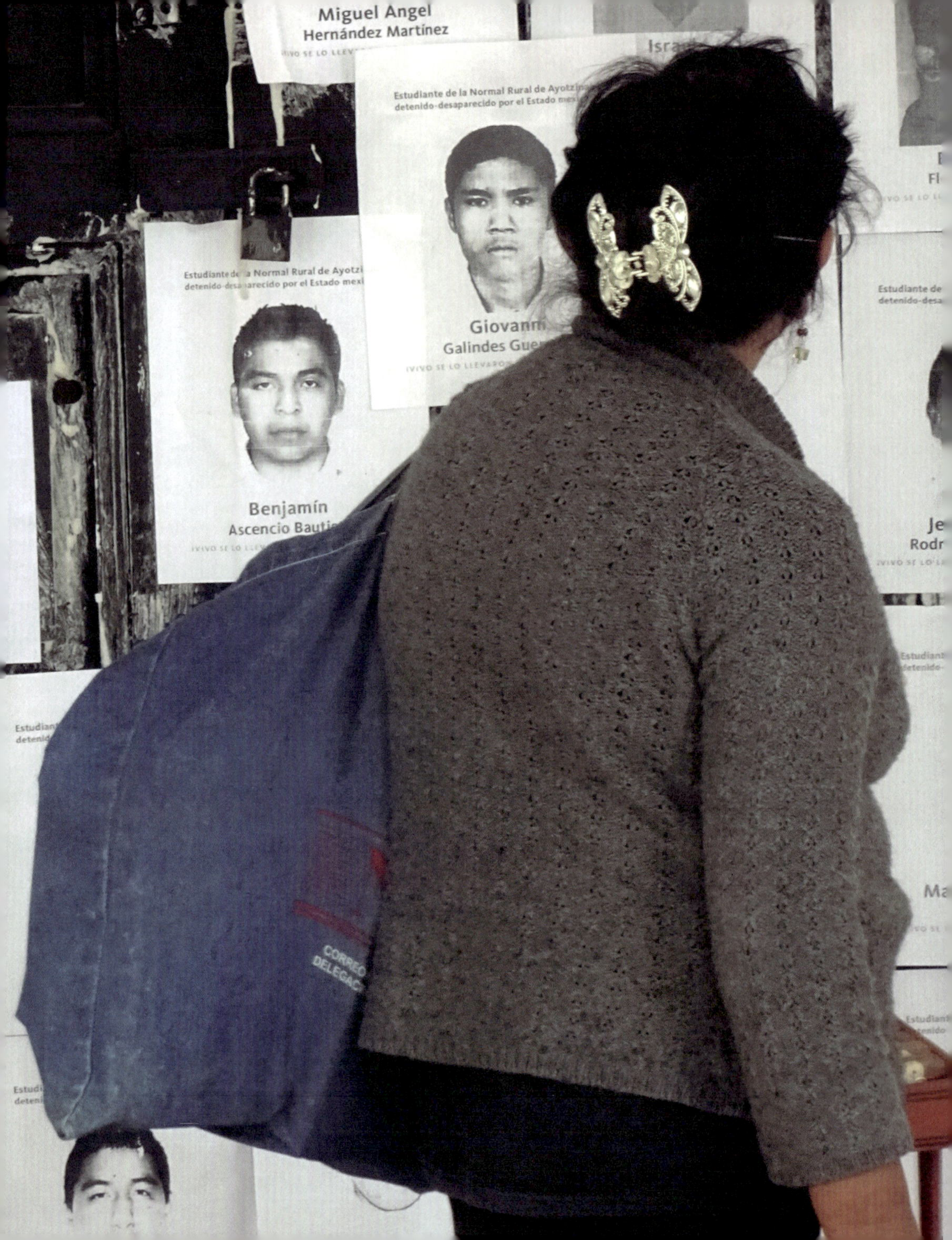
Miguel Angel
Hernández Martínez
Benjamín

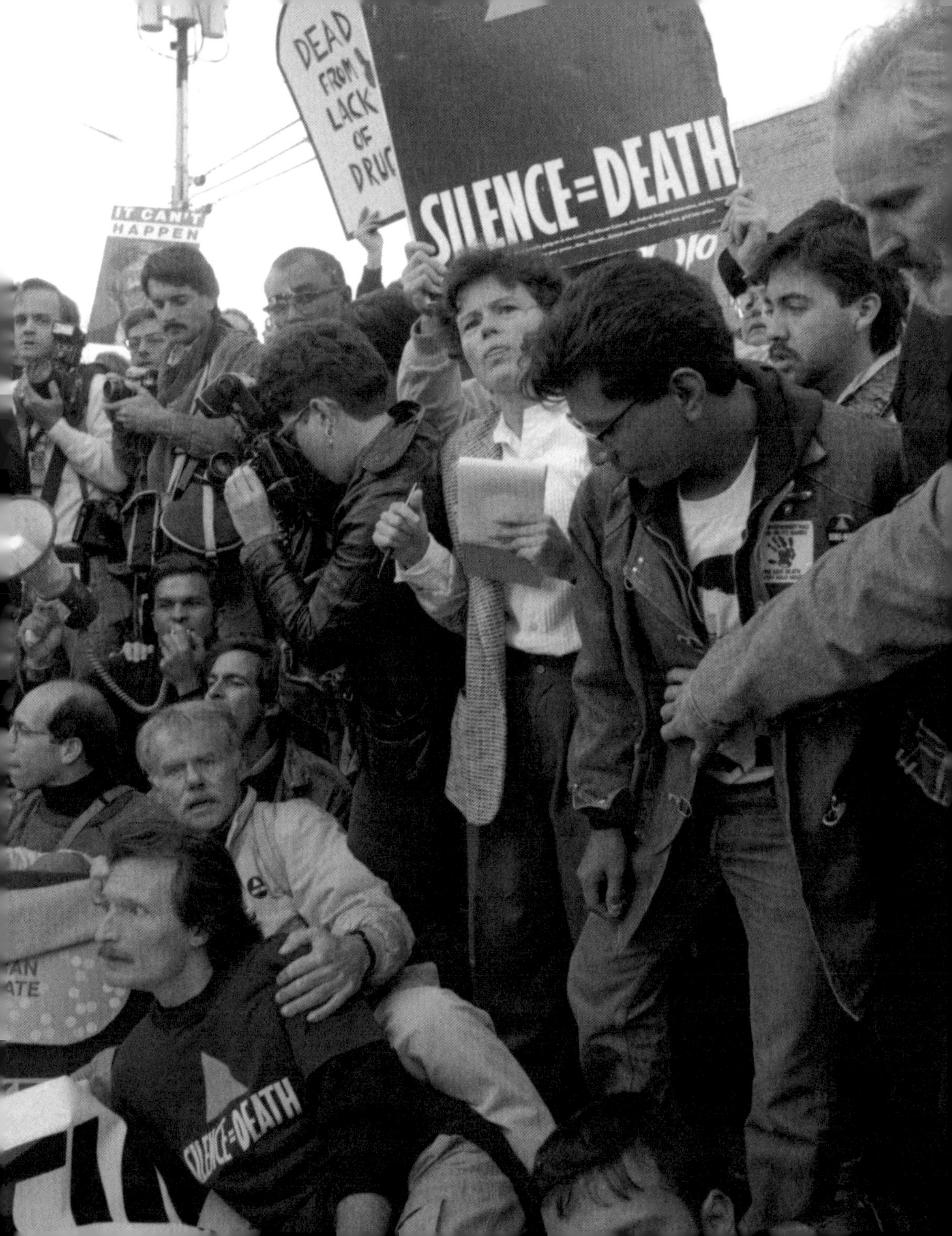
DEAD FROM LACK OF DRU
SILENCE=DEATH
IT CAN'T HAPPEN
SILENCE=DEATH

Pratibha Parmar

Memory Pictures, 1989
Video, color, sound
Running time: 24 minutes
Courtesy of Kali Films

Pratibha Parmar (British, b. 1955) is a filmmaker, writer, and artist whose work and humanitarian activism have brought attention to marginalized groups of people worldwide. Born in Nairobi, Kenya, she was raised in the United Kingdom, where she attended Bradford University for her BA and the Center for Contemporary Cultural Studies, Birmingham University, for graduate school. Parmar has made a number of award-winning films, including *A Place of Rage* (1991), about African American women's role in the civil rights movement, which was named Best Historical Documentary by the National Black Programming Consortium. Her acclaimed feature film, *Nina's Heavenly Delights* (2006), won the Wolfe Award for Best Feature Film at the Fresno Film Festival, Best Feature Film at Cineffable (France), and Best International Feature Film at the Tampa International Gay & Lesbian Film Festival. Her feature documentary film *Alice Walker: Beauty in Truth*, a definitive biography of the Pulitzer Prize–winning author Alice Walker, was screened on American Masters (PBS) and by the BBC, and has won several film festival awards. Parmar is Associate Professor in the Film Program at California College of the Arts, San Francisco, and is currently working on a hybrid documentary film on Andrea Dworkin.

THAT MOMENT OF EMERGENCE

by Pratibha Parmar

One of my concerns as a filmmaker is to challenge the normalizing and universalizing tendencies within the predominantly white lesbian and gay communities—to assert the diversity of cultural and racial identities within the umbrella category of gay and lesbian. There is a need also to redefine *community*, and just as there isn't a homogeneous black community, similarly, there isn't a monolithic lesbian and gay community.

In my video *Memory Pictures,* and my films *Flesh and Paper* and *Khush,* I interrogate Asian gay and lesbian identities in ways which point to the complexities that we occupy as lesbians and gays of color. I explore our histories of diaspora, the memories of migration and upheaval, the search for an integration of our many selves, and the celebration of "us," our differences, and our eroticisms.

It is a condition of these postmodernist times that we all live heterogeneous realities, constructing our sense of selves through the hybridity of cultural practices, and this is inevitably reflected in the aesthetic form employed in my work. The form itself needs to be interrogated as much as the content, and by using a combination of styles and narratives—for instance, documentary realism, poetry, dramatic reconstructions, experimental, autobiographical—I attempt to enunciate the nuances of our subjectivities in my work. Furthermore, the influences of the mass media and popular culture inevitably find their way into the work in a self-conscious way. The four-minute video *Bhangra Jig,* commissioned by Channel 4 as a "television intervention" piece to celebrate Glasgow as the cultural capital of Europe for 1991, borrows unashamedly from advertising codes and pop promos.

In the film *Khush,* which I made for Channel 4's lesbian and gay series *Out on Tuesday,* one of my strategies was to use a diverse range of visual modes. So, for instance, my reworking of a classical dance sequence from an old Indian popular film utilizes the strategy of disrupting the given heterosexual codes. In the original film the female dancer's act is intercut with a male gaze, but for *Khush* I reedited this sequence and took out the male gaze. I reused this sequence with scenarios of two Asian women watching and enjoying this dance. The gaze and the spectator became inverted. Clearly, postmodernist interest in reworking available material gives us an opportunity to use strategies of appropriation as an assault on racism, sexism, and homophobia. It is these politicized appropriations of dominant codes and signifying systems which give us powerful weapons in the struggle for empowerment.

This hybrid aesthetic, as it has come to be known, works with and against the "tools of the master" because these are tools which we, as cultural activists and artists, have appropriated and reformulated with our diasporic imaginations. In *Bhangra Jig* this was precisely my aim: to allude to Glasgow's history as the second biggest city of the British Empire, as reflected in the city's architectural signs and symbols. At the same time, I juxtapose against these memories of the colonial carnage the vibrancy of our cultures of resistance: Bhangra music and dance as signifying practices of Asian youth culture, crossovers of reggae, soul, and traditional agrarian Indian music and dance. For *Bhangra Jig* to be shown several times within one week on British television (known for its history of stereotyping and the invisibility of self-determined imagery of Asian people) not only disrupts dominant ideas of European culture, but also offers new meanings of what constitute national cultures and identities.

Just as much as I distance myself from any notion of an essentialist lesbian or black aesthetic, so, too, do I reject the idea that I am forever relegated to the confines of an outsider looking in. Lesbians of color around the world are asserting our visions through film and video, and our creative efforts can only but grow in the twenty-first century as the map continues to be redrawn with our imaginations.

Pratibha Parmar, excerpt from "That Moment of Emergence," first published in *Queer Looks*, edited by Martha Gever, Pratibha Parmar, and John Greyson (New York; London: Routledge, 1993), 9–11.

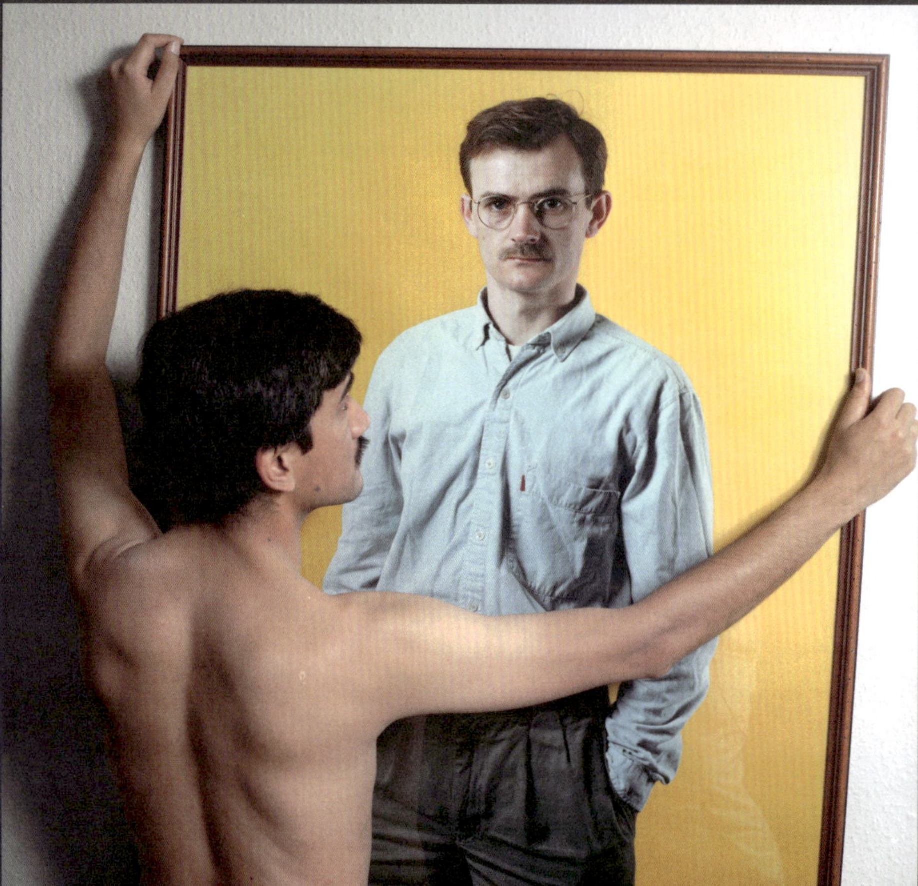

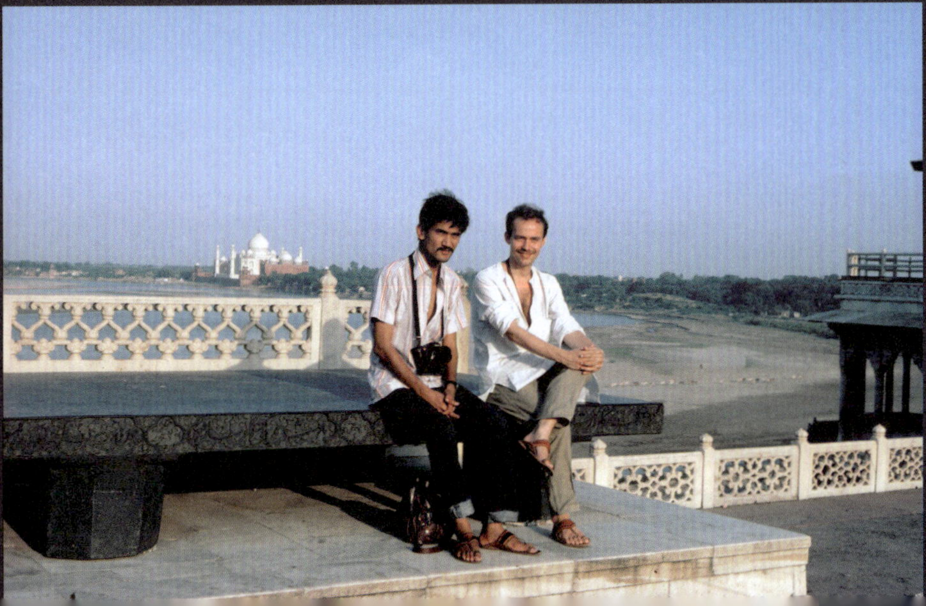

Dara Birnbaum

Tiananmen Square: Break-In Transmission, 1990
Five-channel video, color, four channels of stereo sound, surveillance switcher, and custom-designed support system
Running time: looped
Courtesy of Marian Goodman Gallery, New York

Dara Birnbaum (American, b. 1946) received a bachelor of architecture from Carnegie Mellon University, Pittsburgh, and a BFA in painting from the San Francisco Art Institute. A retrospective exhibition of her work was organized in 2009 by the Stedelijk Museum voor Actuele Kunst, Ghent, Belgium, and also traveled to Museu Serralves, Porto, Portugal. Her work has been exhibited at the Whitney Museum of American Art, New York; the Museo Nacional Centro de Arte Reina Sofia, Madrid; the Museo d'Art Contemporani de Barcelona; Kunsthalle Wien and Museum Moderner Kunst Stiftung Ludwig Wien, Vienna; The Metropolitan Museum of Art, New York; Moderna Museet, Stockholm; the National Museum of Modern Art, Tokyo; the Museum of Modern Art, New York; the Museum of Contemporary Art, Los Angeles; the San Francisco Museum of Modern Art; Centre Georges Pompidou, Paris; Castello di Rivoli, Turin; and Tate Gallery, London. She has participated in Documenta 7, 8, and 9, Kassel. She is the recipient of numerous awards, including a Certificate in Recognition of Service and Contribution to the Arts, Harvard University (1988); TV Picture Prize, International Festival of Video and Electronic Arts, Locarno, Switzerland (1991); the American Film Institute's Maya Deren Award for Independent Film and Video Artists (1987); and several National Endowment for the Arts awards.

CONVERSATION: DARA BIRNBAUM AND HANS ULRICH OBRIST

HANS ULRICH OBRIST: It would be interesting if you talked a little bit about your *Tiananmen Square: Break-In Transmission* (1990). . . .

DARA BIRNBAUM: *Tiananmen Square: Break-In Transmission* came after *Rio Videowall.* In *Rio* we have this television box as one of twenty-five units. Thus, you could symbolically relate the box to a pixel as well as a television: microcosm and macrocosm. The television image now breaks through its "frame." Previously, the image was contained within an individual box, an individuated frame; now the image was being pushed out into a multiframe matrix, stretching past its previous boundaries.

For *Tiananmen Square,* it was almost the opposite. I made very small boxes, a landscape of imagery formed by LCD monitors, which present an image that you can see only frontally, and if you go to the side, it ghosts out. That's the mechanics of it. At first you see the small monitors as if they were lights hanging from the ceiling, as if information is coming down at you—it's not putting video work on a pedestal. I think I had the impulse to hang it like this because the feeling was already, as it was with *Transmission Tower,* that the information is coming from out there. At first, museums and institutions chose to contextualize video by building a platform for it, a base for a sculptural event. You turn the monitor on, you see the image. But here it was coming like lights—I thought they had to be small and similar to utility lights. At a distance, you only see light. Only when you come closer do you see image. Given this necessary proximity of the viewer, he/she has to travel through that space to see many small images.

There is, from my point of view, no "eyewitness news." A slogan from Channel 7 in New York, ABC, one of the biggest networks in the United States, goes, "We bring you Eyewitness News." No, you bring to me, obviously, a mediated portion of news. So here you would more appropriately say ABC's version of the news of Tiananmen Square. They own that news; you have to buy it from them. If you go and say, "I really want to do this work and rerepresent the news," they say: "Oh, who will you make it for? Will you make it for the state of New York? Then we will charge you one rate per minute. Will you make it for the whole of the United States? Oh, you also want to go to Europe? Which countries?" You even have a rate now for the cosmos, for the universe. The networks already know where this is all going. I think the most important thing for me in my work has been to uncover the mechanism of television. To question it and then to look at this larger mechanism developing—the communication, the networking. Television has projected itself into space already. In the United States there's some good science fiction about what happens when it goes out there. *Wonder Woman,* you know, will eventually reach someone on a distant planet who will see the show in a different time and space than our own. So I think with the work *Tiananmen Square,* it was to say, "You've made an awfully large image of this event for me on television." I have to deal with that size, and with the fact that there's really no unity in that image.

HUO: So in *Tiananmen Square: Break-In Transmission,* you show different views of the events?

DB: Different views, from a "garagey" song composed by the students, "The Wound of History," to the exact moment that for me was a very important moment in the history of television—when CNN and CBS were taken off the air, when they were told, "You will cease to exist in this way." The Chinese government shut down satellite transmissions, knowing that they would eventually crack down on the students. The major networks knew that any minute these demonstrations would go violent. That's what everyone was waiting for, the rupture. Dan Rather is there. They have the image of him, headphones on, a big satellite dish in the background. What he's hearing in his headphones is, "They just broke off transmission of CNN." And he's hearing from their field reporters, "We're getting the first images of violence, of the police cracking down on people." At CNN's headquarters, when I show you that imagery, rerepresent it, you see that in the newsroom, when the government comes in to stop the broadcast, the news team tries to push the government representatives back out; they're trying physically to say: "No, what are you doing? You can't stop us!" At CBS, Rather makes it a diplomatic moment. He stalls. He says to the government as they come in: "I'm sorry, I don't understand. Oh, you need to shut us down." What he's doing is buying time. He bought one-sixteenth of a second or so, just enough time to get out the first images of violence to audiences worldwide. That's my interest—to look at historic moments and how they affect us. I think I want to leave behind a kind of totem. I want to leave behind pieces of the history of this crazy, industrialized telecommunications system that affects all of us. Maybe it's the telecommunications that are making the envelope-like membrane we were talking about earlier.

HUO: I thought *Tiananmen Square* is also like a parkour, but a parkour where there isn't any given path. It's a parkour where every viewer finds her or his own path.

DB: That is true. Each viewer can find the images he or she wishes to look at. But dominating the small images—the loops—there is a large monitor in the background, and there is a surveillance switcher. The surveillance switcher is going around the room, taking grabs from these small images and randomly putting them up on the large monitor. So if you're viewing an image, that image may be taken by the surveillance switcher. It can be taken away from you and all of a sudden put on to the large monitor, as TV. The work is about control. When are you in control of your own representation, or when is it out of your control? Do you have the ability to control it?

This text was excerpted from "Conversation: Hans Ulrich Obrist and Dara Birnbaum," *Dara Birnbaum: The Dark Matter of Media Light*, edited by Karen Kelly, Barbara Schröder, and Giel Vandecaveye (Munich: Del Monico Books/Prestel, 2010), 23–24. The interview was previously published in German in *Dara Birnbaum* (Vienna: Kunsthalle Wien, 1995) and in English in *Art Recollection: Artists' Interviews and Statements in the Nineties* (Danilo Montanari, Exit, and Zona Archives, 1997).

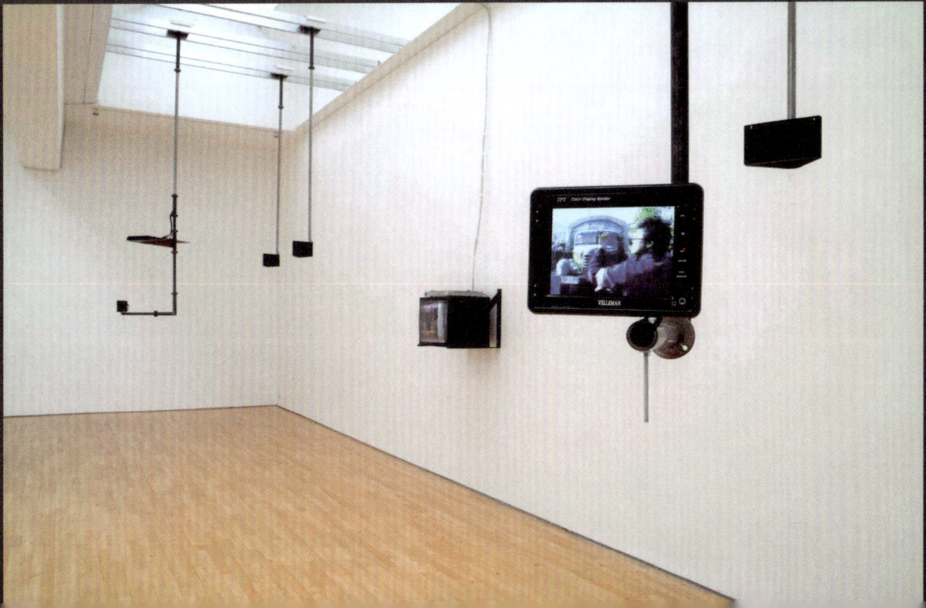
VELLEMAN

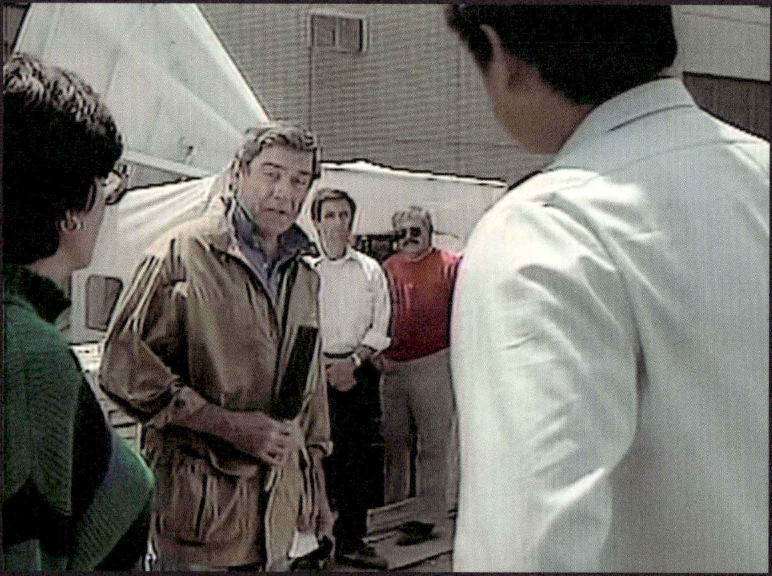

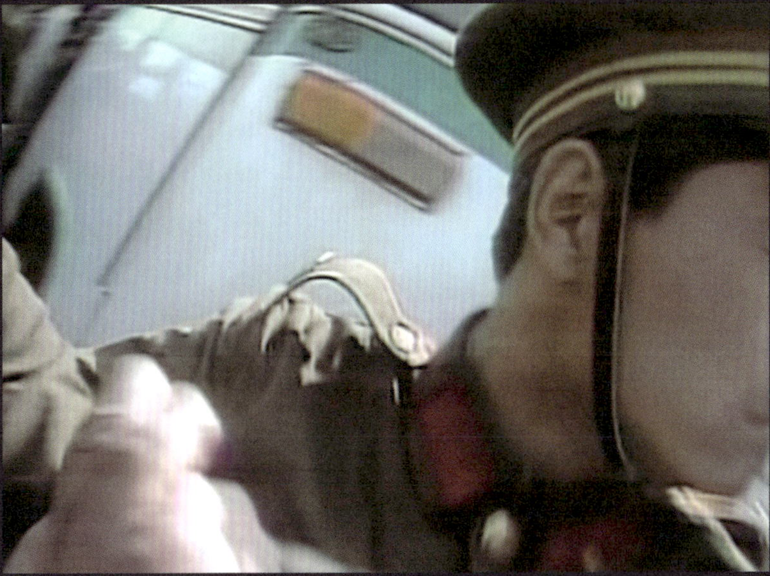

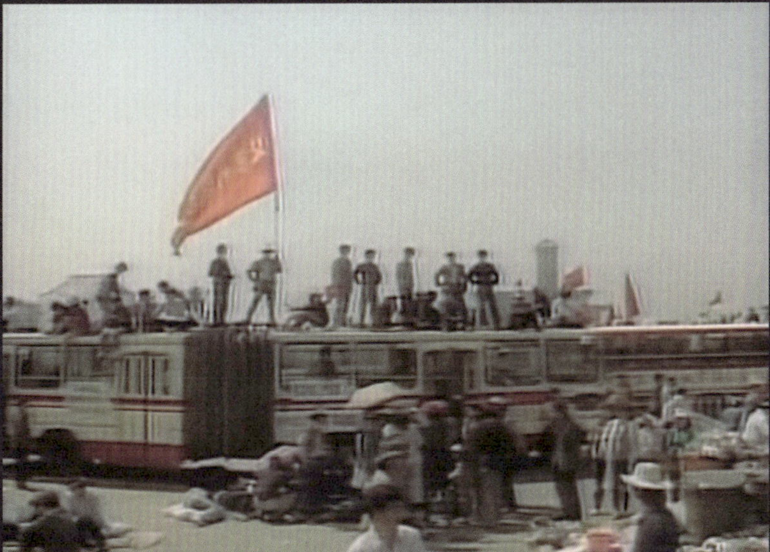

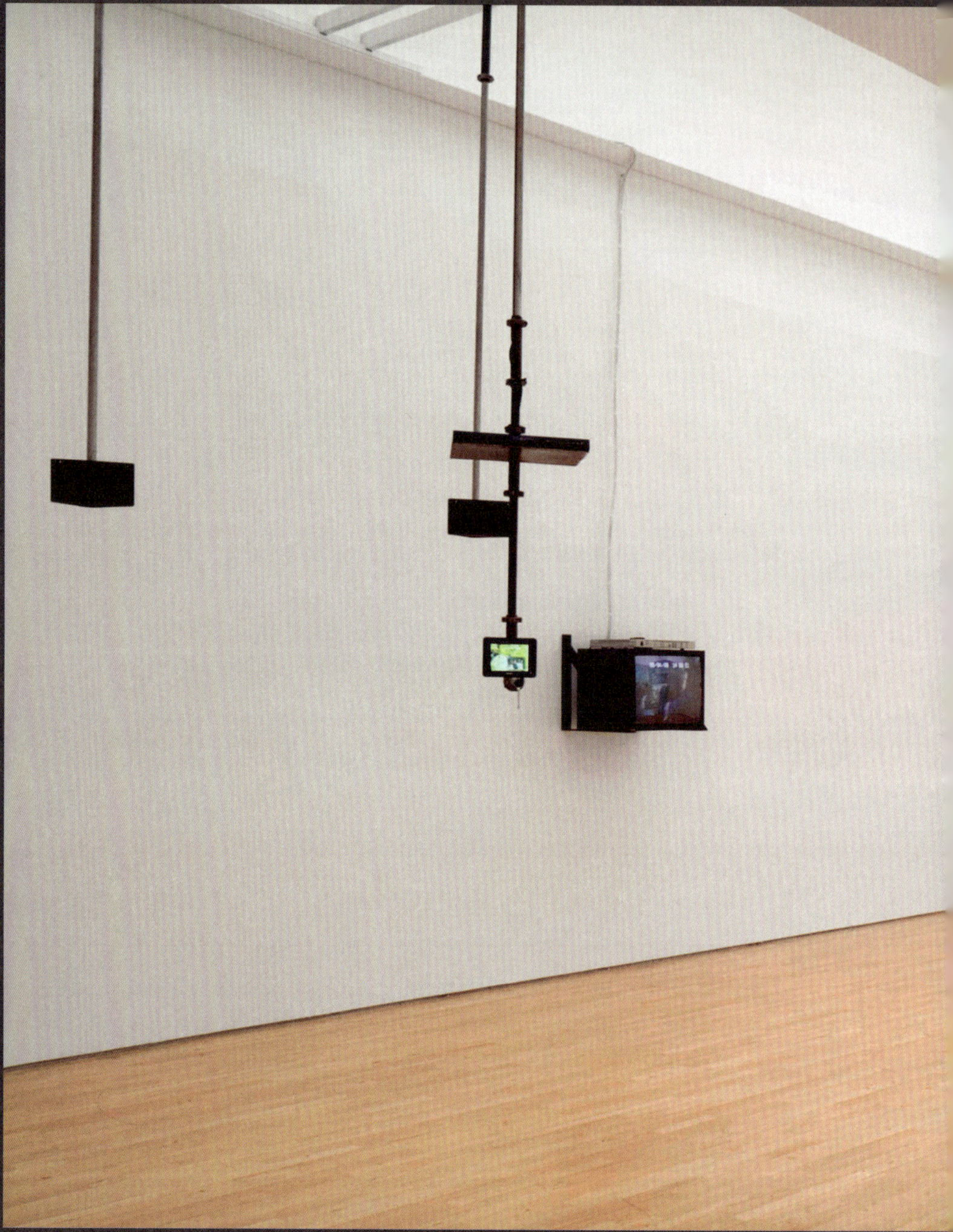

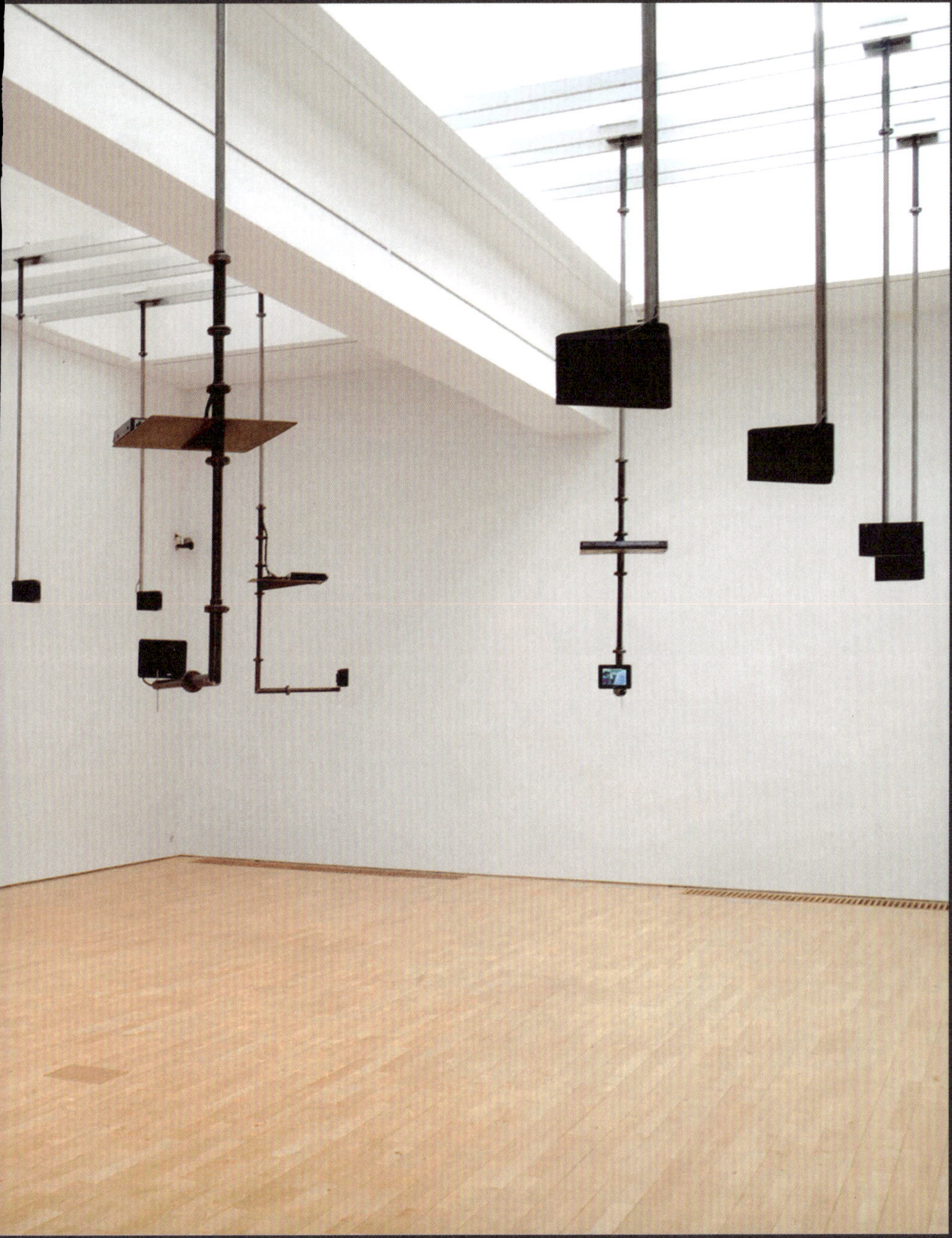

Catherine Gund and Zoe Leonard

Keep Your Laws off My Body, 1990
Video, black and white, sound
Running time: 13 minutes
Courtesy of the artists, Aubin Pictures, and Hauser & Wirth, New York

Catherine (Saalfield) Gund (American, b. 1965) was born in Geelong, Australia, and is a New York–based, Emmy-nominated filmmaker. She is a graduate of Brown University and the Whitney Independent Study Program. In 1989 she cofounded the media collective DIVA TV, which documented the AIDS activism of ACT UP in New York. In 1996 Gund founded Aubin Pictures. She has produced and directed many films, including *A Touch of Greatness* (2004); *What's on Your Plate?* (2009); *Born to Fly* (2014); *Dispatches from Cleveland* (2017); and *Chavela* (2017), which have been screened around the world in festivals, theaters, and schools, and on PBS, the Discovery Channel, and the Sundance Channel.

Zoe Leonard (American, b. 1961) was born in Liberty, New York. Leonard has had solo exhibitions at institutions such as the Museum of Modern Art, New York; Dia:Beacon, Beacon, New York; the Chinati Foundation, Marfa, Texas; Pinakothek der Moderne, Munich; the Camden Arts Centre, London; and Kunsthalle Basel, Switzerland. She was included in Documenta 9 and 12, Kassel; as well as Whitney Biennials in 1993, 1997, and 2014. Leonard received the Anonymous Was A Woman award (2005) and the Bucksbaum Award from the Whitney Museum of American Art, New York (2014).

INTERVIEW WITH CATHERINE GUND

by Sarah Schulman

SARAH SCHULMAN: Tell me about *Keep Your Laws off My Body*.

CATHERINE GUND: It was 1989. *Keep Your Laws off My Body* was a place where the Whitney Independent Study Program and ACT UP [AIDS Coalition to Unleash Power] came together for me. I made the installation in collaboration with Zoe Leonard, who was not in the Whitney program and hadn't even finished college, but was also feeling liberated by these modes of expression: photography, video, and reading. And she was so smart and so hungry for stuff. We made one project, a video project, together, called *Keep Your Laws off My Body*, that was black-and-white film footage that she'd shot on a Super 8 camera downtown at the Target City Hall demonstration. It was basically just footage of rows and rows and rows of cops. They were in such abundance. And they were so organized. And it was so intentionally intimidating. But when Zoe started filming them, it was just sort of like, *Oh, there's another one.* They were all wearing rubber gloves—dishwashing gloves—things like that, which made them start to appear silly. Ridiculous even. One of my favorite chants was "Your gloves don't match your shoes."

So Zoe and I intercut that footage with us rolling around in her sparse, white-painted loft, or apartment, with a white bathtub, and we were sort of on her bed and kissing. And my hair was blonde and very short, so unless you knew it was two women you might not even have realized that. The footage is softly focused and handheld. We actually filmed it ourselves while we were rolling around. And then, throughout, there is graphically imposed text of different laws that affected bodies, not only laws about HIV or AIDS, but also about gay and lesbian issues, about reproductive rights, about pornography. We tried to make it not-too-boring legalese, but instead, a brief sentence stating, for example, what the Hyde Amendment was.

Then we created an installation [for *The Center Show* at the New York Lesbian and Gay Community Center], so we silk-screened all these laws onto the bed sheets of a single cot. There was a flash of interest from the Home section of the *New York Times*, [but we were told] "you'd have to make a lot of them," for not very much money [in order] to sell them. But I did like this idea of people actually sleeping in these sheets, with all these laws about their bodies. I thought that would have been really cool.

We had the video playing on a big television set on the floor by the cot with the sheets, and there was a surveillance camera pointed down on the bed and another monitor playing the images from the surveillance camera. So if anybody got on the bed, got under the sheets, or read the sheets, or touched them, or stood near them, they would see themselves in the layers.

We were trying to make broader connections. For most of us, it was already a broader issue than drugs for people with HIV manifested in ACT UP's demonstrations and among the constituents. This was one example of the broader issues coming to play.

SS: Looking back, what would you say was ACT UP's greatest achievement?

CG: I guess the greatest achievement, for me, was being part of something that was about people speaking for themselves, and people with HIV getting to have a voice and insinuate themselves into the decisions that were affecting their lives.

This text was excerpted from "Interview of Catherine Gund, April 20, 2007," 53–54; 63–64. Courtesy of ACT UP Oral History Project: Sarah Schulman and Jim Hubbard. Revised 2017.

INTERVIEW WITH ZOE LEONARD

by Sarah Schulman

SARAH SCHULMAN: Were you politically active in any way before ACT UP [AIDS Coalition to Unleash Power]?

ZOE LEONARD: No. No. No, because I didn't go to—I had this idea about social justice. I had a sort of idea of personal ethics, as we talked about with my family, and that was really clear. But I didn't go to college, and so I didn't have any idea of organized political resistance. I'd heard about the civil rights movement, of course, and I'd grown up in New York in the sixties and seventies, so I understood what Malcolm X was and all that. But I'd never been to a protest. I'd never been to a march. I'd never been to a meeting. I didn't know what any of that was. I'd never read any political—I didn't know *Robert's Rules of Order,* and I didn't know words like *hegemony*. I was totally—that was all new to me, and ACT UP politicized me.

SS: But you were in this world of innovative artists, which was also a mixed queer world, and at a time when both of those things were highly politicized, even though not in an organized way.

ZL: Right.

SS: Were you having those conversations, the "art and queer" conversation and the "queer and political" conversation, with your friends?

ZL: In my teens and really early twenties, I was just kind of a punk rocker. We were just nuts, and that is deeply a political movement. Punk and new wave and no wave all came out of a certain kind of political stance, but it wasn't about organizing—it was about being mad, and really good music. So I think I was antiestablishment in a really deep and comfortable way, like that's what felt right to me, but I didn't have an organized sort of political mind. I didn't understand about organizing.

In terms of having those conversations around queer, I wasn't having those conversations about being a maker. I was making my work, and I wasn't really thinking about the politics in my work and the queer political potential in my work. I think some of it was there just because it was part of my gaze, but it wasn't something that I was consciously nurturing or bringing out. I think it was embedded rather than being consciously worked out.

When I first went to ACT UP, it was unlike anything I'd ever experienced before. I didn't know that language; I didn't know that way of thinking. I wasn't at home as an activist looking for a cause. I was at home, and my friends started dying, and I became political, and then I understood there was this whole form that people used to resist, but I hadn't really understood that. I'd been attracted to counterculture images of the sixties, but in my own experience, no, I had a different relationship to being an artist.

Also, there are things that came up for me through ACT UP. I just finished this retrospective show, and it was really interesting to look back over the thirty years of my work so far and to remember that there was this moment while I was in ACT UP when I realized there was this incredible chasm between the work that I was making in my studio and the work that I was doing in ACT UP, and that there was some sort of trajectory that I was on [that] got really interrupted in a way and felt really inappropriate. I was taking aerial photographs. I was really interested in a very different set of issues.

Being in ACT UP and having the experience, not just being in ACT UP, I mean the more base thing of having so many friends with AIDS and so many friends dying and then being in ACT UP and understanding the politics of that, made me want to understand how to apply my voice in a different way as an artist, and it took me a while to figure out how to do that. There were so many artists, like Adam Rollston and Don Moffett and Gran Fury, of course, and all the individuals in Gran Fury, whose work was inherently connected. I can see his face, and I'm skipping his name right now. Vince Gagliostro. And my voice felt really different, like the work that I made wasn't graphic in that way. I didn't use tacks, I didn't use silkscreen, I didn't use acid colors. My work was much, much quieter. It took me a few years to understand how to develop my individual voice into a politicized queer voice, and that happened through ACT UP.

SS: Had you ever collaborated as an artist before ACT UP?

ZL: Not really. Not formally, no.

SS: I just want to ask you one more question about the pre-AIDS era and yourself. Because, first of all, in ACT UP you were involved in so many different things, and you come from urbanity, from being an artist, you come from a lot of things that fed into ACT UP. So you were on your own artistic trajectory and you had your own sense of politics that was not organizational. What about queer identity or the condition of the American queer pre-AIDS? Do you know where you were in that regard?

ZL: Yes, yes. That's a good question. I considered myself bisexual pretty much instantly in my teens. I had boyfriends and slept with men or boys and also slept with girls really early on, and that just kind of felt like my identity. Then I fell in love, when I was twenty-three, with a woman, and I was like: "Oh, I get it. I'm gay. I'm queer."

Sort of throughout—it's so hard to create language around that, because in my life I've had relationships, as you know, with Gregg [Bordowitz]. During the ACT UP years I had relationships with both men and women. So, at the time, I think really shortly before ACT UP, I think I was twenty-six when I first went to ACT UP, and I was with Simone for two years, and then we split up. So although I'd been identified as bisexual and I'd been active with women for a while, I hadn't really come out until I was twenty-three and really been like, "Oh, there [are] all these lesbian books to read and there's all this lesbian culture." The culture that I'd been a part of was a kind of queer culture, because it was just a radical culture, like the Mudd Club and punk rock and art. There were the Bush Tetras and there were queer bands, but I hadn't really been a part of a separate gay culture. I hadn't really known about it. I hadn't been particularly attracted to it. It was a much more heterogeneous kind of situation, and I think in my early twenties, maybe like twenty-one, I started going to the Cubbyhole and investigating more of an explicitly gay or queer identity.

So when I walked into ACT UP, I identified as—I don't think anybody identified as queer then. I identified as gay, so as a dyke, as a lesbian. So, yes, just the whole language and perception, I think, of identities was so different then. And it's so interesting now, the term *queer* and that whole terminology that came out of ACT UP and came out of the work that we did and is being reconfigured by a new generation now. Actually, that definition and the multiplicity that it allows for feels like the definition that would have worked for me all along. It's really interesting, and I love what has come out of the work that we did and the issues that we kind of hammered out.

SS: So you created the context that you needed.

ZL: Yes, I think we did, yes.

This text was excerpted from "Interview of Zoe Leonard, January 13, 2010," 9–13. Courtesy of ACT UP Oral History Project: Sarah Schulman and Jim Hubbard.

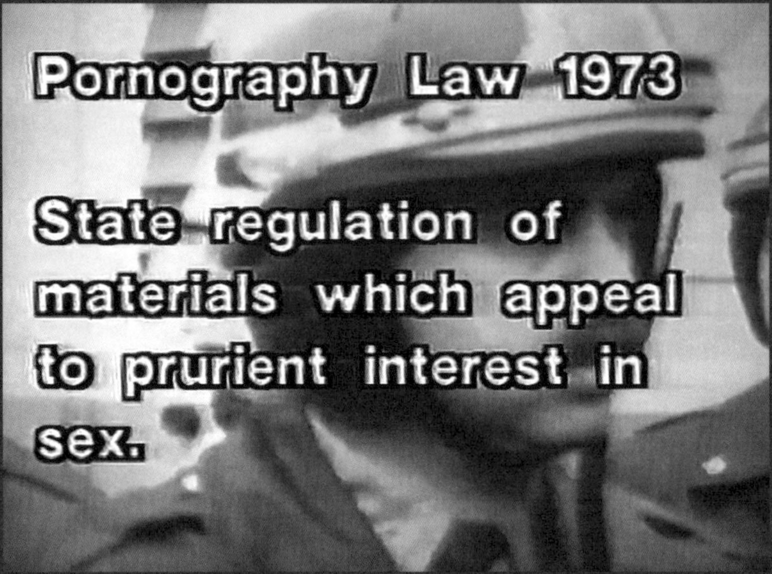
Pornography Law 1973
State regulation of materials which appeal to prurient interest in sex.

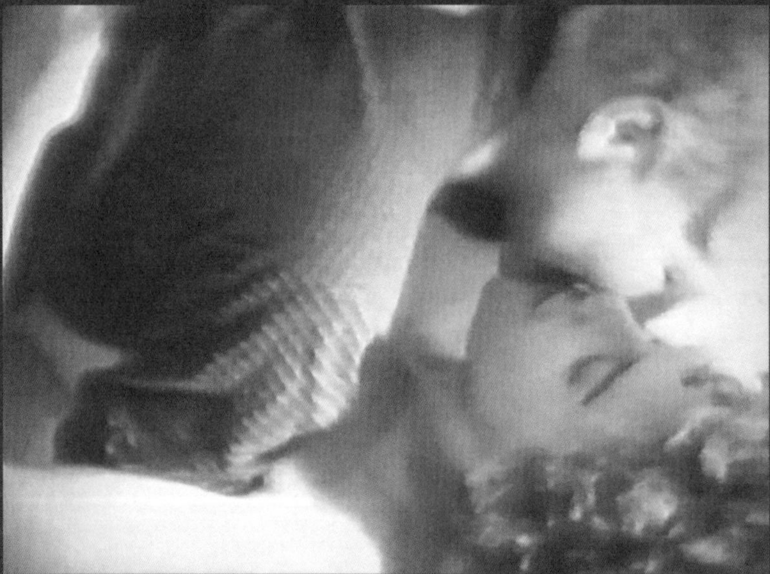

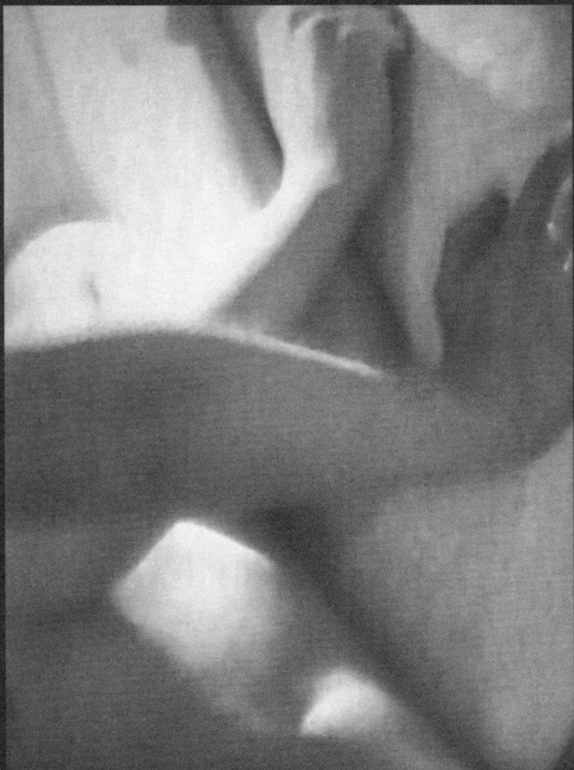

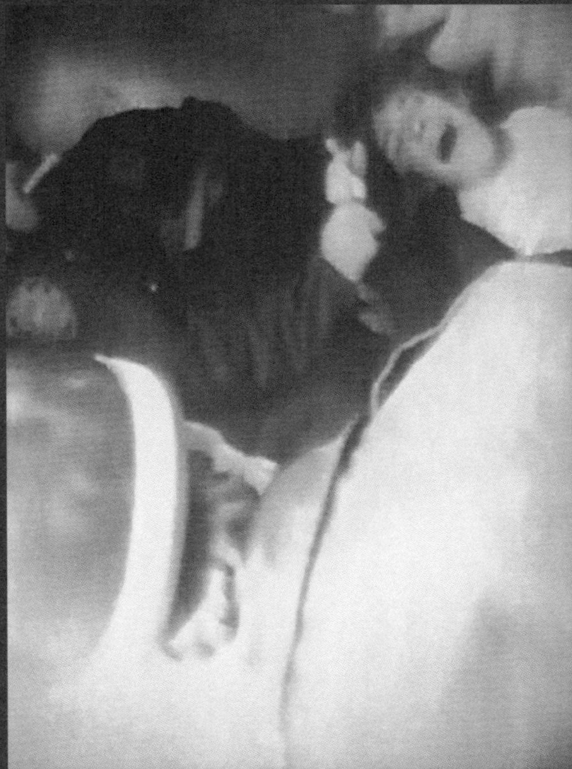

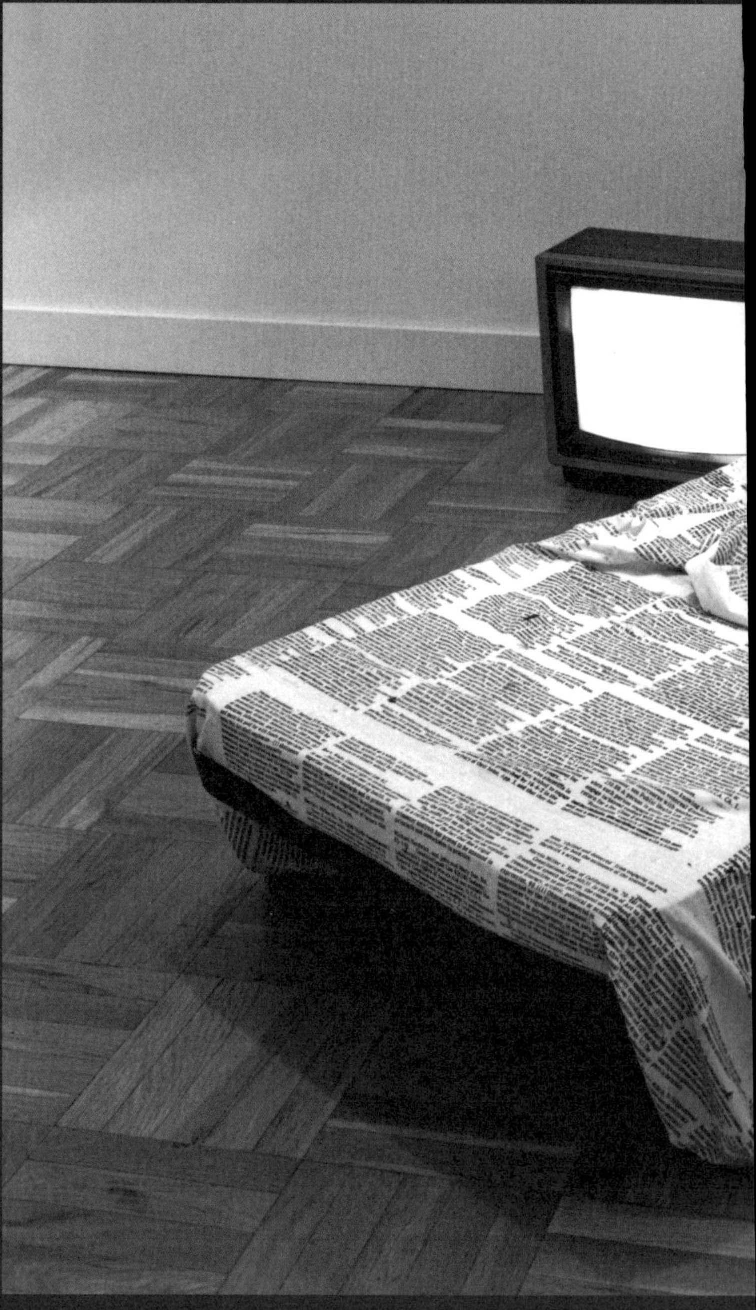

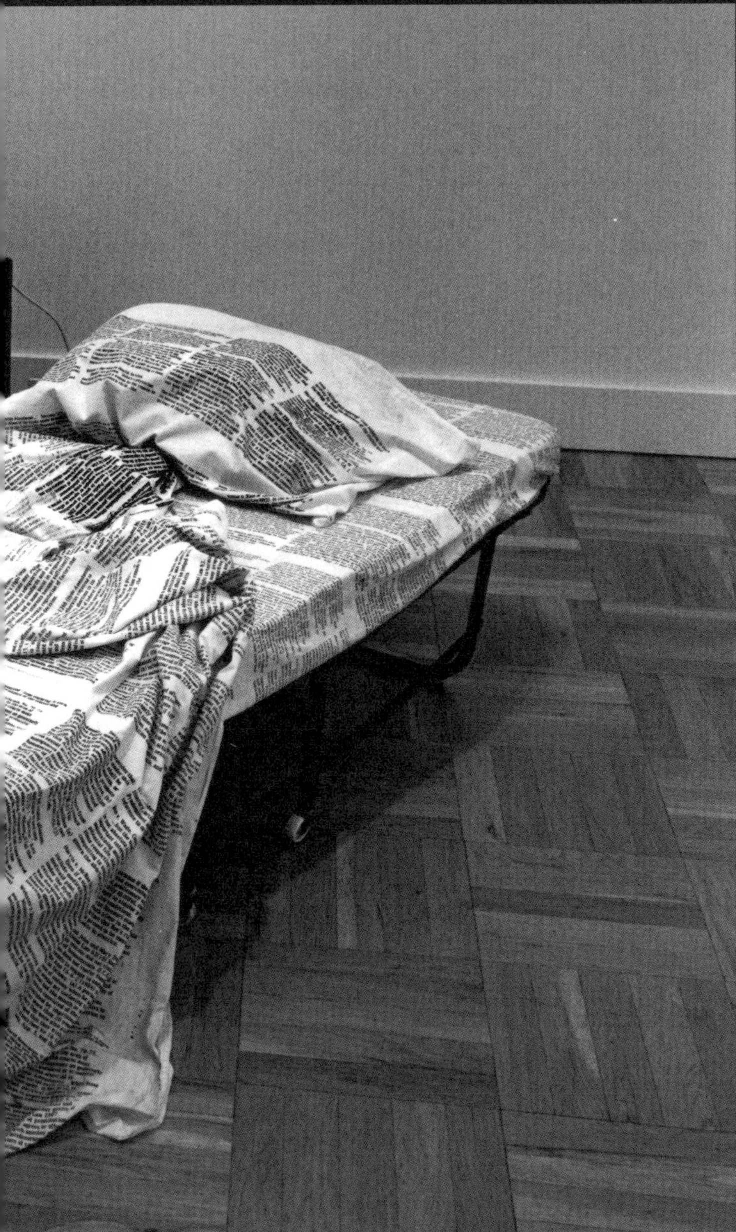

Coco Fusco and Paula Heredia

The Couple in the Cage: A Guatinaui Odyssey, 1993
Video, color, sound
Running time: 31 minutes
Courtesy of Video Data Bank and Alexander Gray Associates

Coco Fusco (American, b. 1960) received her BA from Brown University in 1982, her MA from Stanford University in 1985, and her PhD in art and visual culture from Middlesex University in 2007. Fusco is the Andrew Banks Endowed Professor of Art at the University of Florida and author of numerous publications. She was included in two Whitney Biennials (1993 and 2008), *All the World's Futures* at the 56th Venice Biennale, and at the Göteborg International Biennial for Contemporary Art (2015). She received the Greenfield Prize in Visual Art (2016), a Guggenheim Fellowship (2013), and the Absolut Art Award for Art Writing (2013).

Paula Heredia (Salvadoran, b. 1957) is a filmmaker based in New York City. She studied at the University of Costa Rica, New York University, and the State University of New York. Heredia has worked on films and television series including *Finding Christa* (1991); *Unzipped* (1995), for which she received an American Cinema Editors Eddie Award; *In Memoriam, NYC 9/11/01* (2002), for which she received an Emmy; *Alive Day Memories: Home from Iraq* (2007); *Africa Rising* (2009); *Sleepless in America* (2014); and *Beyond Borders* (2016). Heredia is the head of the international committee of New York Women in Film and Television and a member of the board of advisors of the Tribeca Film Institute's All Access program.

INTERVIEW WITH COCO FUSCO AND GUILLERMO GÓMEZ-PEÑA

by Anna Johnson

COCO FUSCO: When we created [*The Couple in the Cage: A Guatinaui Odyssey*], our original intent was not to convince people that the fiction of our being Amerindians was a reality. We understood it to be a satirical commentary both on the quincentenary celebrations and on the history of this practice of exhibiting human beings from Africa, Asia, and Latin America in Europe and the United States in zoos, theaters, and museums. When we got to Spain, more than half the people thought we really were Amerindians. Then there were others who came to watch those who were taking us seriously. There were people who were not sure whether to believe that we were real. Other people were absolutely convinced that they understood Guillermo's language, which is virtually impossible because it's a nonsense language. One man in London stood there and translated Guillermo's story for another visitor. We had a lot of sexualized reactions to us. Men in Spain put coins in the donation box to get me to dance because, as they said, they wanted to see my tits. There was a woman in Irvine who asked for a rubber glove in order to touch Guillermo and started to fondle him in a sexual manner. There were several instances where people crossed the boundaries of expected sexual behavior. I think that was provoked by us being presented as objects, by their sense of having power over us. . . .

GUILLERMO GÓMEZ-PEÑA: The boundary between ethnography and pornography. To add to what Coco has said, this endemic dual perception of the Other, as either noble savage or cannibal, has existed at the core of European and American relations since the very first encounters. We try to play very much with these dualities. When we appear in the cage, I am the cannibal; I am the warrior, this threatening masculine Other who causes fear in the viewer. Coco performs the noble savage, you know, the quiet, subdued innocent. The response people have toward her is either one of compassion or one of sexual aggression.

CF: The most hysterical reactions we had to the piece happened when we appeared at the Smithsonian. One alarmed person called the Humane Society. The Humane Society told that person that human beings were out of their jurisdiction.

The responses we had from Native Americans and Latins were more interesting. They tend to find fault with the hybridity of the contents of the cage, while Anglos take this as a sign of our lack of authenticity. In Washington, for example, there was a Native American elder from the Pueblo tribe of Arizona who was interviewed by a Smithsonian representative. He said that our performance was the most real thing about the Native Americans displayed in the whole museum. He said the installation and performance ought to be permanent to give people a very clear idea of the Native American experience. Then there was a man from El Salvador who pointed to the rubber heart hanging in the cage and told everybody, "That heart is my heart."

ANNA JOHNSON: In your performance, you presented artifacts from a fictional land, including a laptop computer, video, a bottle of Coca-Cola—poking fun at the idea that you were authentic savages from a foreign place. Could you talk about your idea of authenticity and ethnic identity?

CF: We were trying to blast this myth that the non-Western Other exists in a time and place that is completely untouched by Western civilization or that, in order to be authentic, one would have to be devoid of characteristics associated with the West. It's reasonable to say that non-Western cultures have a better understanding of Western civilization than Western civilization has of other cultures. In any case, we introduced into the cage some elements that shocked and bothered many people and became the focus of a lot of questions put to the zoo guards. People said: "How could [he] be authentic if he smokes Dunhills? How could she really know how to use a computer if she is from this undiscovered island? Why is she wearing Converse high-tops?" Everything they viewed as part of their world, they didn't want us to have. That would mean that we were inauthentic. However, if you see Conchero dancers in Mexico City, they do wear Converse high-tops and Adidas and Nikes. They probably listen to hard rock when they are not dancing to traditional music. We wanted to make fun of this very Eurocentric notion that other people operate in a pristine world untouched by Western civilization.

GGP: To me, authenticity is an obsession of Western anthropologists. When I am in Mexico, Mexicans are never concerned about this question of authenticity. However, when I am in the United States, North Americans are constantly making this artificial division between what is an "authentic" Chicano, an "authentic" Mexican, an "authentic" Native American in order to fulfill their own desires. Generally speaking, this authentic Other has to be preindustrial, has to be more tuned with their past, has to be less tainted by postmodernity, has to be more innocent, and must not live with contemporary technology. And most importantly, must have a way of making art that fulfills their stereotypes; in the case of Mexico—magical realism.

CF: This fetish about authenticity is connected to an idea that the non-Western being doesn't have a sense of reflexivity about him- or herself. I think, for example, of the videos being made now by Kayapo Indians in the Amazon. I was at a conference this year where American academics questioned the Kayapos' interest in filming themselves filming and editing. They want to talk about the process while they're making it, and that blows American academics away.

GGP: The bottom line is they don't want us to be part of the same present or the same time. They want us to operate outside history.

CF: The Kayapos aren't allowed to be self-conscious. If you can be ironic, if you can be reflexive, it's because you can think. Ethnography and anthropology have consistently negated that dimension of non-Western cultures. It would threaten the veracity of the Western observer's "information."

This text was excerpted from "Guillermo Gómez-Peña and Coco Fusco," an interview commissioned by and first published in *BOMB* magazine, no. 42 (Winter 1993), 37–38. The *BOMB* Archive can be viewed at www.bombmagazine.org.

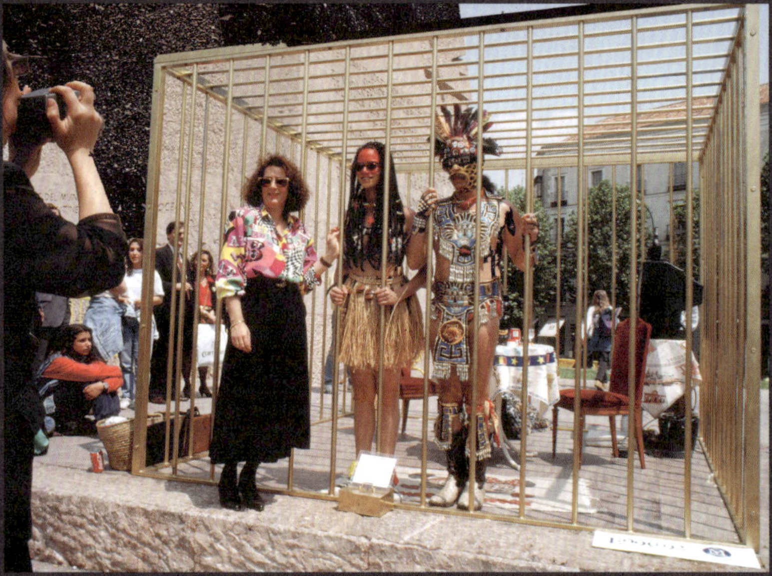

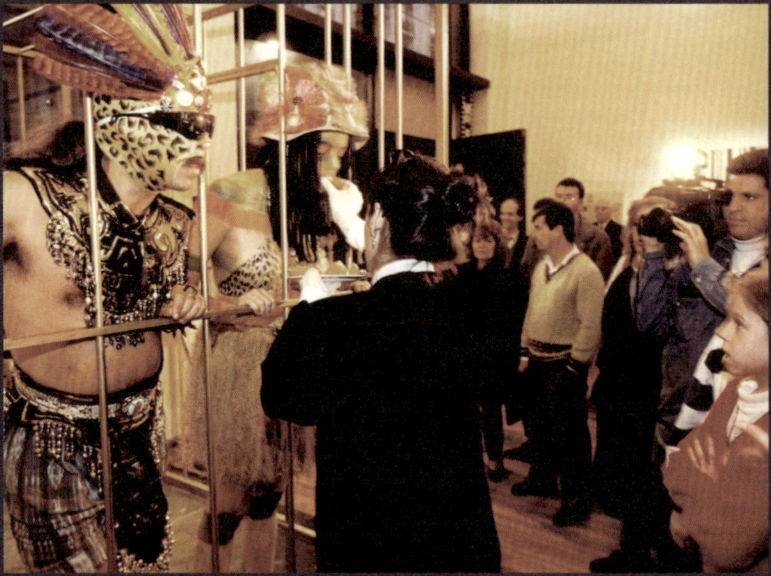

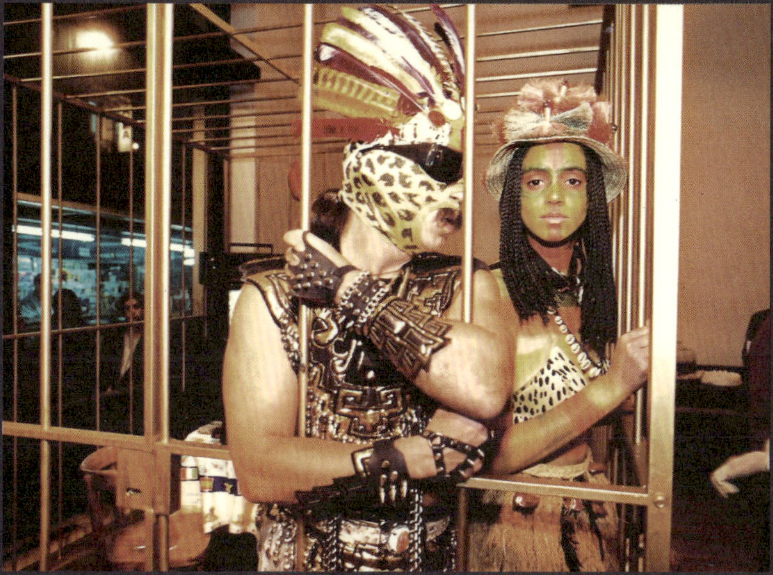

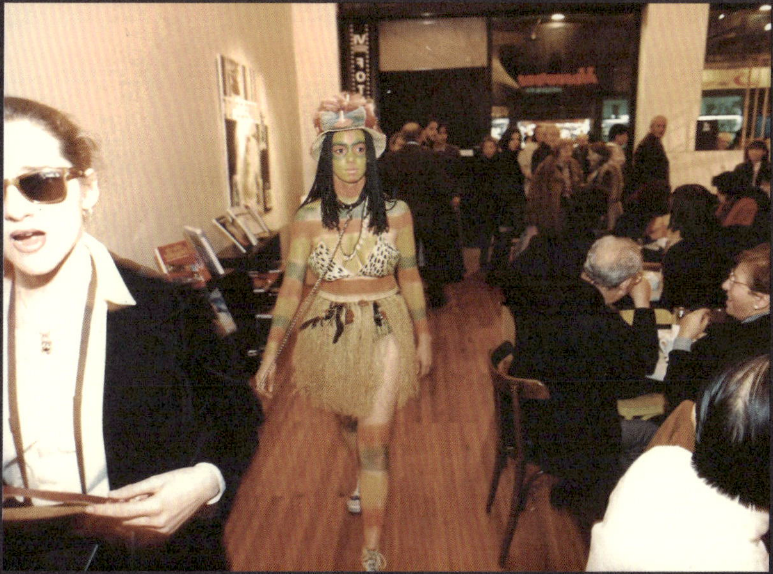

Rosemarie Trockel

Zum Beispiel Balthasar, 6 Jahre (For example, Balthasar, age 6), 1996
Video, color, sound
Running time: 9:15 minutes
Dallas Museum of Art, anonymous gift, 1998.45

Rosemarie Trockel (German, b. 1952) was born in Schwerte, Germany, and attended the Werkkunstschule (School of Applied Arts) in Cologne. The major exhibition *Rosemarie Trockel: A Cosmos*, organized by the Museo Nacional Centro de Arte Reina Sofía, Madrid, traveled to the New Museum, New York, and Serpentine Galleries, London (2012–2013). Solo exhibitions have been held at the Moderna Museet, Stockholm (2001); Dia Art Foundation, New York (2002–2004); the Museum of Modern Art, Frankfurt (2004); MAXXI, Museo nazionale delle arti del XXI secolo, Rome (2006); and Pinacoteca Giovanni e Marella Agnelli, Turin (2016). Trockel was awarded the Kunstpreis der Kulturstiftung der Stadtsparkasse München (Art Prize) for her exhibition at the German Pavilion, the 48th Venice Biennale (1999); the Kaiserring der Stadt Goslar (2011); and the Roswitha Haftmann Prize (2014).

ROSEMARIE TROCKEL

by Ulrike Groos

When Rosemarie Trockel showed her first videos in 1990 at the Michael Werner Gallery in Cologne, [Germany], she still regarded them as commentary, supplemental to her other works. Two exhibits in Geneva and Vienna (1994) presented her videos as a comprehensive body of work in their own right for the first time.[1]

Although Trockel had already experimented with the "new medium" during her course of university studies in the 1970s, she had nonetheless never considered herself a video artist. Instead, she viewed her work with the video camera as parallel to her other work, which consists of drawings, pictures, and sculptures. Today the artist still employs the medium as she would a pencil, devoting herself to it in varying degrees, treating it either centrally or tangentially. The themes examined in her videos are apparent throughout her oeuvre, ultimately indicating a sense of unity among her works.

The principal subject matter of the videos shown in the project room of the Hauser & Wirth Collection in Saint Gallen, Switzerland (August 18–September 9, 2000), includes topics such as personal identity, memory, and time, or revolves around role reversal between the child's world and that of the adult.

CUT AND CLOSE-UP: Ulf, Doro, Peter, Gitta, Moni, Otto, Geli, Rosi, Pia, Jan, and others swing and sway comfortably along, turning and rocking to the rhythm of a faintly audible song; although they occasionally nudge each other gently, they remain undisturbed.

The first and longest take in the black-and-white, one-minute video *Ei-Dorado* [literally, Egg Dorado, but a play on the mythic El Dorado] (1993) reveals several eggs in continuous, gentle motion, bearing the names mentioned above. The scene's subtle aesthetic radiates an idyllic sense of ease, the entire room bathed in an indefinite, diffuse illumination, the eggs casting soft light-dark shadows. However, an impression of fragility and threat gradually insinuates itself. The eggs roll around on a piece of cloth, which drops away to the rear of the picture. They seem to be increasingly agitated by the movement of the cloth and are forced to hop and jump with escalating aggressiveness. The cloth becomes a slide where the eggs tumble down, reducing their number. Two swiftly ensuing sequences show the rapid, blurred movement of the high-speed free fall of the eggs into the depths. The last take shows an egg hitting the ground and shattering. This freeze-framed final image remains for a few seconds as a black-and-white composition of broken eggs—a mixture of light egg white, dark yolk, broken shells, and the fragments of the names. The scenes are accompanied by Janis Joplin's barely audible song "Cry Baby," which is almost completely drowned out by the indistinct sound of rushing water. The climax of the song embellished by the singer's screamed words coincides with the impact of the egg on the floor.

The egg, in many cultures as well as in Christianity, here symbolizes fertility and life, inasmuch as Trockel wanted to express her opposition to abortion through this video. Based on the artist's commentary, the water noises suggest womb sounds, the idyllic opening scene of the fertilized, labeled eggs corresponds to the affirmed El (*Ei*) Dorado in the title, a dreamland and paradise suddenly and brutally obliterated by abortion.

CHANGE OF SCENE—CHILDREN'S PROGRAM: In the intervening years, Trockel has produced a substantial number of videos in which children perform. In the realm of television and cinema, it is [arguably] simple to differentiate between films made for children and films in which children merely appear.[2] With Trockel the boundaries between the world of the adult and the world of the child become quite deliberately blurred, memories and wishes become entangled, cross-references and a sense of déjà vu emerge, time and place detach themselves from their customary frames of reference.

Accordingly, both puppet shows presented in the project room, *Mohn gegen Strom* (Poppy against electricity) (1989/2000) and *Sigi gegen dicke Frau* (Sigi against thick woman) (2000),[3] provide a puppet theater spotlighting discussions conducted either by the devil or by "Sigi" [Sigmund] Freud on topics such as drugs, [going] cold turkey [withdrawals], the id, the ego, and the superego.

In Marguerite Duras's love and family story *Summer Rain* (1991), the twelve- to twenty-year-old Ernesto, second eldest son in a large family, speaks these words to his mother: "I'm not going to school anymore, because in school they teach me things I don't know." For her video *Julia, 10–20 Jahre* (Julia, 10–20 years) (1999), Trockel was inspired by the story and character of Ernesto, who assumes the burdens of his unemployed parents, in particular, responsibility for his siblings. The title itself indicates a period of time to be bridged. The girl, Julia, approximately ten years old with a well-mannered hairstyle of braids and bangs, appears in the video in a neutral room, sitting at a table, speaking to the camera, and singing. A distinctive, timeless aura, evoked by the diffuse brightness of the white tablecloth, the white wall in the background, and her white blouse, seems to envelop the girl. Due to the rigid frontal camera position aimed directly at the girl and because of the lack of story line, the viewer concentrates on her words and on the few movements in the picture: the observer becomes aware of Julia's mobile mouth, the reductive mimicry, the nervous, embarrassed gestures.

The sharp video cuts—making the girl's face or the soda bottle in front of her shift abruptly—indicate that between her sentences, which are mainly answers, questions posed by a second, off-screen person have been cut, with the result that Julia's answers, with all their taciturnity and abrupt change of topic, irritate and annoy. The child's comments are delivered sometimes in a childlike fashion, sometimes precociously and perfectly formulated, and sometimes unemotionally and without understanding what has been said ("A cloned person is also a person"). The contrast between childlike chatter and rehearsed answer, between naturalness and synthetic construction, is also apparent in one of the most striking visual changes, namely, at the moment Julia undoes her braids, thereby achieving the transformation into a teenager not only verbally, but also physically.

Because of their sobriety and objectivity, the images call to mind scientific, psychological, or criminological interrogations. Here is a study relating to growing up, occasionally enriched by a very private moment through the remarks of the interrogated. Julia parallels the artist's search for a girl embodying the potential of both childlike and adult attributes. At their first meeting, Julia wore old-fashioned nylon stockings, suggesting an outdated notion of an adult outfit. Although Trockel prefers an open arrangement and intuitive process for most of her videos, and she highly prizes spontaneity, randomness, and unpredictability during the onetime shoot, this method was not immediately accessible to Julia. The girl was unable to spontaneously reproduce in her own words the artist's preformulated answers. Consequently, the filming proceeded gradually while difficult "adult" answers were discussed.

In general, Trockel is not concerned with elaborate scenes based on a refined, detailed, and finalized screenplay, but rather with the elucidation of her own ideas and conceptions. The chief concern is not acting ability or blending into the role, but rather the quick, spontaneous reaction to her shouted instructions. This method, resulting in short filming sessions [that are also a consequence of using] the simplest technical equipment and lending the video projects a somewhat imperfect and unpolished appearance, allows the viewer considerable scope for association.

SLOW MOTION AND CUT: A comical example of unpredictability resulting directly from minimal plot instructions and affecting both the filming itself and the actor is the video *Mutter, Mutter* (Mother, Mother) (1992). In this black-and-white, one-minute video, the significance of duplication is not only evident in the title, but also comprises the subject matter of the entire project. Trockel's sister plays a woman moving purposefully through a house to a cellar room, where she takes a rug beater from the wall in order to swat two sizable spiders lying motionless in front of her. With the exception of a wistful Italian song copied by the artist from a film, there is no sound, neither of the woman's progress through the scene, nor of the forceful swatting of the spiders. The visual impression is intensified by the mute rendering and the use of slow motion, while the brutality of the action is attenuated by the gentle melancholy of the song. The absurdity of the performance is further heightened by the abrupt end, as the camera shifts from the spiders on the floor and glides off into nothingness. Trockel's description of the filming provides an explanation for this severance: although both sisters have suffered from a spider phobia since childhood, the mood during the filming shifted rapidly and quite astonishingly for both into hysteria, which also explains the advancing panic and loathing in the sister's face.[4]

The use of slow motion in *Mutter, Mutter* is a frequently employed stylistic approach in Trockel's videos, facilitating a slower and more intense scrutiny of the scenes and their details. The artist herself quite pragmatically cites two reasons for its application: the banality of the filmed episodes, which acquire a certain degree of suspense through slow motion, and the technical drawbacks of an unsteady handheld camera.

CLOSING SHOT: An effect bordering on kitsch is created by the slow-motion effects in *Zum Beispiel Balthasar, 6 Jahre* (For example, Balthasar, age 6) (1996), a video exploring the theme of religion. The work opens with a close-up of a boy's laughing face and subsequently follows two children, accompanied by their two dogs and loaded down with a suitcase and backpack, traveling through an idyllic landscape. Following a short, threatening moment when a predatory bird appears in the sky, the children approach a church. They enter, and the boy grasps the bell rope and rings the bell. The scene changes. The laughing boy hanging on the rope is now in a gymnasium; the action has been converted into a sports activity. The last shot shows the boy standing in front of a playground merry-go-round. This poetically and idyllically laden chain of association proceeds from devotion to details and appreciation of the images implemented by the slowing down of events. The impression of intentional borderline kitsch is sustained by the minimalist, emphatically melancholy, and repetitive music, composed by Christoph John, who was commissioned [to compose the score] specifically for the video.[5] On the one hand, Trockel characterizes these scenes as fictional childhood memories. On the other hand, she invariably sees religion as a substitute for something else, hence the connection to the notion of a sports club. The bell, in sacral usage the call to prayer, pealing fully only on Sundays and holidays, thereby retaining its solemn significance, is here playfully reinterpreted as an item of sports equipment. The remembered moment and the reference to the past are enhanced by the sepia tint of the video material: a sentimental "antique touch," customary for pseudo-old, color-treated photos.

Ulrike Groos, "Rosemarie Trockel," first published in a brochure on the occasion of Rosemarie Trockel's exhibition *Drehmomente* (Turning points), at the Hauser & Wirth Collection, Saint Gallen, Switzerland, August 13–September 9, 2000.

Notes

1 In the Centre d'Art Contemporain in Geneva, videos from 1993 and 1994 were augmented by thematically related works; in the MAK-Galerie, Österreichisches Museum für Angewandle Kunst/Gegenwartskunst, Vienna, only videos were shown.

2 Classics such as *Le ballon rouge* (The red balloon) (1956), by Albert Lamorisse, and *L'argent de poche* (Small change) (1975–1976), by François Truffaut, were quite clearly made for children. Films such as *Los olvidados* (The young and the damned) (1950), by Luis Buñuel; *Au revoir les enfants* (Goodbye children) (1987), by Louis Malle; or *Lord of the Flies* (1963), by Peter Brook, were not filmed for a young audience.

3 The puppet show *Sigi gegen dicke Frau* (Sigi against thick woman) in the video *Der Löwe* (The lion) is only one in a series of sequential stories including the topic of wool as a kind of common thread.

4 Psychology claims that spider phobia results from a poor relationship of the subject to his or her mother, an explanation to which Trockel gives no credence. For the video *Yvonne* (1997) the artist even overcame her fear and visited a spider trainer. Spiders and other apparently unpopular "pets," such as maggots and moths, frequently appear in Trockel's videos, e.g., in *Parade* (1993) and *Á la motte* (The clod) (1993).

5 The music in Trockel's videos, always carefully selected by the artist herself, deserves to be considered on its own merits. Sometimes it is a song copied from a film *(Mutter, Mutter)*, often it is compositions commissioned by the artist from musicians Christoph John, Carlo Peters, and Kurt Hoffmann. Another alternative is the use of well-known rock or pop songs. Such is the case when the girl, Julia, in the video of the same name, herself chose the Toni Braxton song "Unbreak My Heart." Other examples are Janis Joplin's "Cry Baby" in *Ei-Dorado* or Jimi Hendrix's "Are You Experienced?" in *Mohn gegen Strom*.

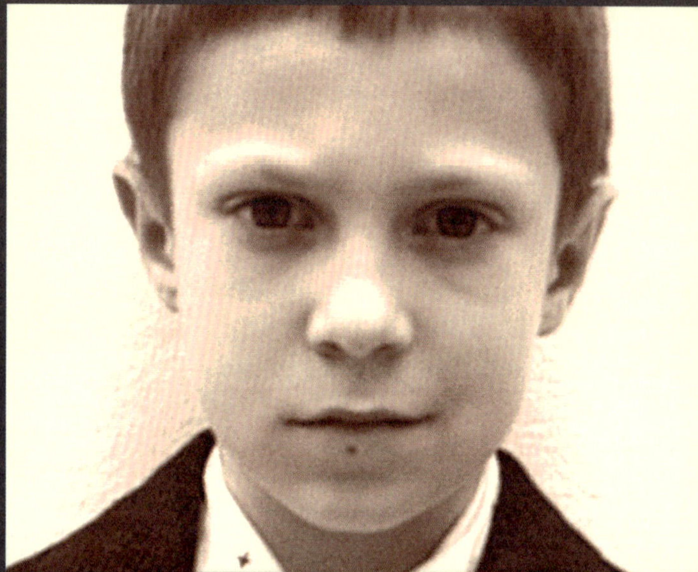

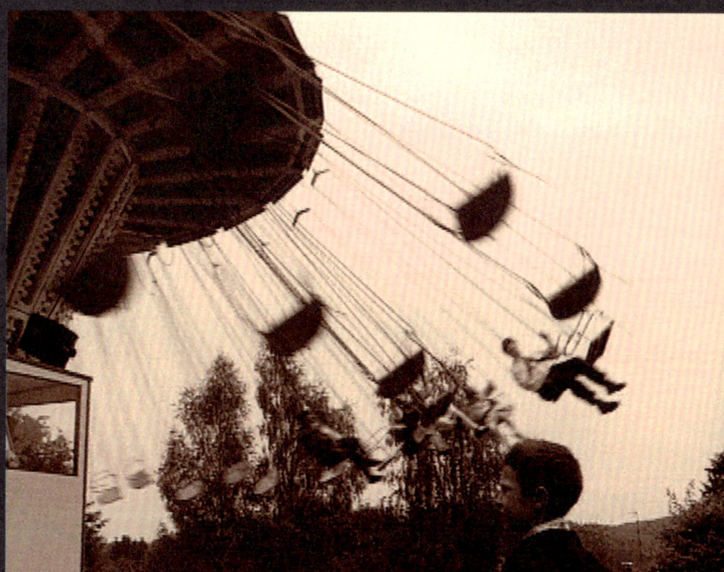

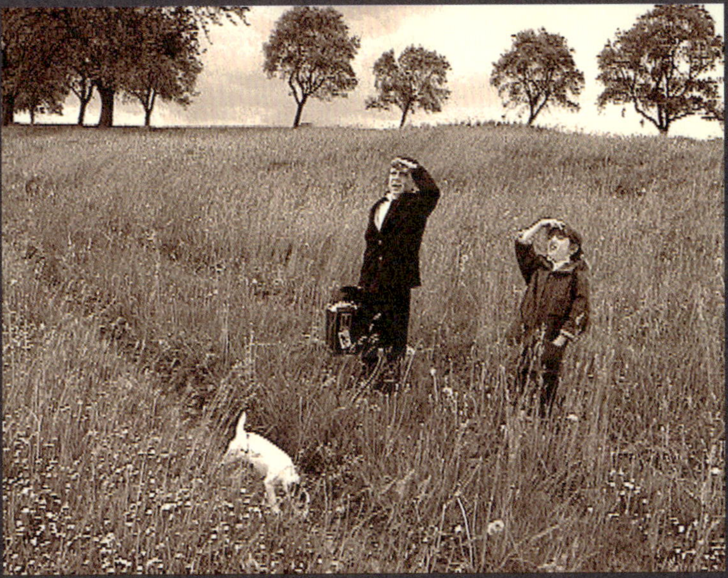

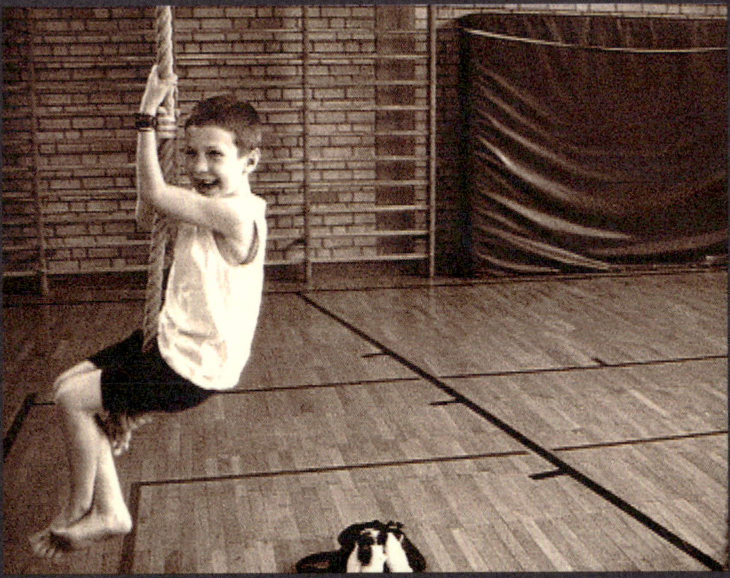

Anri Sala

Intervista, 1998
Video, color, sound
Running time: 26 minutes
Dallas Museum of Art, Lay Family Acquisition Fund, 2002.37

Anri Sala (Albanian, b. 1974) was born in Tirana, Albania, and now is based in Berlin. Following his studies in video at the École nationale supérieure des arts décoratifs, Paris, and in painting at the National Academy of Arts, Tirana, Sala took postgraduate courses in film directing at Le Fresnoy, Studio national des arts contemporains, Tourcoing, France. Major solo exhibitions were held at the Dallas Museum of Art (*Concentrations 41: Intervista*, 2002); Louisiana Museum of Modern Art, Humlebæk, Denmark (2012); the 55th Venice Biennale (*Ravel Ravel Unravel* in the French Pavilion, 2013); Haus der Kunst, Munich (*The Present Moment [in D]*, 2014); and the New Museum, New York (*Answer Me*, 2016). He earned the Best Documentary Film Award at Filmfest in Tirana (2000), the Young Artist Prize at the 49th Venice Biennale (2001), and the Vincent Award in The Hague, Netherlands (2014).

ANRI SALA: UNFINISHED HISTORIES

Interview by Massimiliano Gioni and Michele Robecchi

MASSIMILIANO GIONI AND MICHELE ROBECCHI: In your videos the absurdity of violence and history comes across through the simple means of juxtaposition. You alternate past and present, like in *Intervista,* or you present two characters who apparently have nothing to do with each other, like in *Nocturnes*; it's as though your work were merely a matter of editing.

ANRI SALA: The juxtaposition of different stories is extremely important: alternating past and present, moving to different places, from here to there, overlapping narratives. . . . This alchemy of images and sounds helps to create a simulacrum of reality, an alternative present time, which is the time of a projection, and which could actually be more real than what we think reality is.

MG&MR: There is a strange mistrust toward reality in your work, even though everything you do seems informed by the language of television and documentary films.

AR: Maybe, I don't know. I think there are no such direct influences. Television and cinema were never really part of my everyday life. In Albania the only television program we had started at eighteen hundred [hours] and ended at twenty-two [hours], mainly airing the same news program and fiction film three times a day. Everything was so unreal that I remember the only realistic thing was the weather forecast.

At the end of the film *Intervista* my mother says, "I think we passed to you the ability to doubt, in the sense that you always have to question the truth." This is part of the mistrust toward reality that we inherited; people had to believe in a reality that didn't exist, and they had to act as if they saw it every day. It was like *The Matrix*, the film—have you seen it? You didn't have the choice to believe or not, and lots of the people probably didn't want to have one, either. Actually in *The Matrix* there is a great scene I absolutely love. In this scene they ask Neo, the One, if he wants to go "our way or the highway?" And Neo opens the door of the car he's sitting in and tries to leave. Trinity stops him and says, "Neo, please, you have to trust me." Neo answers, "Why?" Trinity: "Because you've already been down there, Neo. You already know that road. You know exactly where it ends. And I know that's not where you want to be." Neo closes the door. When I saw the film, I thought, This road could be every street in Tirana, and I couldn't stop thinking of all the people there trying to find a way out.

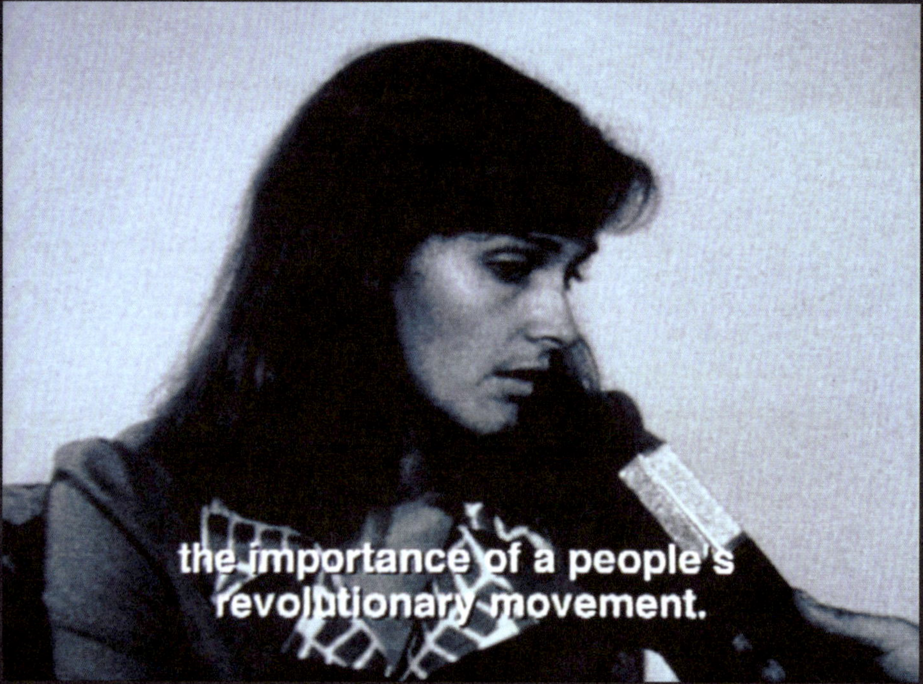
the importance of a people's
revolutionary movement.

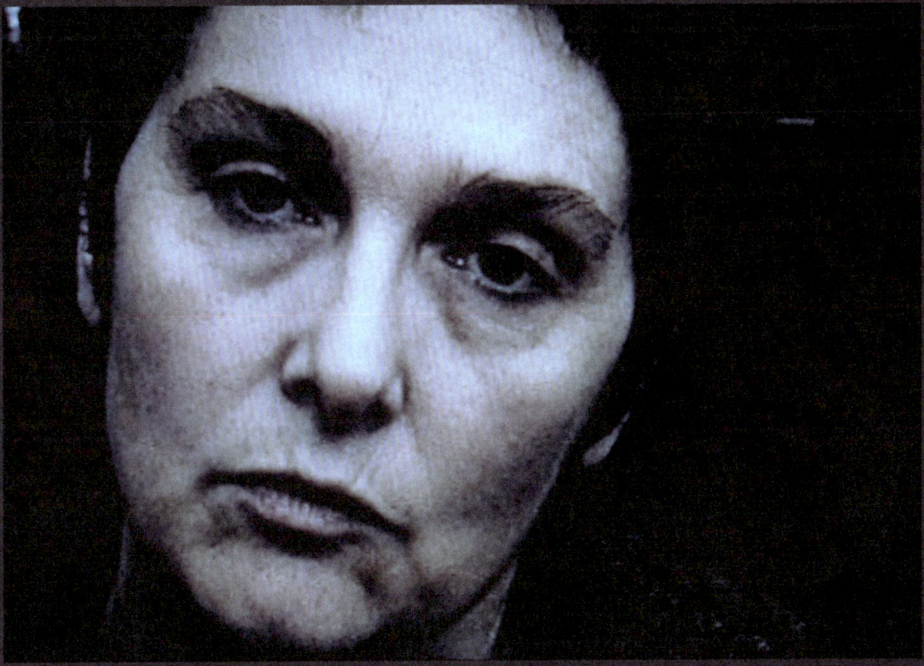

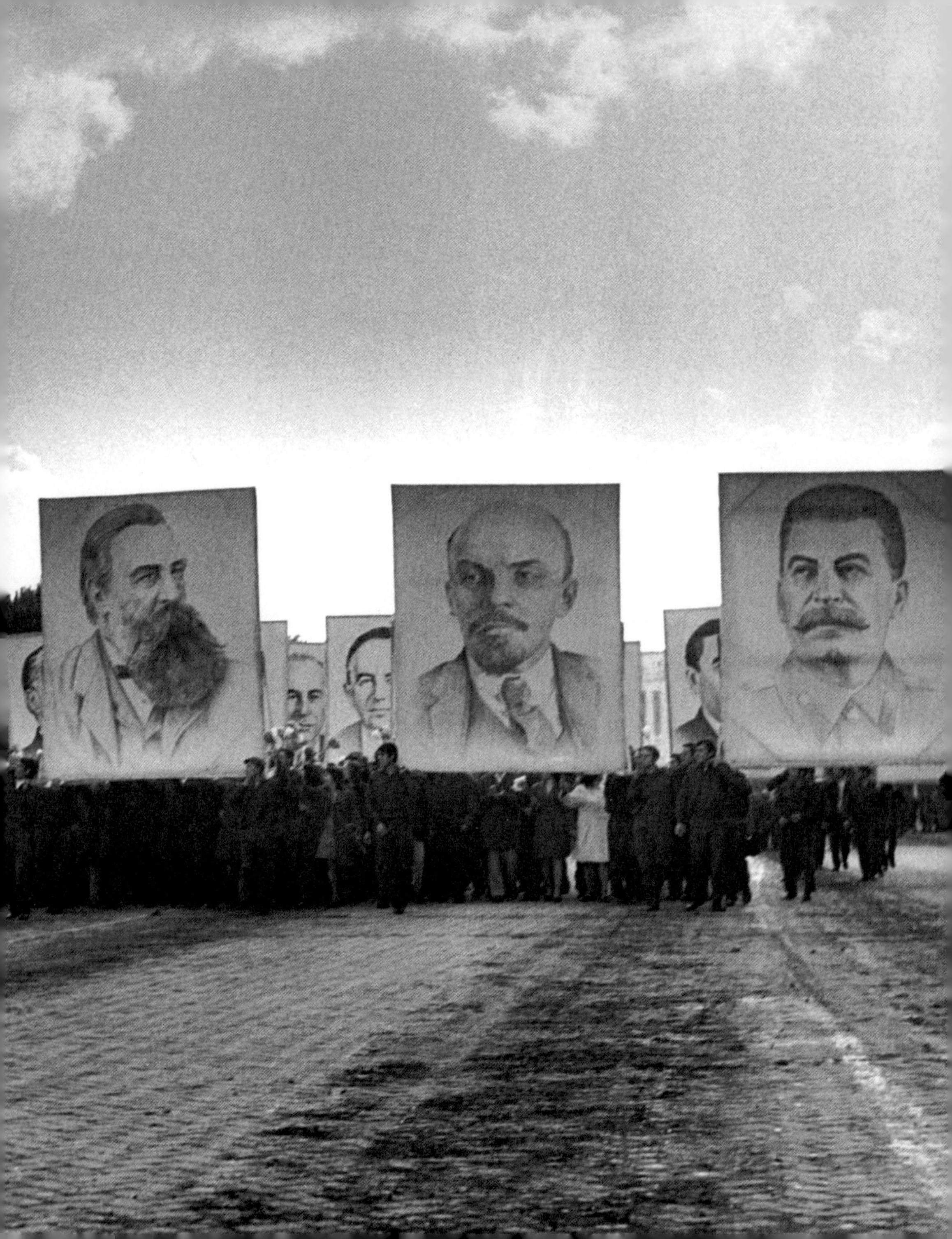

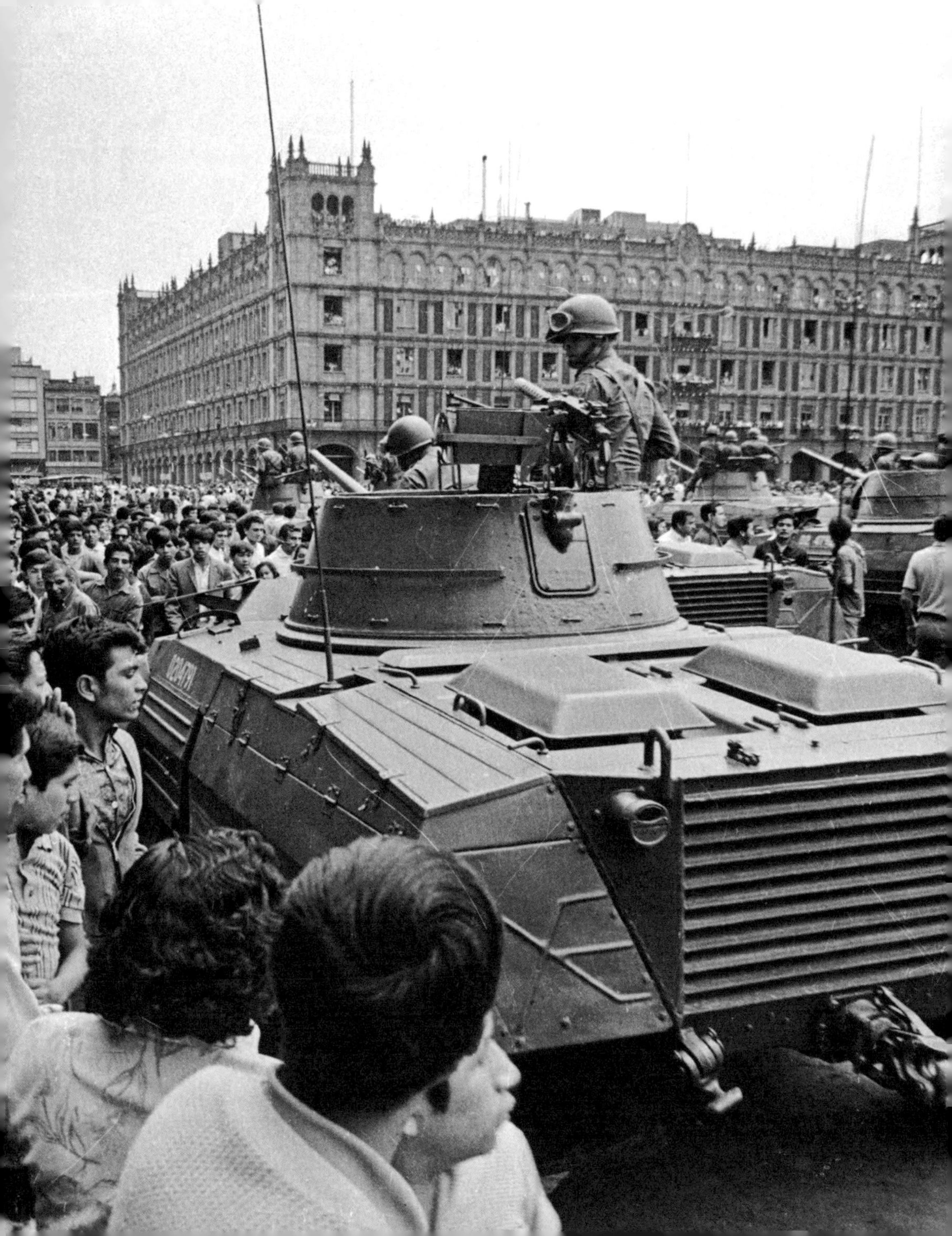

Shirin Neshat

Soliloquy, 1999
Two-channel 16 mm film transferred to digital video, color, stereo sound
Running time: 17:33 minutes
Dallas Museum of Art, the Contemporary Art Fund: Gift of Mr. and Mrs. Vernon E. Faulconer, Mr. and Mrs. Bryant M. Hanley, Jr., Marguerite and Robert K. Hoffman, Howard E. Rachofsky, Deedie and Rusty Rose, Gayle and Paul Stoffel, and two anonymous donors; the Lay Family Acquisition Fund; and the TWO x TWO for AIDS and Art Fund, 2000.320.A-B

Shirin Neshat (Iranian American, b. 1957) was born in Qazin, Iran, and moved to the United States in 1974 to study art, receiving a BA, an MA, and an MFA from the University of California, Berkeley. In 1983 she moved to New York City, where she worked at the nonprofit gallery Storefront for Art and Architecture. Since the early 1990s Neshat's photographs and videos have explored the position of women in postrevolutionary Iran. She has had a number of solo exhibitions at venues including the Museo de Arte Moderno, Mexico City; the Hirshhorn Museum and Sculpture Garden, Washington, DC; the Stedelijk Museum, Amsterdam; the Dallas Museum of Art; the Walker Art Center, Minneapolis; the Art Institute of Chicago; the Serpentine Galleries, London; and the Hamburger Bahnhof, Berlin. Neshat has also participated in the Whitney Biennial, New York (2000); Documenta 11, Kassel (2002); and the Venice Biennale (1999, 2009, and 2017). Her film *Turbulent* won the 48th Venice Biennale Prize (1999), and she received the Silver Lion for Best Director at the 66th Venice Film Festival for *Women Without Men*. She received the Lillian Gish Prize (2006) and the USA Artists Rockefeller Fellowship (2016).

GERALD MATT IN CONVERSATION WITH SHIRIN NESHAT

GERALD MATT: Your work is frequently presented in the context of projects or exhibitions concerned with a dialogue between different cultures. Having been raised in Iran and living in the US, you not only stand between two cultures, but also take your artistic inspirations from these very divergent cultural backgrounds. At the same time, you do not have a certain audience in either of the two cultures, as Hamid Dabashi put it. To what extent do you consider a dialogue between the poles of exoticism—how your work is perceived in the West—and provocation—how your work is seen in Iran—to be at all possible?

SHIRIN NESHAT: When I am in the process of making a work, I try to focus on the importance of the concept within its own cultural context, as opposed to its connections with other cultures or my position as a cross-cultural artist. It is absolutely critical for me to present the subject within its own terms, to retain purity, and not become bogged down by the pressure of cross-cultural parallels. The point is how to address culturally specific issues, which are heavily based on particular sociopolitical agendas, in a way that is of universal value on an emotional, intuitive level. The challenge lies in the balance I have to strike between the originality of an idea and the thread of universality.

GM: Different cultures impose different boundaries. Referring to Iranian filmmakers and censorship in Iran, you once said that the existence of borders enforces a need to get to the core of things. Which are the limitations that you are subject to as an artist, and what is their influence on your work?

SN: When I began to focus on the traditional and philosophical ideas behind Islam, particularly in relation to women, I decided to remain within the framework of the social, cultural, and religious codes, to maintain the given boundaries, as I believe to have done otherwise would have been disrespectful and simply reactionary. Once I had established this pattern, I was faced with an incredibly reduced number of elements of representation. This reduction offered me a sense of clarity, of simplicity, that seemed to imply the possibility or penetrating more deeply into the subject.

I have often referred to the Iranian cinema after the Islamic revolution as a major inspiration in how it has created a language that, although remaining within the confines of the social codes, so profoundly expresses the cultural subtleties that would have been otherwise extremely difficult to detect. The approach is simple, concise, poetic, minimalist, and powerful, as it criticizes society without claiming to do so. I think that these filmmakers have discovered a new approach that thrives on the very poverty of the possibilities and creates works of great substance with a universal meaning.

GM: So far, the criticism and reception of your work has focused primarily on the questions you have raised about feminism and fundamentalism. However, the veiled woman wearing a chador is no mere victim. She enters the picture with a direct gaze, as a strong, active personality. Your work highlights the complexities of Islamic womanhood and poses questions about issues ranging from patriarchy to colonialism. Aren't you concerned with putting the system of values and the viewers' conceptions to the test rather than with making political statements?

SN: I see my work as a visual discourse on the subjects of feminism and contemporary Islam—a discourse that puts certain myths and realities to the test, claiming that they are far more complex than most of us have imagined. It is very important to point out, however, that I don't see myself as an expert on this subject. Rather, I consider myself a passionate inquirer. I prefer raising questions, as opposed to answering them, as I am totally unable to do otherwise, and I am not interested in creating works that simply state my personal political point of view. Some of the questions my works raise with regard to Islamic societies, particularly in Iran, have been addressed in recent academic discourse. But while academic analysis obviously results in a purely factual and theoretical dialogue, my approach as a visual artist fuses facts and the subliminal. This method in a way universalizes the subject and allows a more open interpretation.

GM: You are very involved in architecture and, as codirector of New York's Storefront for Art and Architecture, have collaborated with various architects. How has thinking about defined spaces influenced your conceptualization of images? You seem to distinguish between male and female spaces in the world of Islam.

SN: My involvement with the Storefront for Art and Architecture, which lasted for about ten years, was pivotal for the development of my personal work. Apart from the fantastic exposure, Storefront offered me a chance to get to know the latest theoretical and aesthetic developments in architecture; there were several aspects of this experience that particularly grabbed me as an artist. While visual art always remains completely independent and unaffected by other fields, and even functions on a purely intuitive level, architecture only exists within a complex relation with other fields and issues. As the very premise of architecture is building, it cannot remain neutral to the reality of functionality, community, tradition, and cities. Storefront's programs concentrated as much on the presentation of architects' research and developmental processes as on the final results. When I began to formulate my own ideas, I eventually leaned toward a similar methodology where information and research became crucial aspects of my work.

What also continues to fascinate me is the integral relation between architecture and cultural studies. Architecture seems to be a reflection of a culture because it embodies its ideological history. As I became increasingly involved with Islamic topics, it seemed only appropriate to explore space and architecture from the ideological point of view. I came upon interesting parallels concerning the way in which the female body and space are defined, controlled, and coded. *The Shadow Under the Web,* made in Istanbul in 1997, is a project that precisely addresses such issues. It reveals how the division of space has been organized ideologically in order to separate the sexes and clarify their roles in societies. For that matter, public space is considered "male space," while private space is considered "female space." Since the female body represents ideas of sexuality and individuality, which, distracting men from their duties, are considered problematic in a public domain, women must conceal their bodies by wearing a veil to neutralize their presence. In another film project, *Soliloquy*, which I realized in Turkey and in the United States in 1999, architecture is the core of the narrative since it represents two opposite cultures: the East and the West, the traditional and the modern, the communal and the individual.

This text was excerpted from "In Conversation with Shirin Neshat," first published in *Shirin Neshat* (Vienna: Kunsthalle Wien; London: Serpentine Galleries, 2000), 11–15. Courtesy of Kunsthalle Wien and Serpentine Galleries.

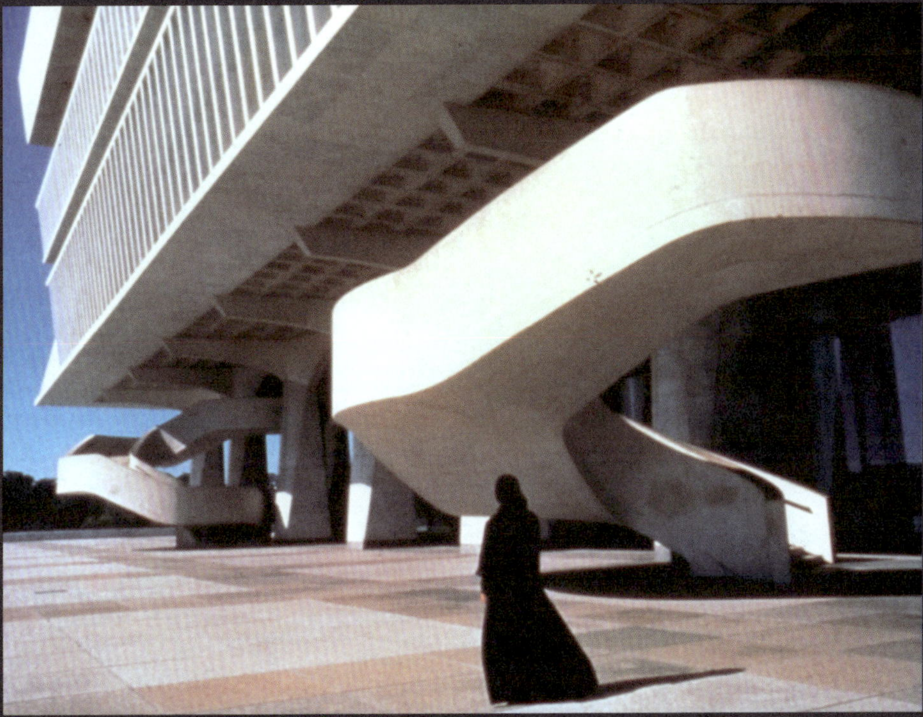

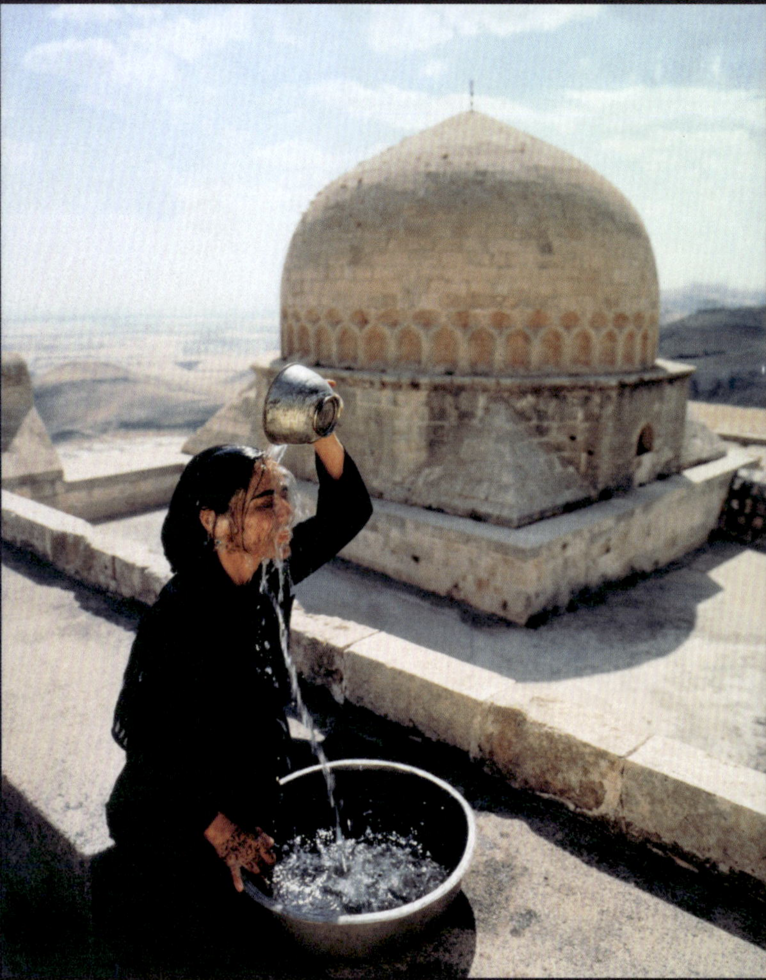

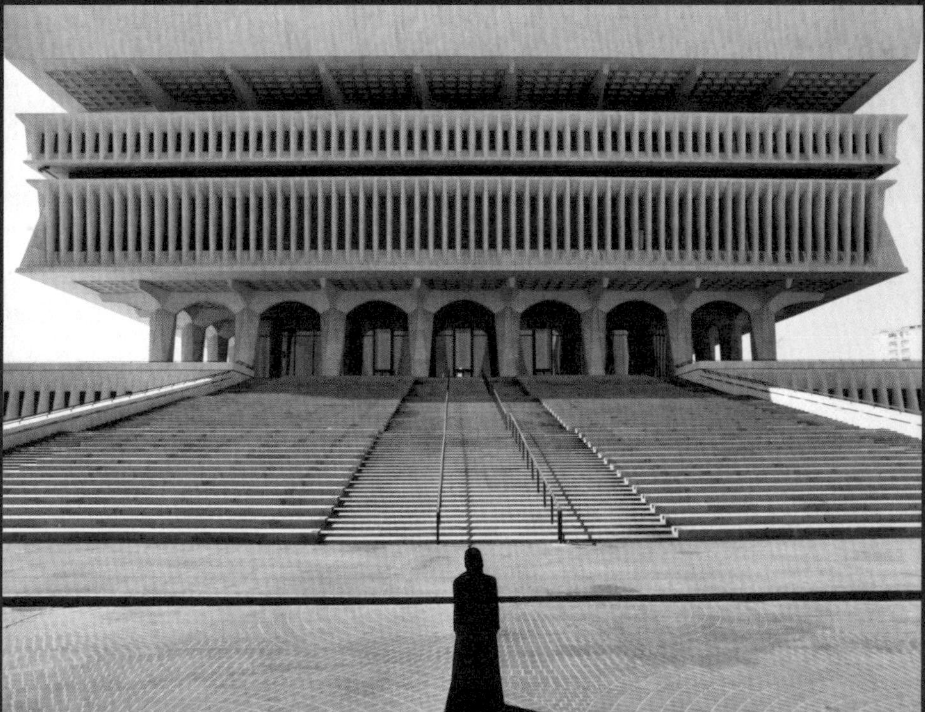

Ben Rivers

This Is My Land, 2006
16 mm film, black and white, sound
Running time: 14 minutes
Courtesy of Kate MacGarry Gallery, London

Ben Rivers (British, b. 1972) was born in Somerset and is an artist and filmmaker based in London. In 1993 he received a BA in fine art from the Falmouth School of Art. His short and feature-length films have been presented in numerous group exhibitions and screened at venues such as the Institute of Contemporary Art, London; the New York Film Festival; the 68th Venice Film Festival, where he won the Fédération Internationale de la Press Cinématographique (International Federation of Film Critics) (FIPRESCI) Prize; and Yerba Buena Center for the Arts, San Francisco. He has also staged solo presentations of his work at Art Statements, Art Basel (2011), where he won the Baloise Art Prize; Camden Arts Centre, London (2015); Kunstverein Hamburg (2016); and the Renaissance Society, Chicago (2016). From 2015 to 2016 Rivers was a Radcliffe–Harvard Film Study Center Fellow.

My interest is in worlds that are not sanitized, clean, and perfect, but that betray some kind of life—not only of the human participants, but also the bacteria, lichens, mineral deposits, dirt, and grain. Film has a tangible nature that mirrors these worlds, particularly when processed in my kitchen and then dried on a piece of string over the bath. Film has always seemed to me less about speed, but rather more about a slower sense of time. For example, there is the delay between filming and seeing the footage that creates an uncertainty about what has been caught on film. I like this tension because I don't want to be at a place constantly looking at what I have just filmed and then immediately responding to that, but instead to feel like I am actually living those moments. This way of working encourages serendipity and accidents. Then, back at home, when I finally see the footage, there are always surprises that change my preconceived idea of the final film.

Film is often associated with the past, but I like to think that far in the future, when humans have no idea what is in all these boxes and containers that store digital data, which will have no doubt been corrupted by then anyway, they will come across films, hold them up to the light, and easily understand what a strip of film does. Some bright spark will rig up a rudimentary projector powered by a dynamo, and in the overgrown cities there will be cinema again.

Ben Rivers, statement first published in *Tacita Dean: Film*, edited by Nicholas Cullinan (London: Tate Publishing, 2011), 114.

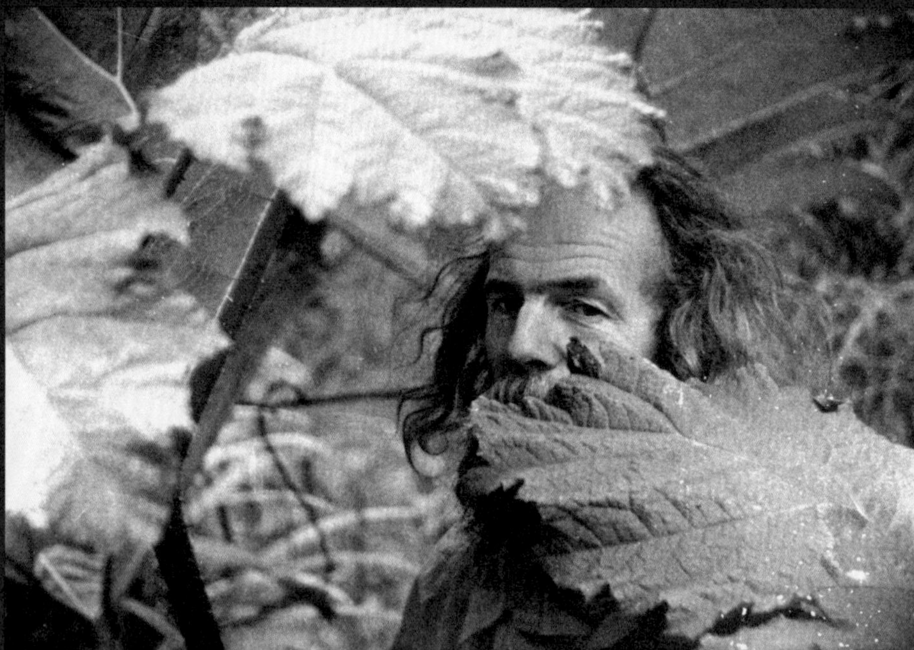

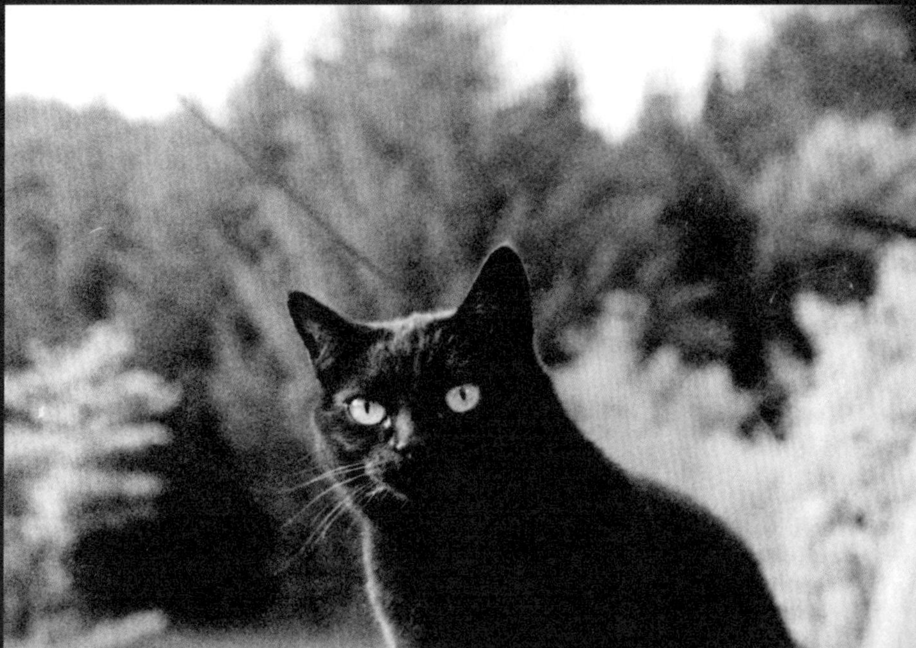

Phil Collins

the world won't listen, 2004–2007
Synchronized three-channel video, color, sound
Running time: 57 minutes
Dallas Museum of Art, Gayle and Paul Stoffel Fund for Contemporary Art Acquisition and gift of Marguerite Steed Hoffman, 2008.12.1-3

Phil Collins (British, b. 1970) was born in in Runcorn, England, and received a BA in English literature and drama from the University of Manchester and an MA in fine art from the University of Ulster, Belfast. He was part of the London-based performance group Max Factory. He is now based in Berlin and Cologne, and his work has been widely discussed and exhibited worldwide, including at the 9th International Istanbul Biennial (2005), the 10th Berlin Biennial for Contemporary Art (2010), and the Manchester International Festival (2017). Solo presentations of his work have been staged at numerous venues, beginning with the Dallas Museum of Art; followed by The Metropolitan Museum of Art, New York; the Museum of Contemporary Art, Chicago; the Gallery of Modern Art, Glasgow; the National Gallery of Canada, Ottawa; the San Francisco Museum of Modern Art; Tate Britain, London; and the Wexner Center for the Arts, Columbus, Ohio. Nominated for Tate's Turner Prize (2006), Collins continues to address the global impact of popular culture and contemporary media in his work.

DON'T BLOW YOUR OWN HORN

by Phil Collins and Suzanne Weaver

SUZANNE WEAVER: Why did you select the Smiths' 1987 album *The World Won't Listen?*

PHIL COLLINS: It could well have been the title, although whatever I picked would have surely provoked a bun-fight among the rarely satisfied, pernickety Smiths fans.

SW: What was your production process? For example, how was the music created for the karaoke machine? How did you solicit Smiths fans?

PC: The re-creation of the album in its entirety was like climbing a mountain. Michèle [Faguet] introduced me to Alejandro Gómez Cáceres Bertel, the guitarist from Los Aterciopelados, Colombia's biggest rock group, who had, I found out by chance, busked "Bigmouth Strikes Again" ten years earlier on the streets of London. What serendipity! Alejo also had squirreled away a dusty copy of *Guitar Player* magazine with an interview with Johnny Marr about his notoriously complicated tunings—which was lucky for us as we hadn't got any sheet music. So we relied on Alejo's magnificent ear and patience to rerecord, quite precisely, each and every guitar line for the entire album, note for note. I don't know if you can imagine what an endeavor it was. (But believe me—it was!)

The album was mixed at Voces e Imagen studio in Bogotá. Drummer, bassist, backing singers—everybody, unbelievably—learned each line by ear and proceeded to lay them down with effortless grace and real dedication. During this period I worked with a couple of video editors to make the visuals. The lyrics would appear at exactly the right moment, line by line. This is a karaoke machine for initiates and devotees, but more importantly, it's a karaoke machine that works like any other, like one you may find down at the local [pub].

Parallel to all this frantic activity, we set out on a publicity offensive. I lectured in any college that would have us—some of that was very memorable for me—and ran a citywide poster campaign with beautiful block-print posters that look somewhere between an ad for a boxing match and one for a political rally. We flyered incessantly at every bar in town until we bored everyone stupid, went on the radio in the evenings and television in the mornings. I wanted to have the widest possible draw for the project and to try at least to offer it to people from all over the city, every age, every background. In the end, we had one participant who flew in from Medellín [Colombia]. And they say the drugs don't work! . . .

SW: There must be a relationship between MTV, *American Idol,* and karaoke machines and the contestants on these shows being so slick. It is just a feeling I have because so many of the singers seem to be trying to be the next Mariah Carey, who I think is terribly uninteresting.

PC: With *American Idol,* there is no real reason for it to be so sickeningly conservative. Why can't we have someone on *American Idol* singing the Cocteau Twins or Tiny Tim? It should be a program that is wide open, but every single season, it is about complete conformity around the idea of the songbook.

Karaoke, of course, is egalitarian by design. If you have had enough to drink and you fancy it, anybody can do it. Except that there is nothing anyone in their right mind would want to sing.

Other people sometimes find karaoke embarrassing or laughable or delusional—the idea that someone gets up and thinks they can sing. But I find it moving and incredibly courageous. As a format, karaoke offers a promise of completion—this act will somehow make me whole—but at the same time it's predicated on the idea of vulnerability and failure, with its countless false starts, its blind terror. The way the pub falls away, and you can clearly see the spot where someone stands. The way they find themselves lost in the middle of a song, but unable to escape until it finishes. It's like a mild form of heroism.

SW: What is the relationship between the karaoke machine and the singer? Is the person who is singing with the karaoke machine wanting to be the performer whose lyrics are being shown on the screen? Or is it something else?

PC: Karaoke is a form of joyful treason in which you quite materially supplant your idol. So it's different from singing into the hairbrush in your bedroom. And the beauty of this kind of treachery is that for the first time you are not singing along, you are in fact the singer, suddenly thrown into the spotlight without a guiding voice, which makes for all kinds of uncertainties and mistakes. In that very simple sense, it's what makes it so compelling for me. Karaoke also raises all the issues of the "original" and the "copy," but who is to say which is the most valid? Is a South American performance of a desperate northern English love song any less, or more, valid than a northern English performance? If the Smiths symbolize a sense of prototypical Englishness, then this Englishness is in no way in and of itself stable. The Smiths themselves were, of course, all from Irish families.

This text was excerpted from "Don't Blow Your Own Horn," *Phil Collins: the world won't listen* (Dallas: Dallas Museum of Art, 2008), 88–91.

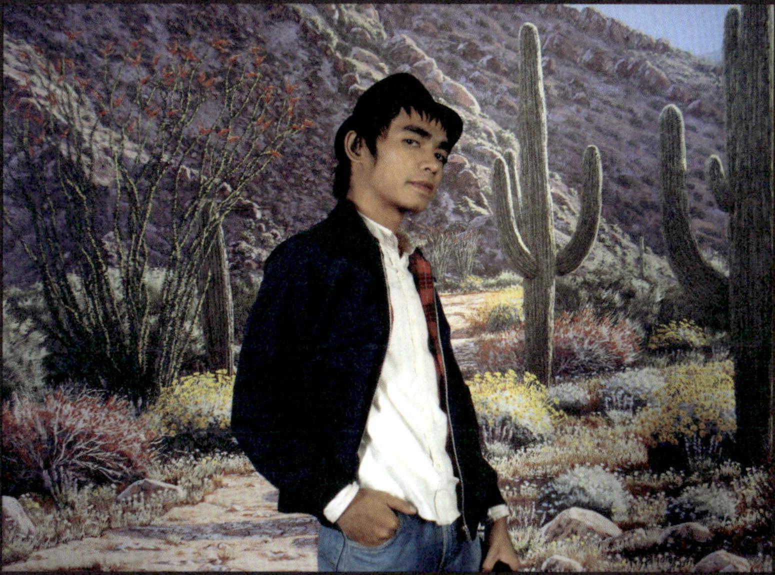

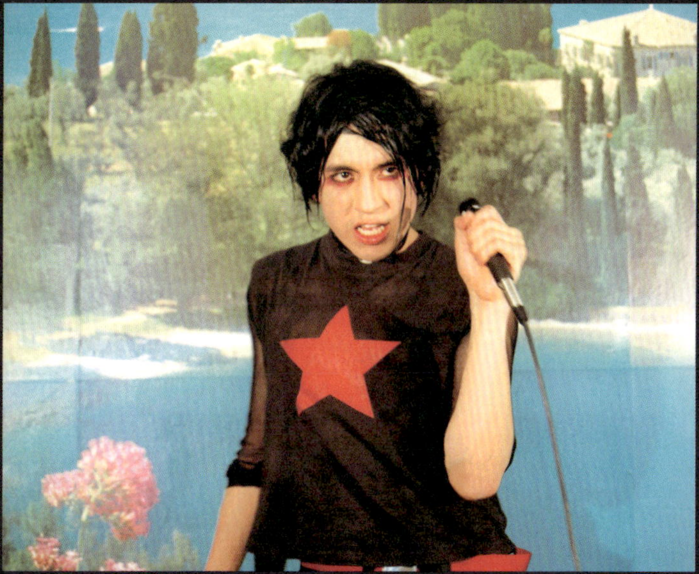

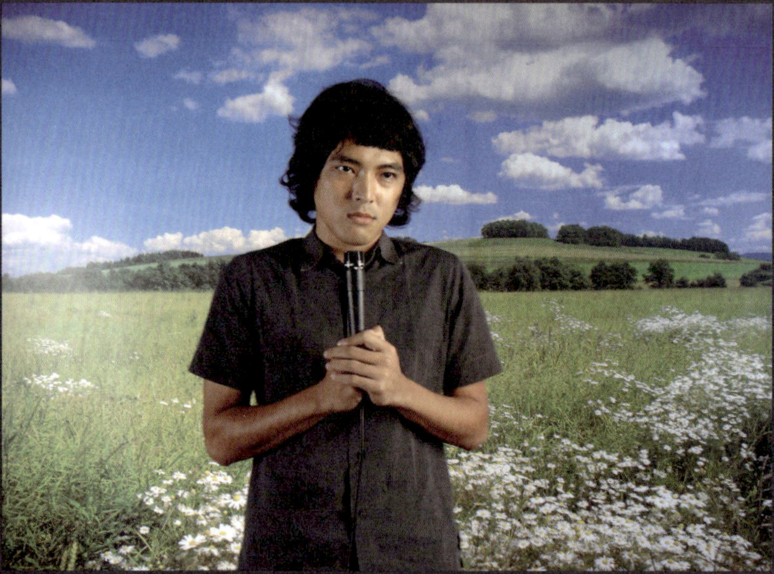

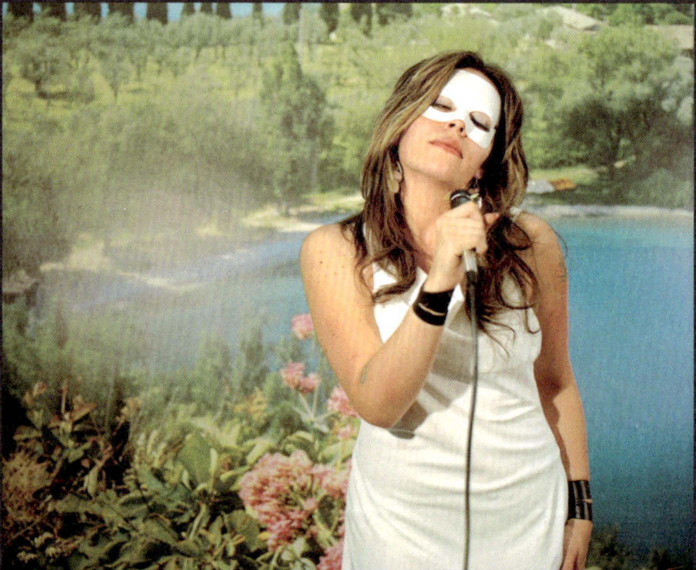

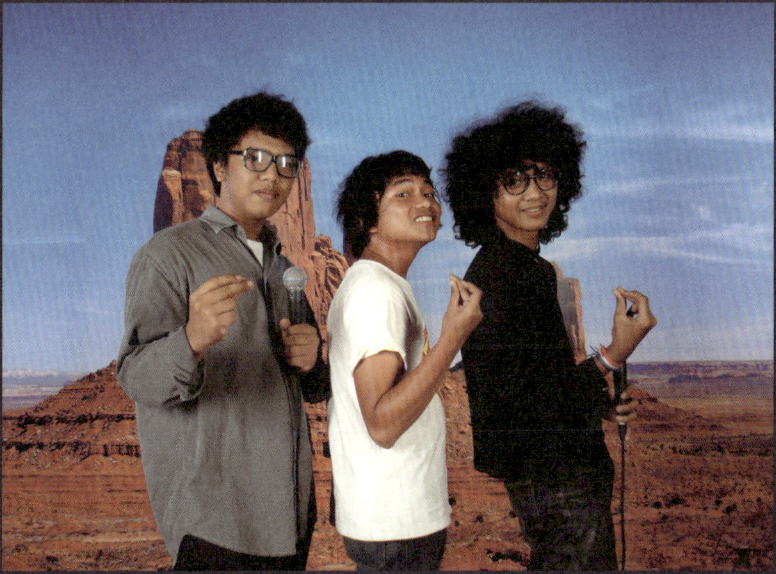

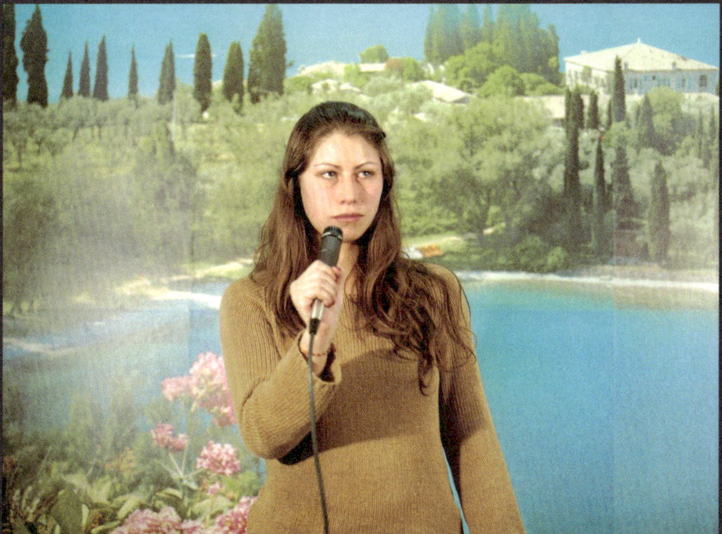

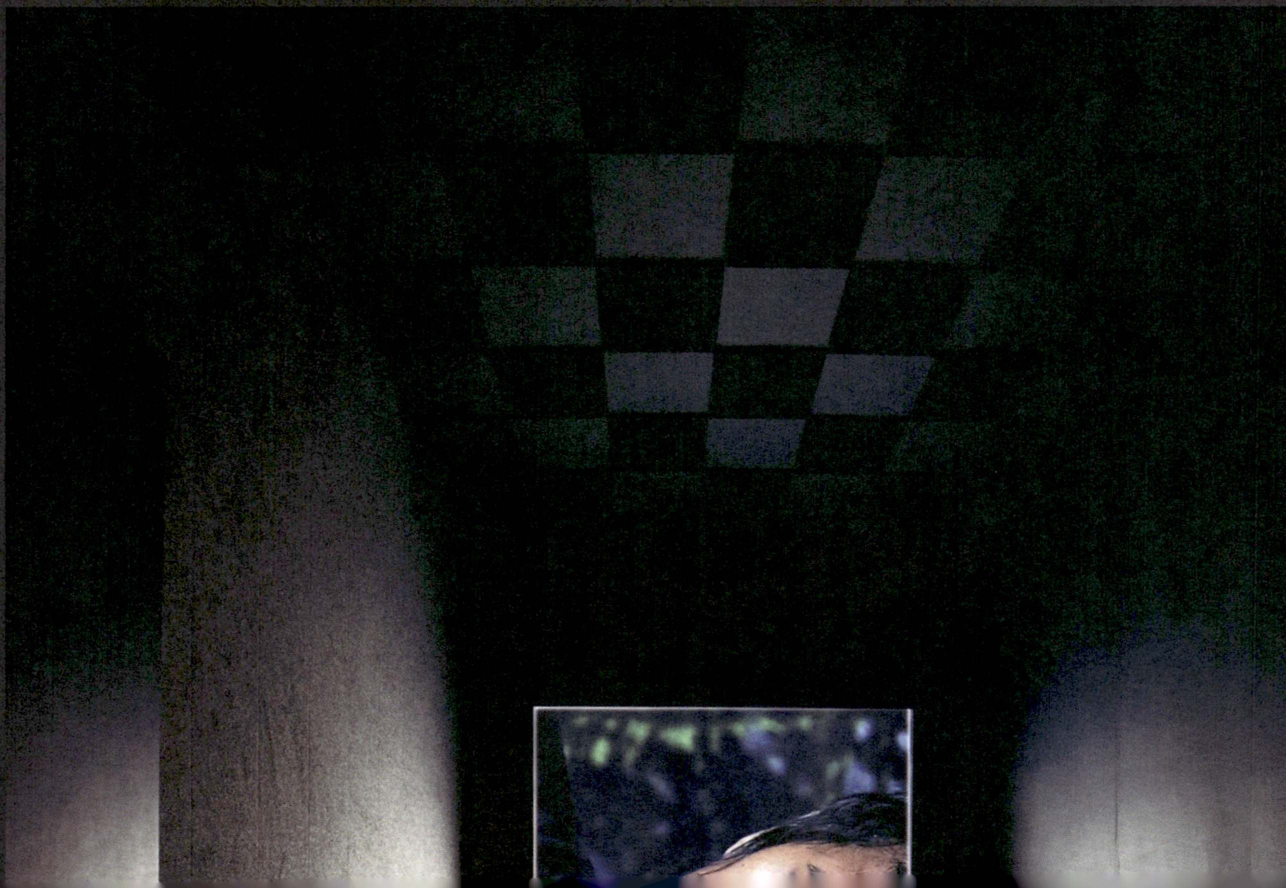

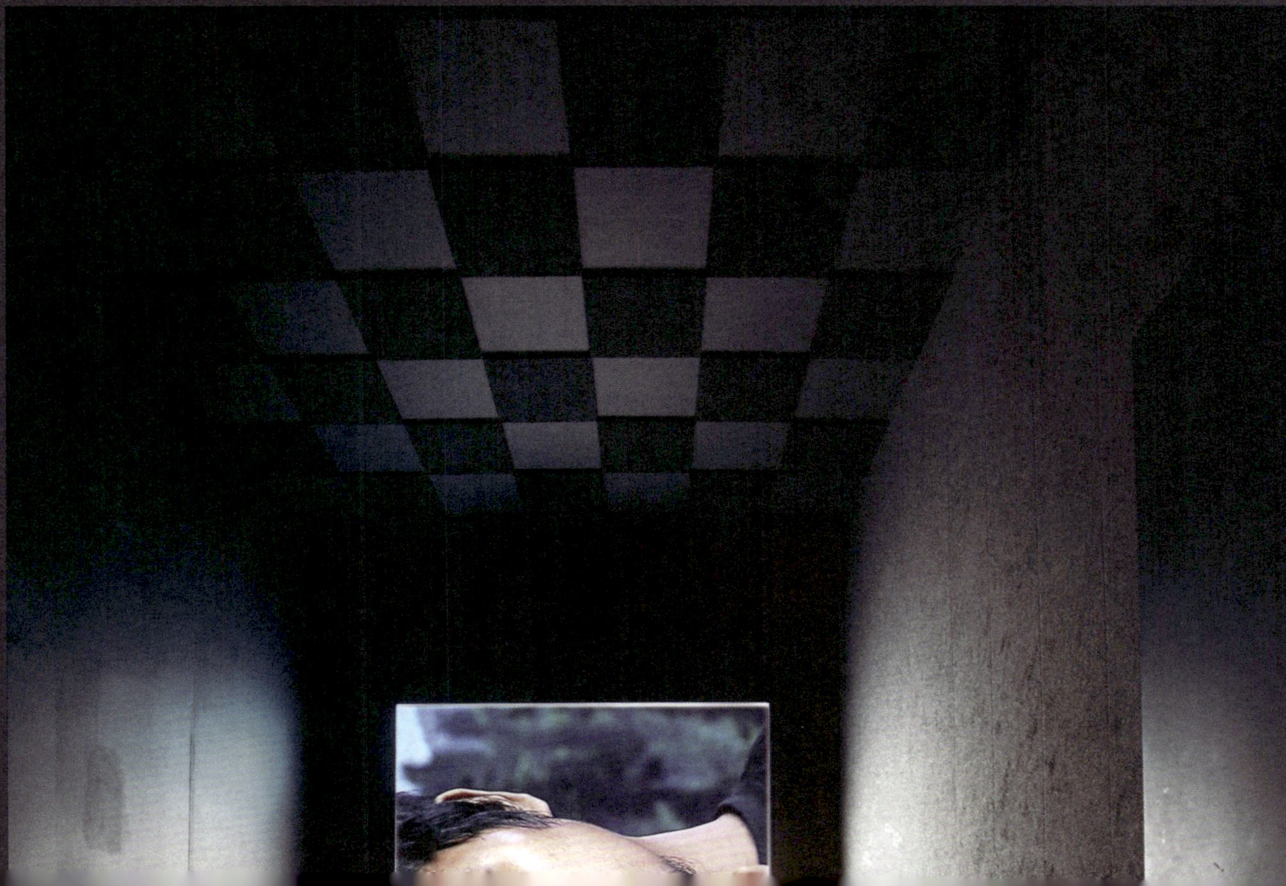

Willie Doherty

Ghost Story, 2007
High-definition digital video, color, sound
Running time: 15 minutes, looped
Dallas Museum of Art, TWO x TWO for AIDS and Art Fund, 2008.11

Willie Doherty (Irish, b. 1959) studied at Ulster Polytechnic in Belfast. For three decades, his films and photographs have explored aspects of landscape, trauma, and political turmoil in his native city of Derry, Northern Ireland. His work was included in the Carnegie International, Pittsburgh (1999); the Bienal de São Paulo (2002); the 52nd Venice Biennale (2007); and Documenta 13, Kassel (2012). Doherty has also had solo exhibitions at art institutions worldwide, including the Dallas Museum of Art; the Irish Museum of Modern Art, Dublin; the Renaissance Society, Chicago; Museum of Modern Art, Oxford; and Art Gallery of Ontario, Toronto. He was nominated for Tate's Turner Prize in 1994 and 2003.

REQUISITE DISTANCE

by Charles Wylie

Slowly, one could say stealthily, the art of Willie Doherty enters the eye and mind with a disorienting power and precision. Doherty creates art that is at once unsettling and beautiful, an art shaped by the background of the Troubles in his native Northern Ireland but that communicates across all borders to any receptive viewer. Taking no sides in a highly demarcated face-off, Doherty has unstintingly portrayed through photography and media installations the intense, often crushing psychological and physical effects of that conflict and the part that words and images have played in those effects. Doherty's subjects are those who lived through and succumbed to the Troubles, the land on which the conflict has taken place, and the language and imagery that have been used to define, obscure, influence, and sway. Yet, for all its specificity, his art exists outside the boundaries of determinant historical conditions; it conveys states and places of mind and existence independent of any context save that of being human.

In this exhibition [*Willie Doherty: Requisite Distance* at the Dallas Museum of Art, May 23–August 16, 2009], two types of Doherty's art are presented: a group of eleven photographs, made in the 1990s, and the video installation *Ghost Story,* made in 2007. Both contain the strikingly similar motif of a road, and both find in the land a site of incident and a bearer of meaning. The photographs depict the historically contested, beautiful, yet often disfigured landscape where the borders of Northern Ireland and the Republic of Ireland meet.

Meticulous in their formal composition, featuring dark, unvisited roads with monolithic barriers, what look like remnants of crime scenes, and a few select elements of the storied beauty of the Irish countryside, these large color photographs are purposely hung low and unframed to bring viewers into a closer relationship than conventional images might and to suggest that we experience them as if we were visitors in the country itself rather than visitors in a museum.

Ghost Story presents the same or a similar type of landscape. Here the forms of trees on a riverbank and an unused road act as a unifying visual motif for a series of other sequences: a face from which the eyes are peering back at the past, seeing the future, or witnessing events that we are spared; a series of urban settings in which vaguely menacing incidents unfold but do not reach a resolution. Accompanied by a subtly lyric yet potentially disturbing spoken narrative (written by the artist and performed by the actor Stephen Rea) describing apparitions, premonitions, and memories of trauma, *Ghost Story* provides a measured and tensely mesmerizing cinematic experience suffused with melancholic dread and spectral beauty.

Springing from the Troubles, these two bodies of work convey some of the states of mind and emotion that such trauma can produce. Both can be experienced on a profound level, even without any knowledge of the history of the conflict. Thus, in experiencing Doherty's art, one can simultaneously know and not know, a condition at the heart of this artist's formidably intelligent and exacting practice.

One of the challenges of writing about Doherty's art is conveying this sense of opposites, of something that is at once unsettling and beautiful, of something known and unknown, of something not seen but felt. Another challenge is trying to approach the history of the ground from which Doherty's art has arisen, that of the Troubles, with the requisite distance so that, in the service of disinterest and objectivity, one neither overemphasizes nor underplays their impact and does not take sides or even appear to do so. Such hesitancy can overwhelm, however. Language implicates and likely will be misunderstood—one could express something the wrong way and be both true and false in describing a situation from afar. In light of what has happened in Northern Ireland, silence, then, can seem not unreasonable. These very notions are also there, in parts and at various moments, in Doherty's art, but his art is not silent. The work takes no sides, but it *has* come into being and it is there for us to investigate.

The Troubles, which Doherty witnessed (he saw the events of Bloody Sunday on January 30, 1972, in Derry) and which subsided only relatively recently, began in the late 1960s but had their precedents in centuries of political conflict, periods of intermittent violence, and outright warfare between (depending on the histories one consults, and they are legion) English and Irish, Green and Orange, Catholic and Protestant, Ulster and Eire, South and North, Unionist and Republican. There are more of these pairs one could name, but it is worth noting that all of the adversaries are defined by who is on the other side of the *and*. Always, they are locked in combat. . . .

Despite its title, Doherty's *Ghost Story* does not overtly correspond to any of the broadly drawn traditions of the macabre, the occult, and the paranormal to be found in film and literature. There might be precedents in the Irish Gothic of J. S. Le Fanu's *Uncle Silas* and especially in Charles Maturin's *Melmoth the Wanderer,* in which the natural and the supernatural are menacingly intertwined amid a particular pastoral gloom. More to the point, and closer to our age, many of the literary and visual images in *Ghost Story* take their cue from the conventions of the contemporary crime story that, in its infinite varieties, forms one of the major genres of popular entertainment.

Crucially, however, Doherty refuses to honor that genre's (perhaps too easy) dependence on the graphic spoken vernacular or even more graphic violence and splatter effects. Doherty's aim is not to pummel his audiences, but to induce a more concentrated state of sustained tension than popular entertainment ever allows. Here, narrative convention does not reach conclusion but is infinitely postponed: we must construct for ourselves what is around that corner, what that figure standing in the underpass will do, who is in the car we as viewers approach. What we think (perhaps dread) will happen provides the content of these sequences as much as anything that we are shown. While images cut back to the road and to the eyes, *Ghost Story's* narrator tells a tale of wraiths and bodies, of ghosts in the midst of day, and (in one of the more grisly and chilling passages) how a shifting, malevolent liquid spreads on the ground to existentially destabilize all sense of firm foundation.

In many ways, *Ghost Story* can be seen as Doherty's summation of his media work to date. In its formal terms (its icy sheen overlaying saturated, dense color), sophistication of structure (the return to the road between incident and eyes), and interweaving of image and text (the quality of the latter being especially evocative), it can very well claim to be his major work in the genre of the moving image. It is outstanding for all these qualities as a powerful work of art that suggests how events, especially traumatic ones, are remembered through a scrim of pictures and words dimly illuminated by the faulty subjectivity of memory itself.

Charles Wylie, excerpted from *Willie Doherty: Requisite Distance: Ghost Story and Landscape* (Dallas: Dallas Museum of Art, 2009), 33–36.

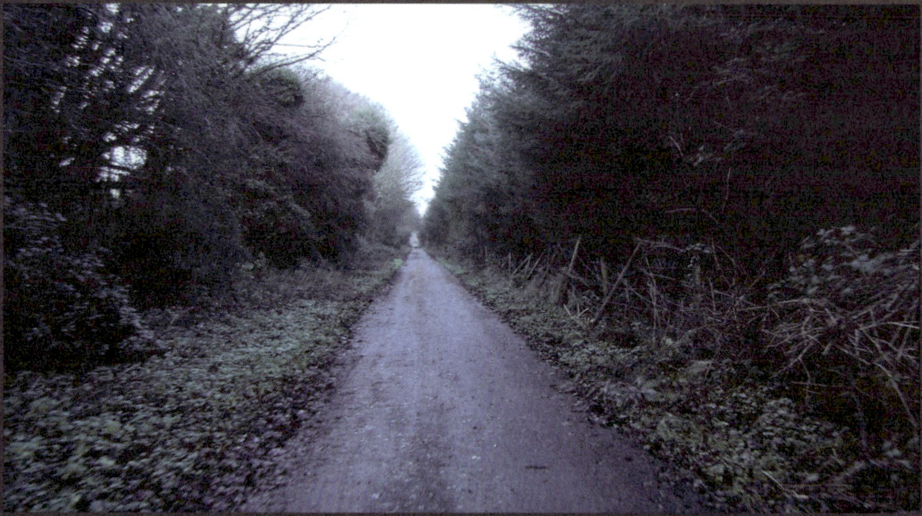

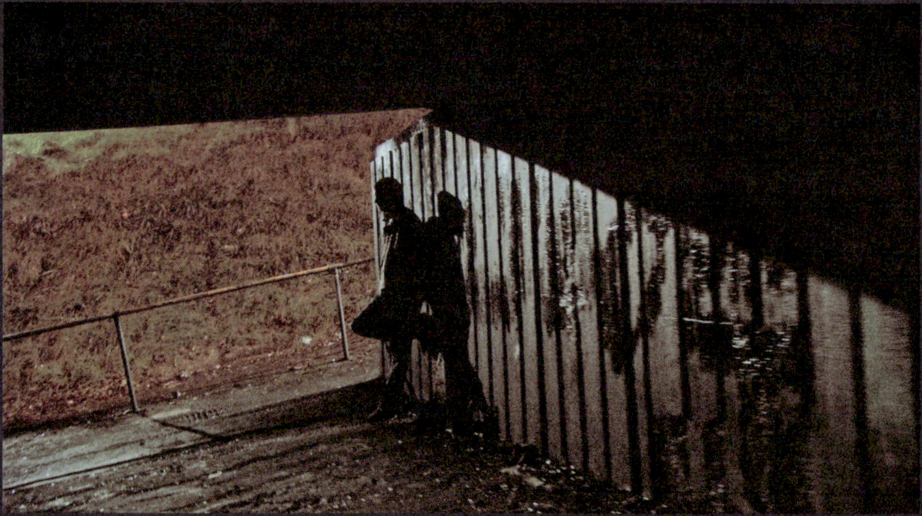

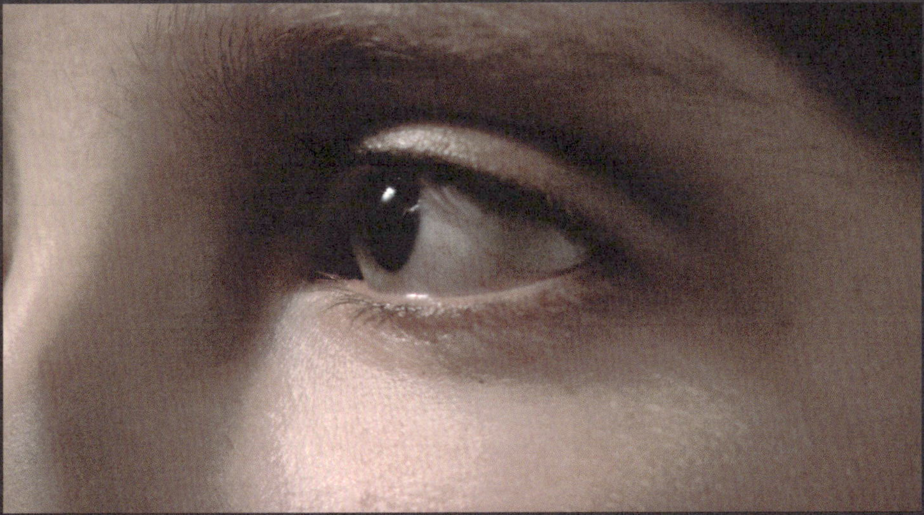

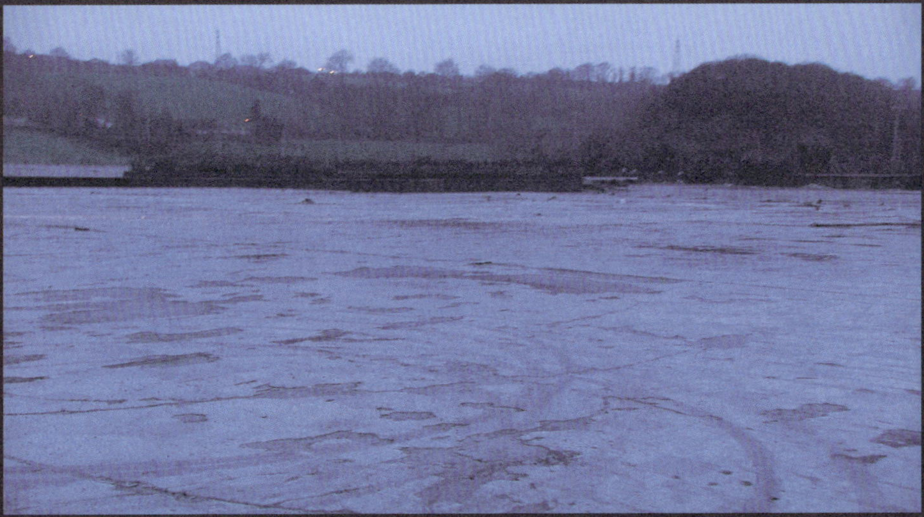

Steve McQueen

Gravesend, 2007
35 mm film transferred to high-definition digital video, color, surround sound
Running time: 17:58 minutes

Unexploded, 2007
Super 8 mm film transferred to digital video, color, silent
Running time: 54 seconds, looped

The Art Institute of Chicago, Through prior bequest of Mr. and Mrs. Joel Starrels; restricted gift of Donna and Howard Stone; through prior gifts of Fowler McCormick and Adeline Yates, 2008.479 and 2008.480

Steve McQueen (British, b. 1969) is an internationally renowned and acclaimed artist and film director whose work spans many different subjects and locations. Born in London, he currently lives and works in London and Amsterdam. Recent solo exhibitions have been held at Espace Louis Vuitton, Tokyo (2014); the Whitney Museum of American Art, New York (2016); and the Institute of Contemporary Art, Boston (2017). An important retrospective of his work was exhibited at the Art Institute of Chicago (2012) and traveled to the Schaulager, Basel, Switzerland (2013). McQueen represented Great Britain at the Venice Biennale (2009). Additionally, he has participated at Documenta 10 and 11 (1997 and 2002), Kassel; and in the Venice Biennale (2003, 2007, 2013, and 2015). He has been the recipient of numerous awards, including Tate's Turner Prize, London (1999); Officer of the Most Excellent Order of the British Empire (2002); Commander of the Most Excellent Order of the British Empire (2011); Best Picture (*12 Years a Slave*), Academy Awards, Los Angeles (2014); Harvard University, W. E. B. Du Bois Medal, Cambridge, Massachusetts (2014); and the Johannes Vermeer Prize, The Hague (2016).

A CONVERSATION WITH STEVE McQUEEN

by Adrian Searle

ADRIAN SEARLE: There are key images in *Hunger*—washing the floor, the light of the cigarette in the snow, the fly at the window—that all take the experience beyond the imperative to drive the narrative forward.

STEVE McQUEEN: These are so familiar to us that we don't really see them in cinema, and when we do, we are immediately put into that moment because they are so recognizable. It's just a case of detail, and it's a case of looking at things. As you said before, it's all a case of looking. When you put something on the screen that's unfamiliar but recognizable it can actually stir an audience and bring them close to the character and bring them close to the narrative.

AS: Close to one's own experience as well.

SM: Absolutely. So you feel a part of something that's very foreign to you. . . .

AS: I am still thinking about an earlier shift in the work, with *Western Deep* and *Carib's Leap:* a very big shift, in terms of locations and narrative.

SM: *Western Deep* was the first time I worked with the cinematographer Sean Bobbitt. My girlfriend, a film critic at the time, Bianca Stigter, introduced me to the film *Wonderland* (1999) and Sean Bobbitt's cinematography. The film was directed by Michael Winterbottom, and there were sequences in that film that were shot in Super 8. They were sped up, and I thought, This is interesting, so I got in contact with him. I told him I wanted to shoot in this South African gold mine, three and a half kilometers underground, on Super 8. He thought I was a bit nuts. We've worked together for twelve years now.

AS: Why Super 8?

SM: I wanted to shoot on something that had grain. I wanted it to stick to the viewer. I wanted something that the viewer could hold on to, that had texture—the texture of the rock, the drilling and mining. I wanted the audience to actually feel the molecules of dust.

AS: Like the graininess of the light.

SM: What's interesting is that you can also translate that into a smell. What I loved about it was that wherever you placed the camera, you could never be wrong. It was like Jacques Cousteau filming underwater. So I said to Sean: "Just shoot it. It can be just here, there, anywhere." Before that, I had always held the camera myself. It was wonderful to be in a situation where I could preempt things before he shot them, and when he got there, I could preempt things again. I think this was almost the first time I was directing. It was extraordinarily thrilling and exciting. Sometimes it was also very, very scary.

AS: I was shocked watching the miners, with thermometers in their mouths, having to do those grueling exercises underground.

SM: That had hardly ever been filmed before. During the apartheid era hundreds of men a week were tested for something like four hours, to check their condition, in a room simulating the temperature and conditions three and a half kilometers underground. Basically what you saw in that film was a test of survival. If you don't pass, you're out. No job. By the time I was there, they only did it for half an hour a day. But it is absolutely inhuman treatment. When we shot it I thought that it was going to cause a stir, people are going to go crazy and say this can't happen. It premiered at Documenta 11 in 2002. Instead, people asked if we'd made it up. There was no outrage. There was nothing. I thought to myself, this is how powerful art is—it doesn't mean anything.

AS: Why did you twin *Western Deep* with *Carib's Leap?*

SM: Caribs' Leap is on Grenada, where my parents came from. I was very interested in the Arawaks, the native people, who were all killed by the Caribs, who arrived from South America. After that the French came and killed all the Caribs. The French bought the Africans. The British came and fought the French a few times, and possession went back and forth. Then the Americans invaded in the 1980s. There you have it. You have the whole world on a little island of less than 345 square kilometers. This little island surrounded by sea is like a prison. As you see in the footage, it's as though there's no escape.

AS: There's nowhere to go. A closed world. Just as the miners are stuck in *Western Deep*.

SM: It's a scrap heap. There's the obvious postcolonial situation but also a kind of sadness.

AS: Which takes us to the Congo, in the film *Gravesend* (2007).

SM: We started in Gravesend, London, where Joseph Conrad's *Heart of Darkness* (1899) begins. Then we went to Walikale, in central Congo, where they excavate coltan. Coltan's in your mobile phone; it's in your computer. It's a mineral that makes a conductor that doesn't overheat. A miracle mineral. What was so fascinating to me about the Congo and coltan was the parallel to the Industrial Revolution. When Prince Leopold "owned" the Congo, that was at the height of the exploitation of rubber and the Industrial Revolution. And now, a hundred years later, with the digital revolution, the mineral coltan is a key element. There was a time in 2001 when a kilo of coltan was worth a hundred dollars or more. So lawyers and doctors were leaving their hats and canes behind to go to the bush, digging this stuff out. It was the new gold rush. It was a bit crazy.

AS: Dangerous?

SM: Yeah, we had seventeen people, two men with AK-47s, marching into the middle of the Congo. In the middle of the jungle we met this guy who was part of the protection of the coltan mine. We had to pay him off. The next day, after shooting, we were surrounded by people in uniform. We had to get the hell out of there quick. Even our guide was crying.

AS: It's a long way from following some guys down Brick Lane. In *Gravesend* you're edging toward a more narrative structure and a more overtly political kind of filmmaking.

SM: I don't know if it was overtly political. It just made sense to me. There was the parallel with a hundred years ago with rubber and coltan. It seemed interesting—but political? I just feel it's so obvious, so in front of your face that it's unavoidable. Even falling in love is political.

This text was excerpted from "A Conversation with Steve McQueen," *Steve McQueen: Works* (Schaulager: Laurenz Foundation, 2013), 201–203. Courtesy of Laurenz Foundation, Schaulager.

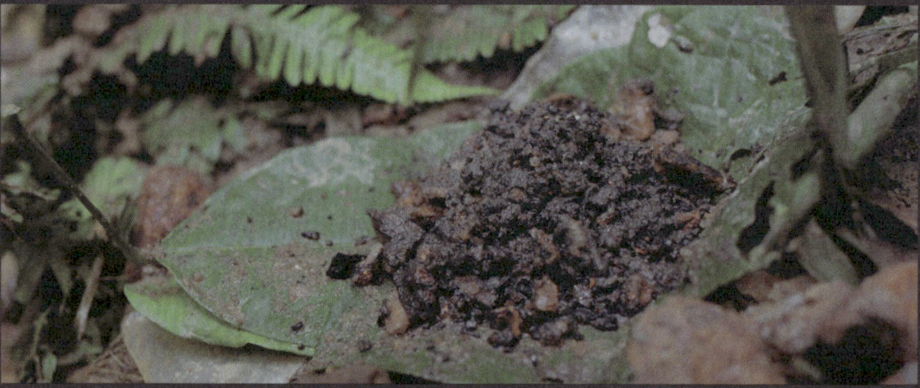

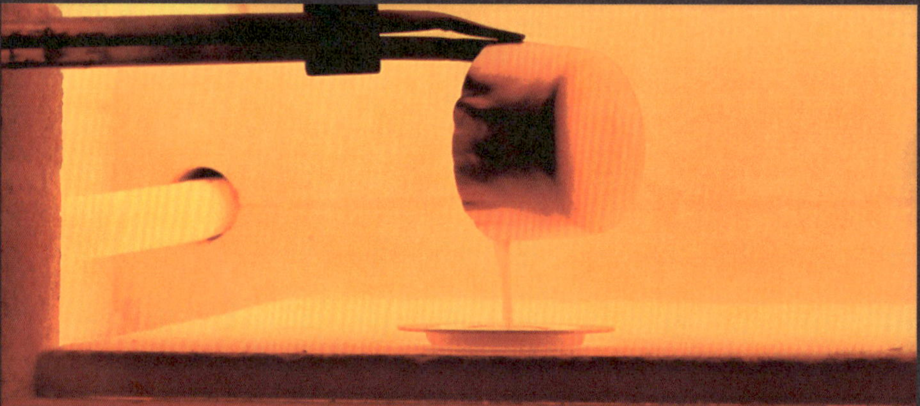

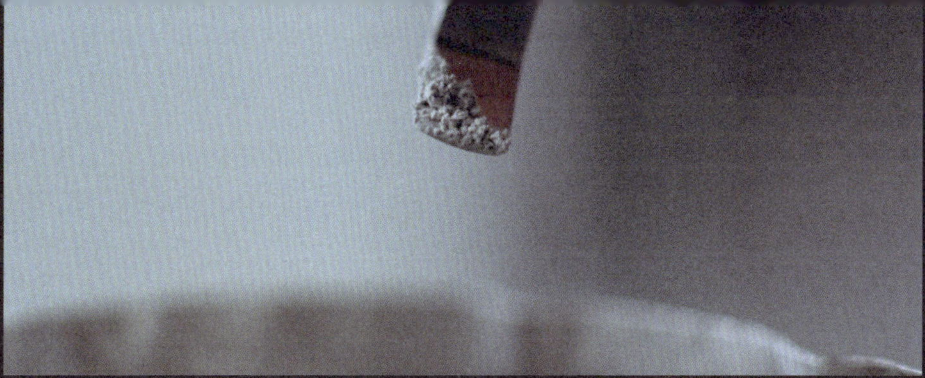

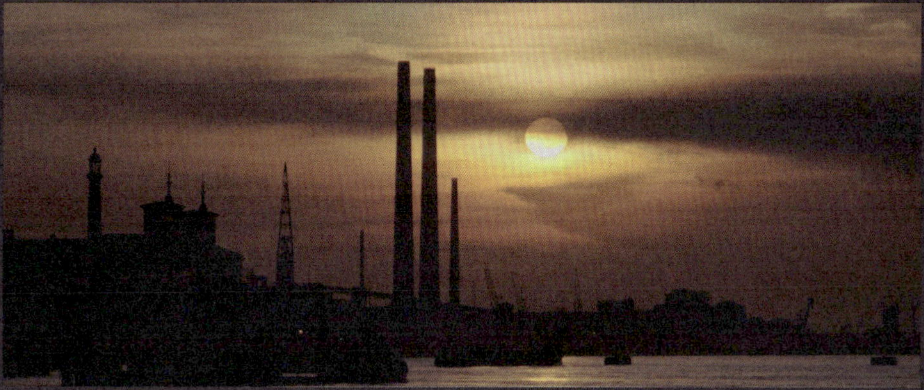

Omer Fast

5,000 Feet Is the Best, 2011
High-definition digital video, color, sound
Running time: 30 minutes, looped
Dallas Museum of Art, TWO x TWO for AIDS and Art Fund, 2011.41

Omer Fast (American/Israeli, b. 1972) was born in Jerusalem and grew up in Israel and New York. He received a BA/BFA from Tufts University/School of the Museum of Fine Arts in 1995 and an MFA from Hunter College in 2000. Fast's video works blend documentary and dramatic narrative, blurring the distinction between reality and fiction. His video installations have been widely exhibited worldwide at venues including the Dallas Museum of Art; the Stedelijk Museum, Amsterdam; Moderna Museet, Stockholm; The Power Plant, Toronto; the Wexner Center for the Arts, Columbus, Ohio; and Tate Modern, London. His work has also been shown at biennials and festivals, including Documenta 13, Kassel (2012); the 54th Venice Biennale (2011); the Sundance Film Festival (2009); and two Whitney Biennials (2002 and 2008). Fast lives and works in Berlin.

ARTIST TALK WITH OMER FAST

Transcribed by Kelly Filreis

AUDIENCE MEMBER: Do you ever think about pursuing documentary filmmaking?

OMER FAST: I read a book many years ago that, for me, packaged a very easy answer to that question, written by someone called Bill Nichols, that deals with documentary as a genre. He claims that every film is a documentary, and that's very much the way that I see it. Even the biggest "*Spiderman Lives Again,*" or whatever is coming out now with *Spiderman,* is in a sense a documentary. It's a documentary of particular wishes at a particular time, the kind of means that are being told to tell this particular story. This is very obvious—viewing or consuming from a critical distance—but I think when you look at films and you're not swallowed entirely by the emotional story that they tell and identify with it, it's very easy to view fictional films as well as documentaries of a particular point of view of a particular culture, a sensibility, and so on. I very much subscribe to that. And I think [Nichols] calls it that—"documentaries of wish fulfillment"—when he describes fiction films. And so, broadly, I do consider myself a documentarian, but the things that I really document are my responses to the stories that I collect at a particular point in time. And that's kind of an evasive answer—perhaps another disavowal—the answer is yes and no. I am a documentarian; I'm not a documentarian in the cliché sense that may not even be really valid of a documentarian in the investigative journalistic way. Obviously not.

AM: Are you saying that the way you ended [your film *The Casting*[1]] by, "It's too long," that you're leaving it with no judgment on whether any of this is true?

OF: No, the judgment, I think, is shifted onto the kind of director, the "voice" of the person who is ostensibly responsible for the piece. What you're doing is you're being shifted in terms of what you consider, whether, "Oh, how terrible—this innocent person was shot." Instead, you're thinking: Wait a second. What is this creep talking about? Why is this story too long? I didn't think it was too long. Or maybe I thought it was too long, but I don't know. But you begin to think about the piece in, I hope, a somewhat more critical way rather than being consumed by these mechanics of forgiveness and identification that I think are very big traps when you are getting into these kinds of stories, which I find nevertheless fascinating and very compelling.

AM: So, it's a judgment?

OF: I don't think so. It's more of a performance rather than a judgment. There is an insertion of a directorial voice, a director who is meant as a foil, as a kind of distraction. And to the degree to which he performs that distraction, the piece presents yet another layer. Now that might be sort of confusing and distracting—that might be another disavowal—but I think that piece really does try to shuffle as many disavowals and keep them in the air and juggle them as much as possible. The degree to which it succeeds, I think, is the degree to which people watch it and then think about it. It's not the degree to which it tells this particular staff sergeant's story in the "truthful" way and says: "How horrible war is. Innocent civilians die; young men get sent to battle; they're not prepared; they don't know what's going on; they shoot people, and you and I are responsible for it." This is obviously the kind of horror that's underlying the piece, but I think what it does is it tries to throw that up into the air in a rather complicated, convoluted set of disavowals.

AM: What was the reaction of the staff sergeant when he saw it?

OF: He was sent to Iraq two weeks after we met and spent the next eighteen months there. So by the time he returned from Iraq, the piece had already been made and shown, and so he wasn't able to see it. Of course, I sent him a link. But I think what the question implies is, in a sense, something that I resist and that is, very often, this notion that I have an ethical responsibility toward my subject matter—the people I interview. And this also gets into sticky territory. I see what I do as exploitation. I see it as exploitation that is mutual. When I meet people, very often I show them work, I explain to them what I'm interested in and what I do, and I don't often ask them what their reasons for participating in the work are. Of course, very often—always—the work is unclear at the beginning. I don't have a very clear sense of what I'm doing and what I'm saying.

But nevertheless when I met with him I did my best to explain that. But I think the people I seek are not this rarified notion of this "virgin storyteller" who has just been pulled away from the world and is telling a story on-camera for the first time just for you. Ron [the staff sergeant] was on *60 Minutes* beforehand. He started a group, Iraq Veterans for the Truth, or, I forget what he called it. He's very much been involved, after his experiences in Iraq, in first and foremost retelling his story, and in retelling his story, he's making very specific moral choices about what he's doing, but he's also agreeing to participate in a public dialogue, and I'm part of that. The work I make, I think, documents that desire to participate in a public dialogue, with all the trappings and misgivings I have about it. But we're not Best Friends Forever; we stayed in touch, and Brandon, the drone sensor operator who was interviewed for *5,000 Feet*, hasn't responded to my e-mails after he's seen the piece, so I can only assume that he either didn't like it or didn't download the link. And they meet with me for different reasons. Very often to get their rocks off their chest or there is an exchange also that's happening, of desires, of time. We spend some time together, we talk, and we go our different ways.

This text was transcribed and excerpted from Omer Fast's artist talk on the occasion of his exhibition *5,000 Feet Is the Best*, Dallas Museum of Art, July 19, 2012.

Notes

1 *The Casting* is a 2007 video in which Fast weaves together a United States staff sergeant's firsthand narration of his experiences in Iraq with a dramatized version of his accounts portrayed by actors. At the end of the video, Fast, functioning as the interviewer/director, remarks to the staff sergeant that his story would be far too long and audiences would lose interest, turning the focus of the video away from the soldier's story and instead questioning the nature of storytelling itself.

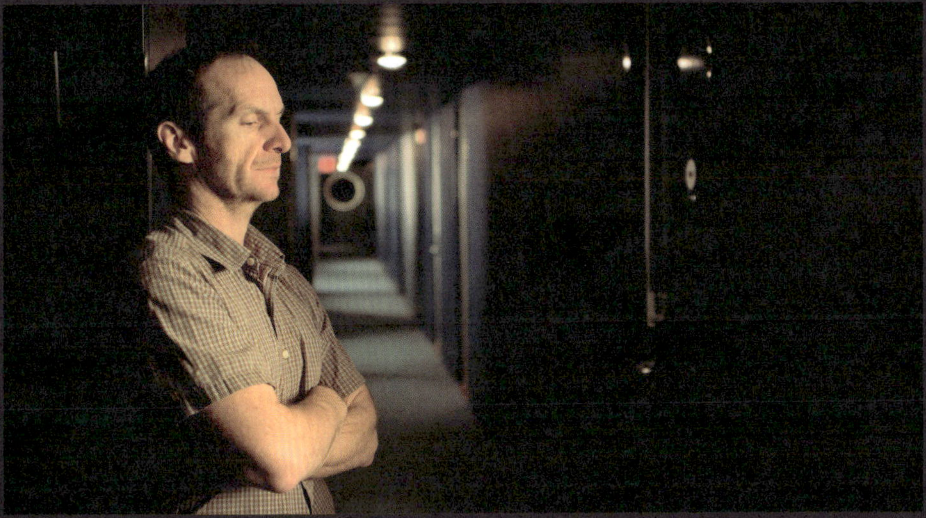

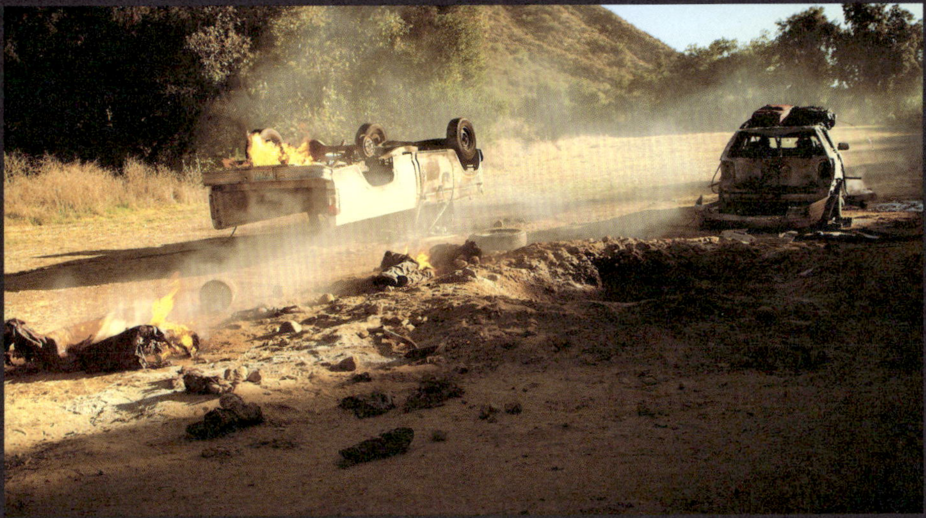

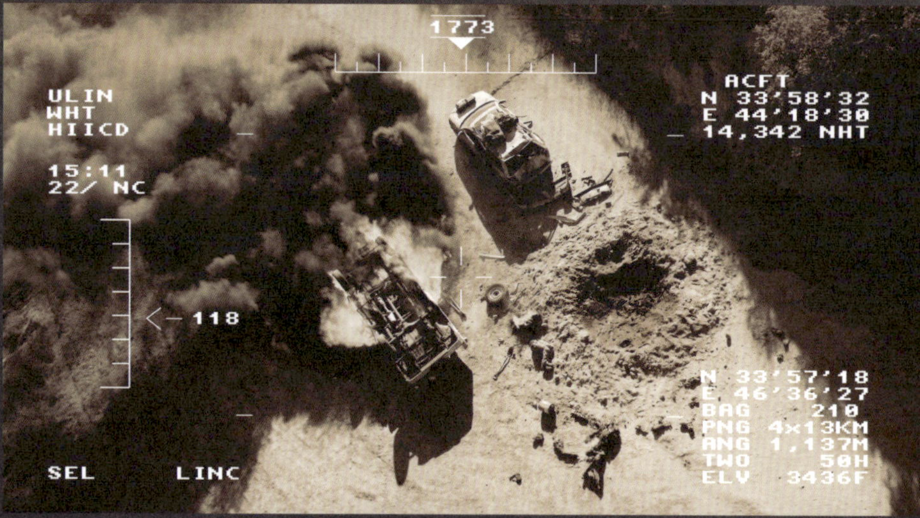
1773
ULIN
WHT
HIICD
15:11
22/ NC
118
SEL
LINC
ACFT
N 33'58'32
E 44'18'30
14,342 NHT
N 33'57'18
E 46'36'27
BAG 210
PNG 4x13KM
ANG 1,137M
TWO 50H
ELV 3436F

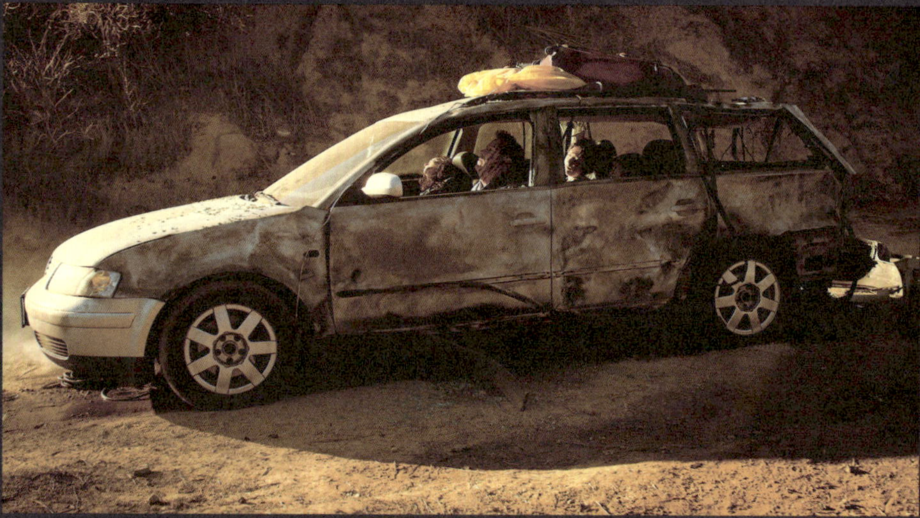

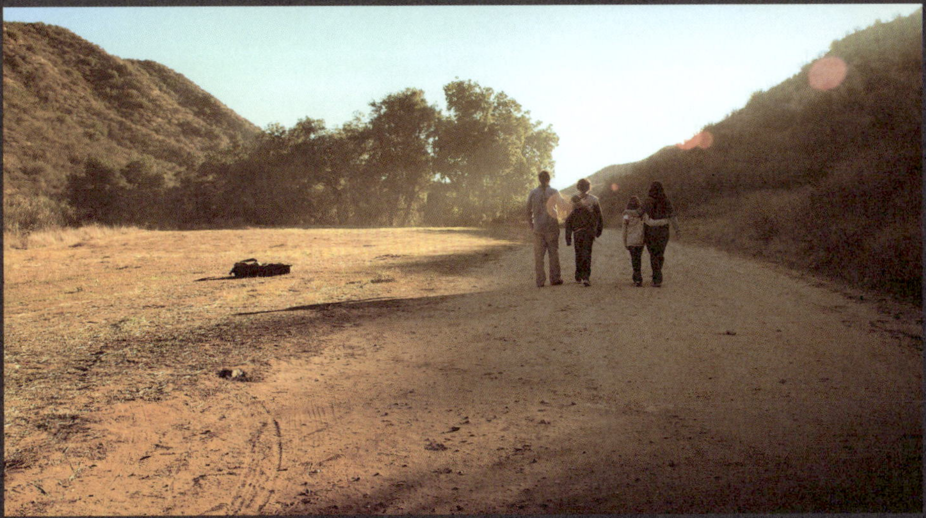

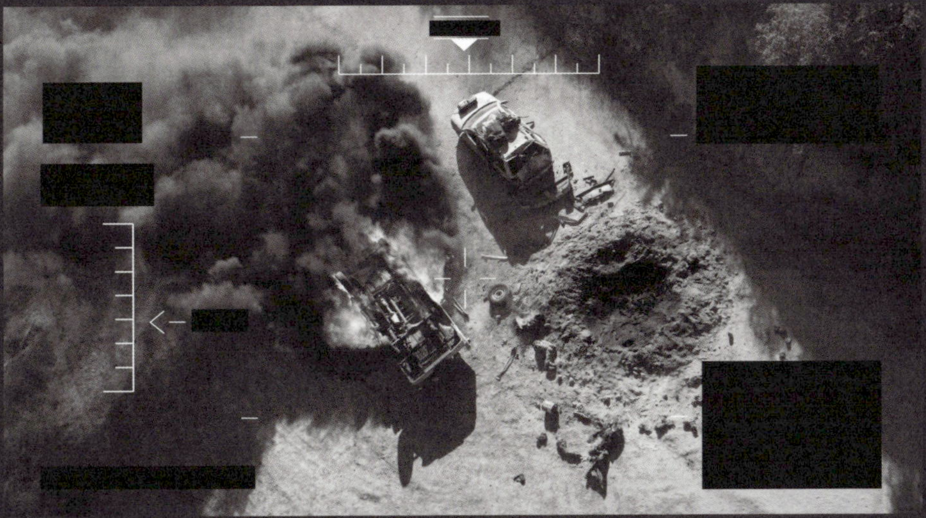

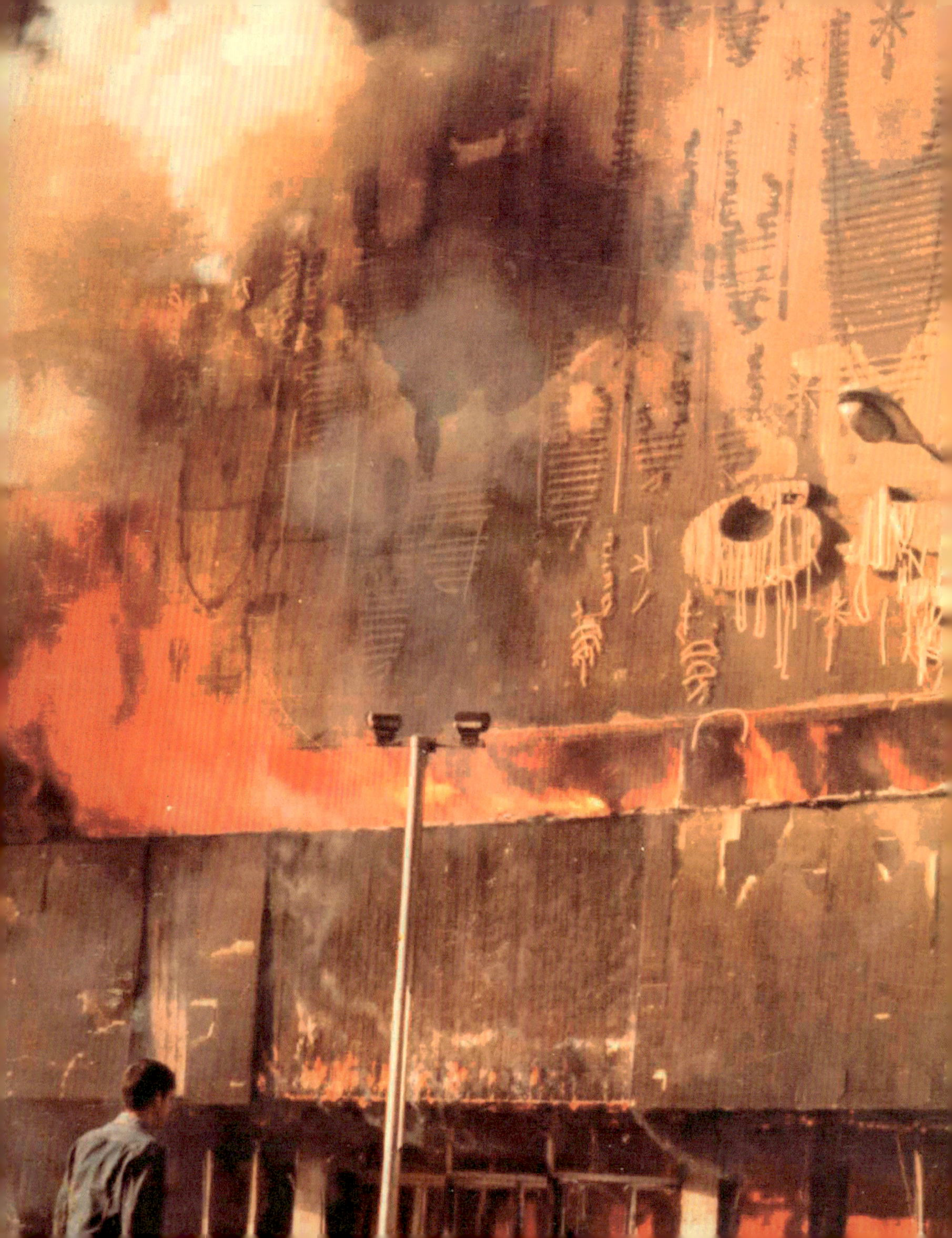

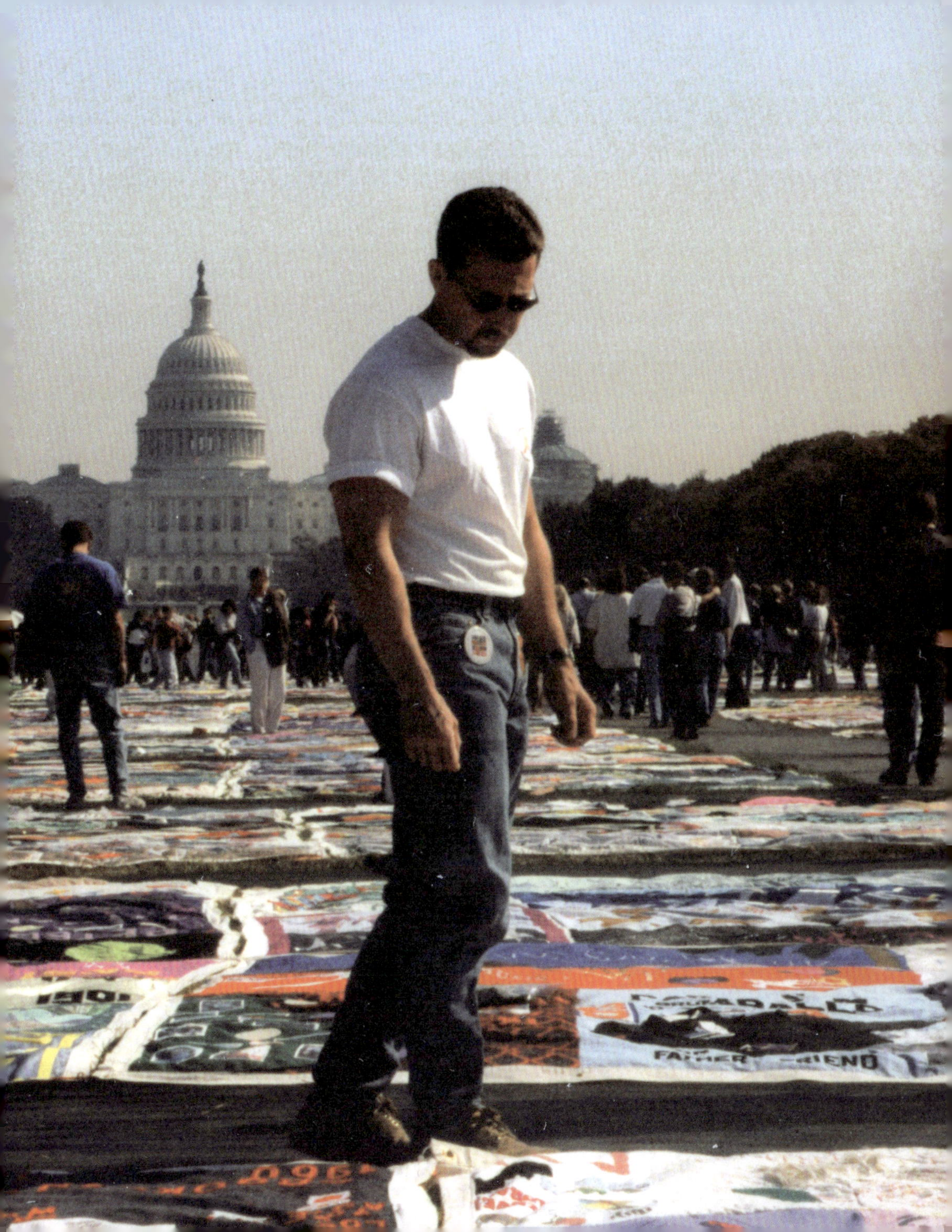
FATHER

James Coleman

Untitled, 2011–2015
LED video installation, color, sound
Running time: looped
Courtesy of the artist and Marian Goodman Gallery, New York

James Coleman (Irish, b. 1941) studied at the École nationale supérieure des beaux-arts, Paris; the Accademia di Belle Arti, Milan; the Central School of Art and Design, London; and the National College of Art and Design and University College Dublin. Coleman represented Ireland at the Paris Biennale (1973) and has participated in Documenta 9, 10, 11, and 12 (1992, 1997, 2002, and 2007), Kassel. He received both the Kurt Schwitters Prize, Hannover, and the Kunstpreis, Munich (2002). Important solo exhibitions have been mounted at the Institute of Contemporary Art, London (1986); the Musée d'Art Moderne de la Ville de Paris (1989); the Van Abbemuseum, Eindhoven, Netherlands (1989–1990); Dia Art Foundation, New York (1994–1995); the Centre Georges Pompidou, Paris (1996); the Palais des Beaux-Arts, Brussels; the Fundació Antoni Tàpies, Barcelona (1999); the Kunstmuseum, Lucerne (2001); the Lenbachhaus Kunstbau, Munich (2002); *James Coleman: Project for Léonard de Vinci: dessins et manuscrits* (drawings and manuscripts), Musée du Louvre, Paris (2003); the Museu Nacional de Arte Contemporânea do Chiado, Lisbon (2004–2005); the Irish Museum of Modern Art, Dublin (2009); and the Museo Nacional Centro de Arte Reina Sofia, Madrid (2012). Coleman lives and works in Dublin and Paris.

THE PLACE OF THE SPECTATOR IN THE WORK OF JAMES COLEMAN

by Jean Fisher

> Plays are normally acted as if the stage had four walls not three; the fourth being where the audience is sitting. The impression given and maintained is that what happens on the stage is a genuine incident from "real life," which of course doesn't have an audience. Acting with a fourth wall, in other words, means acting as if there wasn't an audience.
>
> —Bertolt Brecht
> *The Messingkauf Dialogues*

Brecht's Dramaturg states a condition common to naturalistic theater, commercial cinema, and "narrative" painting, which, while creating a semblance of reality (the Renaissance window on the world), nevertheless situates the viewing subject in an imaginary position outside the real time and space of the action. Brecht recognized that this was an authoritarian mode of representation, which held the audience in a pseudodominant and uncritical relation to it. By contrast, he advocated a *thaëter* which, imitating reality without reproducing the illusions of naturalism, would allow the audience to share actively in its experience. Brecht emphasized the *performance* in which the actor produced an illustration of the *gestus*, a dramatized recitation defining not character motivation but the social significance of the action.[1] I should like to discuss how, in the work of James Coleman, the visual image is an anchor for a dramatized recitation whose psychological implications for the spectator invite certain comparisons with performance art and theater.[2]

In visual art, it was Marcel Duchamp who initially raised the question of the social and psychological status of the art object and the spectator's contribution to its production of meanings. Duchamp's "readymade" gestures, directed against the valorized object of the museums, argued for art that was founded in life: an art that "*obliges* the spectator or reader to become himself an artist or poet."[3] This implied a move away from the object as a self-contained and pregiven reality whose meanings were imposed by the producer, toward art as a *context* in relation to which the spectator introjects and reconstructs his or her own reality; that is, the work itself becomes a "theater" in which the spectator is a "coperformer. . . ."

Performance art, emerging from such diverse trends in the late sixties, encompasses a wide range of activities about which it is impossible to generalize. However, a performance may be broadly characterized as an event of fixed duration executed before a collective audience with the artist as principal executant. While it indeed presents an organized spectacle of live bodies and props, it differs from orthodox theater in two major respects: the action is performed in real time, not the logical time of fictional narrative, and usually the artist functions not as a fictive character whose definition or motivation is the rationale of the narrative, but as a signifier in the production of meaning of the action. The audience's relationship to the performance artist remains, however, ambivalent, since what is enacted is often a narcissistic display which, while it avoids viewer identification with the character typical of theater, nevertheless also fails to provide a reality into which the audience may enter. On the contrary, the viewer is often held at a distance in an exhibitionist-voyeur relationship (one might cite certain performance strategies of Joseph Beuys or Vito Acconci). An ensuing tendency toward the valorization of the artist himself is reinforced through oral dissemination which virtually mythologizes the performer. In such cases, the "fourth wall" remains intact.

James Coleman is not a performance artist. He suppresses his own presence as an "author" in the interests of the text, whose structure as *work* of art restores the spectator's "performance." The work presents a *projection*, an installation, which both draws and comments on the languages of representation using various time-based media with narration and within a defined space. Coleman uses time as a primary signifying element referring directly to the spectator's perceptual and mnemonic faculties. His text unfurls and reveals itself in the real time of one's experience. It is, moreover, a continuous cycle, an endless repetition: a narrative with no implied prehistory, whose inauguration is whichever point the viewer enters its cycle. Thus, unlike conventional narrative, there is no end that would satisfactorily explain a beginning. The spectator's desire for unity—for the resolution or masking of those contradictions that are the contingent reality of one's life and which is the lure of fictional (especially naturalistic) narrative—is not gratified.

Coleman nevertheless exploits repetition, a characteristic of the diegesis: those enigmas and returns of the action which temporarily suspend the forward impulse of the "plot."[4] Repetition, according to the psychoanalytic schema, is a ritual of return whose logic was clarified for Sigmund Freud through his observation of the *Fort–da* [gone–there] game, in which the child—perceiving his mother's comings and goings, and attempting to accommodate this traumatic loss—stages the disappearance of an object to experience the pleasure of its return. But this staging refers to an alienation of the self and the symbolization of its desire for the other through representation.[5] Repetition becomes the symbolized refutation of the moment of loss, an act which thereafter enacts that which, effaced in perception, cannot be remembered, but within which—as Lacan somewhat enigmatically describes it—the subject "is there to rediscover *where it was* . . . the real."[6] The real, the immediacy of an often traumatic lived experience, is what is betrayed by discourse, which henceforth mediates the subject through the agency of the signs of language. This incommensurable difference, or "lost history," of the subject is, however, reenacted in a constant vacillation of repetitions-in-transformation, but an "originary" moment can never be recovered. In much of Coleman's work repetition is presented in changing contexts. One's perception of what is repeated becomes converted into memory, but with each successive recurrence and each new juxtaposition, there is a shift in what is signified. In recognizing this transformation, viewers become aware of themselves as perceiving subjects, which suggests that the work functions in that ungraspable space between perception and its conscious representation: the "space in which the space of the Other is situated, in which the subject is constituted. . . ."[7]

It is . . . in touching on the register of the real, an experience that (as yet) eludes the signifying demands of discursive or symbolic formations, that Coleman's work has its greatest resonance. Despite the assumptions we derive from discourse, language or representation in itself is not transparent; its meaning is not readily available "at a glance" but carried by the context of its use. There is, then, a paradoxical lack of coincidence between the image or work and the thing to which it refers that renders the latter unknowable in its entirety. Coleman's work exploits this aporia of language.

Significantly, his images are not fixed, and in experiencing their narrativity and repetition, one's perceptions become transformed into memory, enabling the building of a spatiotemporal, or "historical," relation with the work, but one nonetheless that does not lead to closure. It is at this juncture that the verbal narration gains resonance, functioning as a relay that extends the spectator's relation to the image into a broader sociohistorical context. The audience's role as listeners is central to the production of meaning here. In speaking of how, in reading, we mentally identify a narrated event, Roland Barthes mentions that while "to read is to name, to listen is not only to perceive a language, it is also to construct it."[8] Such is the essential condition of the spectator's relationship to Coleman's narration, through whose multilayered signs and discontinuities the audience struggles to construct their meanings by connecting with their own past and future, becoming themselves the subject of the text. As Brecht's Actor says, the notion of "continually observing oneself and referring back to one's own experience can easily lead a man to alter the text." To which the Dramaturg responds, "alterations demand a great deal of art"; it is "not the play but the performance that is the real purpose of all one's efforts."[9] Likewise, in the case of Coleman's work, priority lies not with the art object as such, but with the dynamic of reception and the performative potential of language, gesture, and image. Thus it is not outside but *inside* the viewer-listener that the unity of Coleman's "text" is constituted.

In its insistence on attentiveness and response and hence on the immediacy of its experience, the work engages the viewer as a *participant*, not as an observer. This experience is not based in any prior knowledge, which would imply a conscious, speaking subject. On the contrary, in the face of the work's constant slippage away from any determinable referentiality, the viewer experiences a suspension of knowledge, a rendering "speechless," a loss of boundaries between subject and object. In other words, the work induces moments of desubjectivation, a state of uncertainty that can be referred back neither to a subject nor to a psychological state. Nor is it a return to some presubjective state, but it is instead an experience of the condition of our relation to the limits of language itself where it fails to "speak for" us. The spectator is placed in the position of continuously having, as Barthes says, to "construct language," which is to say, to invent meaning. Hence, in its play of indeterminacy, the "place of the spectator" in Coleman's work is the site where an encounter with the real—the ineffable difference between perception and memory (representation), between pure language and discourse—begins to unravel symbolic certitude.

Through meanings established and perpetuated in its discursive systems, society tends to reinforce the imaginary; it emphasizes "sameness" and "difference," playing on the subject's desire to unify itself with an ideal Other—these days most often derived from media personalities. When we speak of our identity, we are speaking not of an independent entity, but of something which is both relative and defined sociohistorically. In this way society binds us to itself, guiding both our perceptions and the meanings we extract from them in order to maintain its own coherence and "truth." It is this disparity between mediated reality and reality as individually lived and perceived that Brecht sought to expose in his alienation effect. In Brecht's *thaëter*, this effect "consists in the reproduction of real-life incidents on the stage in such a way as to underline their causality and bring it to the spectator's attention. This type of art also generates emotions; such performances facilitate the mastering of reality."[10]

Coleman's project is not dissimilar in its aims, because one crucial question asked by it is how we might creatively reinvent a world dominated by "received" information which cripples any sense of subjective agency. In revealing the mechanisms of discursive formations and the ways by which we are inserted into them, Coleman's work exposes the ideological framework at the root of social discourse, drawing us out of our apathetic unawareness of the meanings inherent in it. Thus, his work is "political" not in the conventional sense (it is never "prescriptive," nor does it present a "position"), but in the fact that it challenges the very basis of ideology: those relative, socially determined values projected and reinforced through the representations of culture that ensnare the subject in a system of predetermined meanings and relationships which, because familiar, seem "natural" and unquestionable. If Coleman's work plunges us as spectators into equivocal territory, it is to remind us that even though we may be irrevocably possessed by language, in testing its limits we are better able to understand the nature of this possession. Can one ask more of art than this?

Jean Fisher, excerpted from "The Place of the Spectator in the Work of James Coleman," first published in *Open Letter*, No. 5–6: Summer–Fall 1983. Republished in *James Coleman*, edited by George Baker (Cambridge, MA; London: MIT Press, 2003), 19–35.

Notes

1 Brecht's *gestus* is a combination of gesture and attitude (a play, a person, a sentence can all have a *gestus*); see Brecht, *The Messingkauf Dialogues*, trans. John Willett (London: Eyre Methuen, 1965), trans. note, 46.
2 By "dramatized recitation" in Coleman's work, I mean a kind of dialogical monologue allowing, as in Brecht's *thäeter*, the "subject to be approached from several points of view" (ibid., 106), and in which gesture and props combine to reveal the artifices of the performance as distinct from theatrical naturalism.
3 Octavia Paz, "The Castle of Purity," in *Marcel Duchamp: Appearance Stripped Bare*, trans. Donald Gardner (New York: Little, Brown, 1978), 87.
4 Roland Barthes, *S/Z,* trans. Richard Miller (New York: Hill and Wang, 1974), 19.
5 See Jacques Lacan: *"Fort! Da!"* It is precisely in his solitude that the desire of the little child

has already become the desire of another, of an *alter ego* who dominates him and whose object of desire is henceforth his own affliction." Jacques Lacan, *Écrits: A Selection*, trans. Alan Sheridan (London: Tavistock Publications, 1977), 104.

6 Jacques Lacan, *The Four Fundamental Concepts of Psychoanalysis*, trans. Alan Sheridan (Harmondsworth: Penguin Books, 1977), 45.

7 Ibid.

8 [footnote 21 in source] Roland Barthes, "Introduction to the Structural Analysis of Narratives," in *Image, Music, Text*, essays selected and translated by Stephen Heath (Glasgow: Fontana/Collins, 1977), 102.

9 [footnote 22 in source] Brecht, *The Messingkauf Dialogues*, 74.

10 [footnote 23 in source] Ibid., 102.

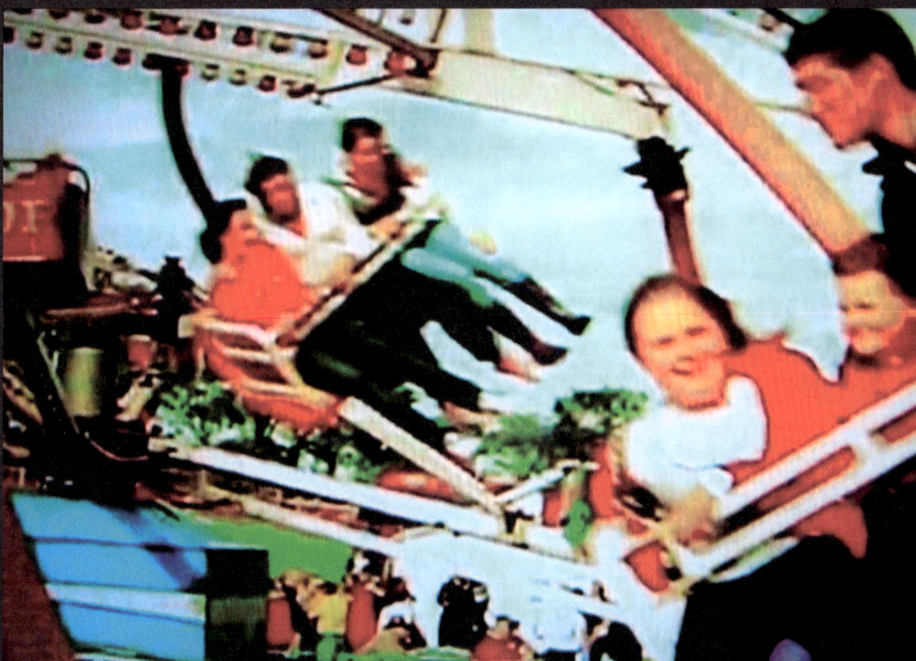

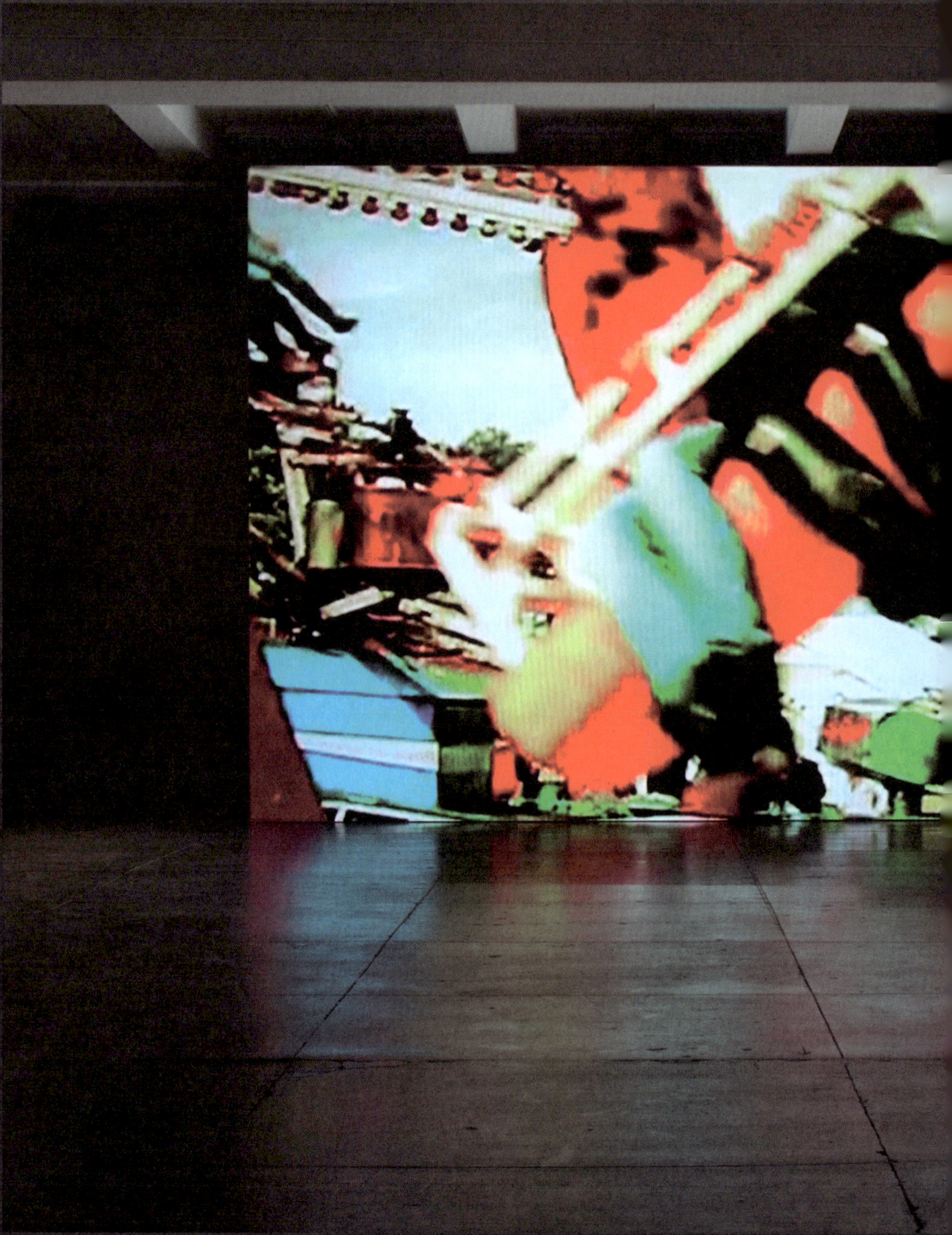

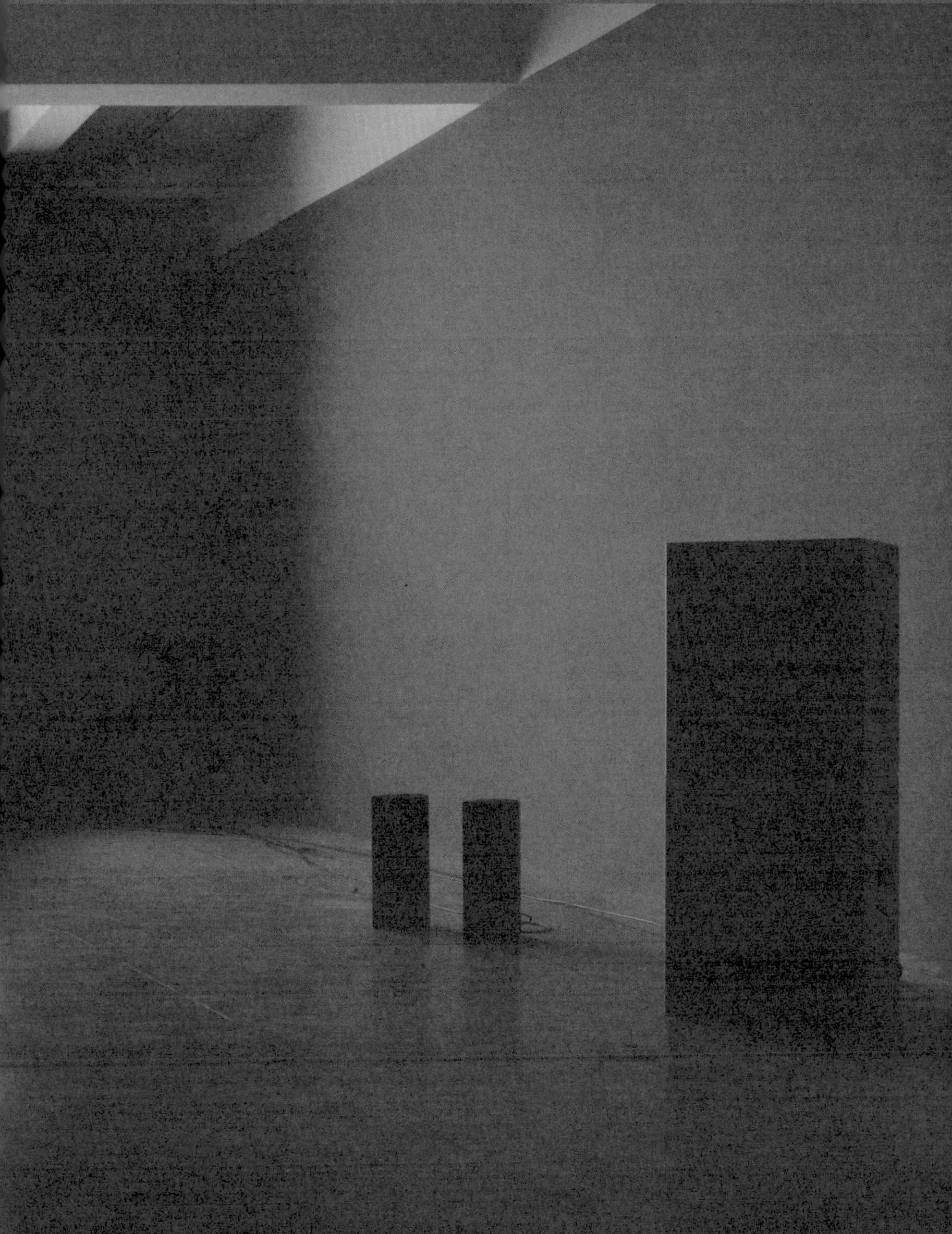

Mark Bradford

Spiderman, 2015
Digital video, color, sound
Running time: 6:03 minutes
Courtesy of The Rachofsky Collection

Mark Bradford (American, b. 1961) was born in Los Angeles, where he continues to live and work. He received a BFA in 1995 and an MFA in 1997 from California Institute of the Arts. Bradford is a recipient of many grants and awards, including the Joan Mitchell Foundation Award, Nancy Graves Foundation Grant, Bucksbaum Award from the Whitney Museum of American Art, New York, and a MacArthur Fellowship (2009). His work—addressing themes of race, sexuality, and the urban environment—ranges from large-scale collage and sculpture to video projection. His work has been the subject of numerous publications and exhibitions at major venues such as the Hammer Museum, Los Angeles; Walker Art Center, Minneapolis; the Los Angeles County Museum of Art; Contemporary Art Museum, Saint Louis; and the Museum of Modern Art, New York. Bradford's first major career survey traveled from the Wexner Center for the Arts, Columbus, Ohio; to the Dallas Museum of Art; the Institute of Contemporary Art, Boston; Museum of Contemporary Art, Chicago; and the San Francisco Museum of Modern Art (2011). Bradford represented the United States in the 57th Venice Biennale (2017).

CONVERSATIONS: MARK BRADFORD AND ANITA HILL, HAMMER MUSEUM, LOS ANGELES

Transcribed by Eric Zeidler and Kelly Filreis

MARK BRADFORD: You talked a lot about content and form. What I realize so much in my work and even in policy: you have to have both. Even in a painting, I will panic if there's no form. I'm good with the content, but if there's no structure and no form, the whole thing falls apart. . . .

ANITA HILL: You use the form not to create some static, but to push the form to include, maybe, more voices, bigger considerations, smaller considerations in this exhibition, and you move from the map—which is to me, the big picture—to the cell.

MB: Yes.

AH: So, tell us about the transition, and why it's important for us to be able to see both in the same exhibit.

MB: Well, cellular—I was thinking about the idea of the body being made up of cells, and the idea that there is a transformation that happens in the body when something is attacking it. And it's very weird because oftentimes the language around it is very military—the "war on cancer," "we're beating the . . . "—it's very military, but in a way, it's almost abstract, looking at cells under a microscope and realizing that those cells are actually in your body. I always find it very strange for me when I go to a doctor and he gives me all these charts and he tells me, "Cholesterol's up here, and this is down here." But I realize that's my *body* I'm looking at in these charts, and I have this disconnect. When I can't feel something, I don't really think it's there [*laughter*]. So, it's this idea of the disconnect between what we perceive and what is actually going on at the same time.

AH: I have a friend who is the head of a women's health program in Massachusetts, and she says that "every cell has a sex." She deals with medicine, and women in particular, and the disparities in treating women—women's health issues—but it seems to me that one of the things that you're saying about HIV is that in order for people to really understand how to deal with the issues . . . not only on a medical level, but on a social and political level, we have got to see the big picture, but we also have to realize that we are talking about human beings.

MB: People.

AH: And we're talking about them at very intimate levels. That, to me, is what the movement from the big map to the cells represents. Getting us to think about individuals as well as the numbers that are out there, the numbers of people who are impacted, which means, really, if you think about it, all of us are. . . .

MB: It's one thing to write a check; it's another thing to go to the women's shelter that you are actually supporting, and sort of volunteering, and seeing people up close. So I vacillate between both. That's probably why I'm an abstract artist. When it gets too hot, I find freedom in abstraction. Race, and what's going . . . and everything . . . the same thing. . . .

AH: What are some of things you think are going on? . . . You just threw that out there: race and . . .

MB: Race, and . . .

AH: HIV is a great place to start because there are conversations that are being omitted. Some of the bigger policy conversations and some of the intimate interpersonal conversations that are being omitted, that the public isn't quite ready to confront, and you've seen that. And when you do the work to put together the pieces, you see that. So what are those things that you think we should be talking about and thinking about as we look at all this work?

MB: I guess the video piece [*Spiderman*] is probably the easiest for me. . . . I sometimes find some stand-up comedians harsh toward women and Otherness; they have a harsh gaze; they kind of stand there with this power and dispense these arrows that to me are kind of hard. I remember seeing the Eddie Murphy [stand-up performance] *Delirious*. I have no problem with Eddie Murphy, but I remember sitting in the audience and thinking: Oh. Gay-bashing has entered into the public domain as being acceptable, because when he started with the "no faggots" and "lookin' at my ass," everybody [was] like, "Ohhh hah hah hah hah." I was like, okay, [it has] entered into the public. So I'm always fascinated when things enter into the public sphere as being okay. At a point they weren't okay, and then they enter in. Fast-forward a little more. It wasn't acceptable at some point to call women bitches and hoes, and then it just entered into the social conversation and was fine. You know, it's just totally no problem.

AH: And ironically it entered in through an artistic form.

MB: Absolutely.

AH: So there was a cover, in a sense.

MB: It sounds like church right around here [*gestures to audience, laughter*]. But those things do fascinate me because there's no protection for those bodies once they're accepted in the public as being okay for abuse.

AH: I was just going to say, that opens the gateway to violence, and it can be based on sexuality, it can be based on gender, and also it opens the gate for excuses, and, "Oh well, it's just a joke, and we should lighten up." And it also gives you an opportunity for people to live in denial about how. . . . We've been talking about all sorts of ways in which this happens. In particular . . .

MB: Bill Cosby?

AH: Were we talking about Bill Cosby?

MB: We were talking about so much stuff backstage . . .

AH: We *were* talking about Bill Cosby, but not only Bill Cosby, but you think about back to 1991. Rather than accept that a very powerful man might be an abuser and a harasser, it was easier to say, "Oh, I'm sure it was not intended that way," or "It never happened," or all kinds of excuses, and fast-forward: it's 2015, and we're hearing some of those same things again.

MB: We had just talked about that, and I think there's always. . . . Race plays a huge part of this kind of equation, oftentimes because you feel this kind of revisionist history for the mass, to make it less messy. But I always find that life is messy, and I don't know why we need to clean it up, because it's the same race. When I in 1991 saw you stand up, and you were the same color and you were speaking your truth, I thought to myself, in my little abused little way, figuring out how to navigate across the schoolyard and not get beat up, I thought, You know, I think I have some of that way deep down inside of me. Even though I didn't want anybody at the time to know. But this idea of standing up—you were—really, it was the first time I saw the same race in opposition on *television*. Girl, you were putting our business out there.

AH: And you say it's messy; race complicated an issue. People really didn't know how to deal with race and gender and abuse of power all in the same sentence.

MB: Not in 1991.

AH: In 1991. And then they have the bodies and also the complications of politics that made it almost impossible for people to deal with, but there are other complicating factors that we deal with, and we talk about race. I've dealt with a lot of groups who have had problems within the community, whether it is a geographic community or a demographic community, where it's always the same response, [which] is, like you said, "You're putting our business out there, and we're not comfortable." I've had it happen in—people come to me and say, "These things are going on in my church, but I have been told that I shouldn't bring it up, because it'll bring embarrassment and shame to our church." On college campuses, when women bring up sexual assault, they are told, "Well, you know, everyone will think that everybody at Brandeis is a rapist if you file this and you go public with it." So these kinds of complications that made things difficult for us as a public to understand are also the very things that we should be working hardest to try to understand. And I'm not trying to rake things, but it seems to me that when we talk not only about race making things complicated, and religion and ethnicity making things complicated, we also have to add that sexuality makes things complicated for us to talk about, so that the intergroup discussion that has to take place around any number of those things is almost impossible.

MB: It feels like sin. Sometimes when you step outside of that narrative, it almost becomes biblical, when you go against the norm or do something outside the kind of static narrative. I always call it. . . . South Central to me was formed kind of around the narrative of *Boyz in the Hood* meets *Menace II Society*, and it kind of stayed at this static moment. And it's interesting. I was just watching, I was thinking about *Menace II Society*, and I was looking for the clip, a part of it: when the man is a crackhead, and he says that he will perform oral sex on another man, and the guy shoots him, but because he's a male, and because it was oral sex male to male, it was totally fine, and they went on to the next scene. But that was the time. Whereas in *Friday*—you guys know, "Bye, Felicia." This saying, this term—"Bye, Felicia"—now that is a strawberry. There [were] strawberries and raspberries. Raspberries were men and strawberries were women. The women were Halle Berry, *Jungle Fever*. The women are always treated like, just dismissed, like: "Go on, girl. Bye, Felicia. Bye, Felicia." Whereas the man was murdered. So this idea of the body and the narrative and sexuality—you pretty much figured out your place real quick. And this idea of "down low" came out of that time. So this idea of speaking, sometimes it *would* feel like sin: "You should *not* have said that. That's *wrong*."

AH: But what we realize is it's not only about interpersonal relationships, it also influences policy.

MB: Absolutely.

AH: Those things that we leave out, that we refuse to address. We stick to a strict narrative that may or may not reflect reality. It reflects what our policies are, and it allows for things like the housing crisis and for "Sexy Cash" [payday loan] enterprises to come into communities, and lack of attention to HIV. And so those are the ways I think that your art can actually get us to look at the reality of our experiences and really can influence policy in ways that maybe a number of policy papers and wonks and statistics cannot do.

MB: Well, I don't know.

AH: [*To audience*] Don't you think so?

MB: I don't know if the painting on the wall's going to influence policy, but I think that maybe the ideas around the work can influence policy. There are artists that mine a very political space, and these ideas can really influence policy. I think that there's a lot of interesting things and a lot of interesting ideas that artists are involved in. It just would be great if we had sometimes larger arenas to have these ideas put forth.

This text was transcribed and excerpted from *Conversations: Mark Bradford and Anita Hill*, held August 2, 2015, at the Hammer Museum, Los Angeles. Courtesy of the Hammer Museum, Los Angeles.

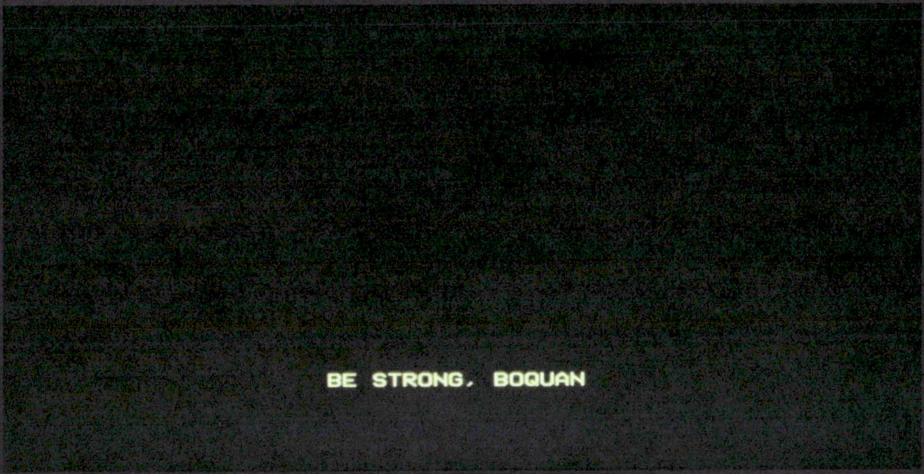
BE STRONG, BOQUAN

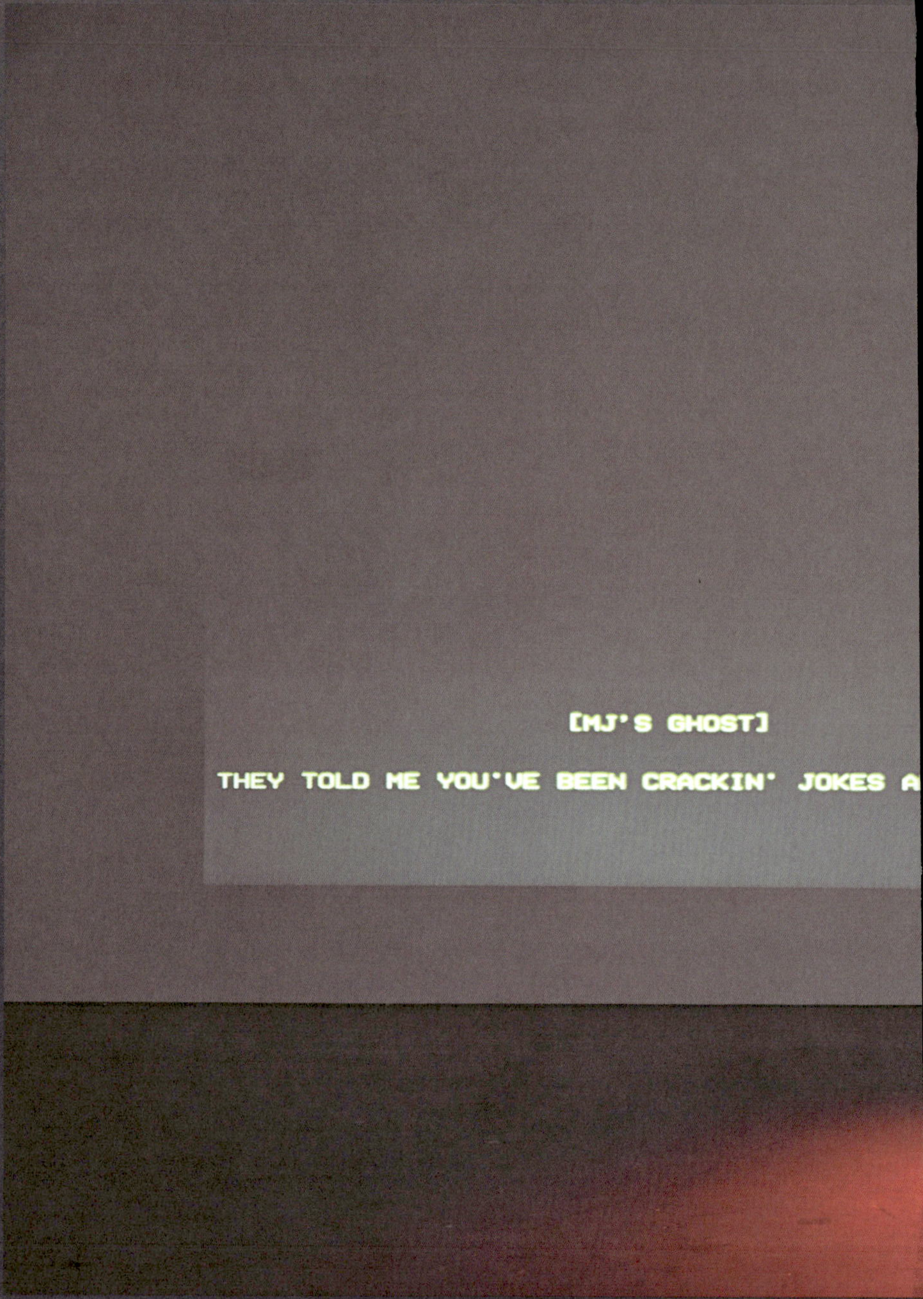
[MJ'S GHOST]
THEY TOLD ME YOU'VE BEEN CRACKIN' JOKES A

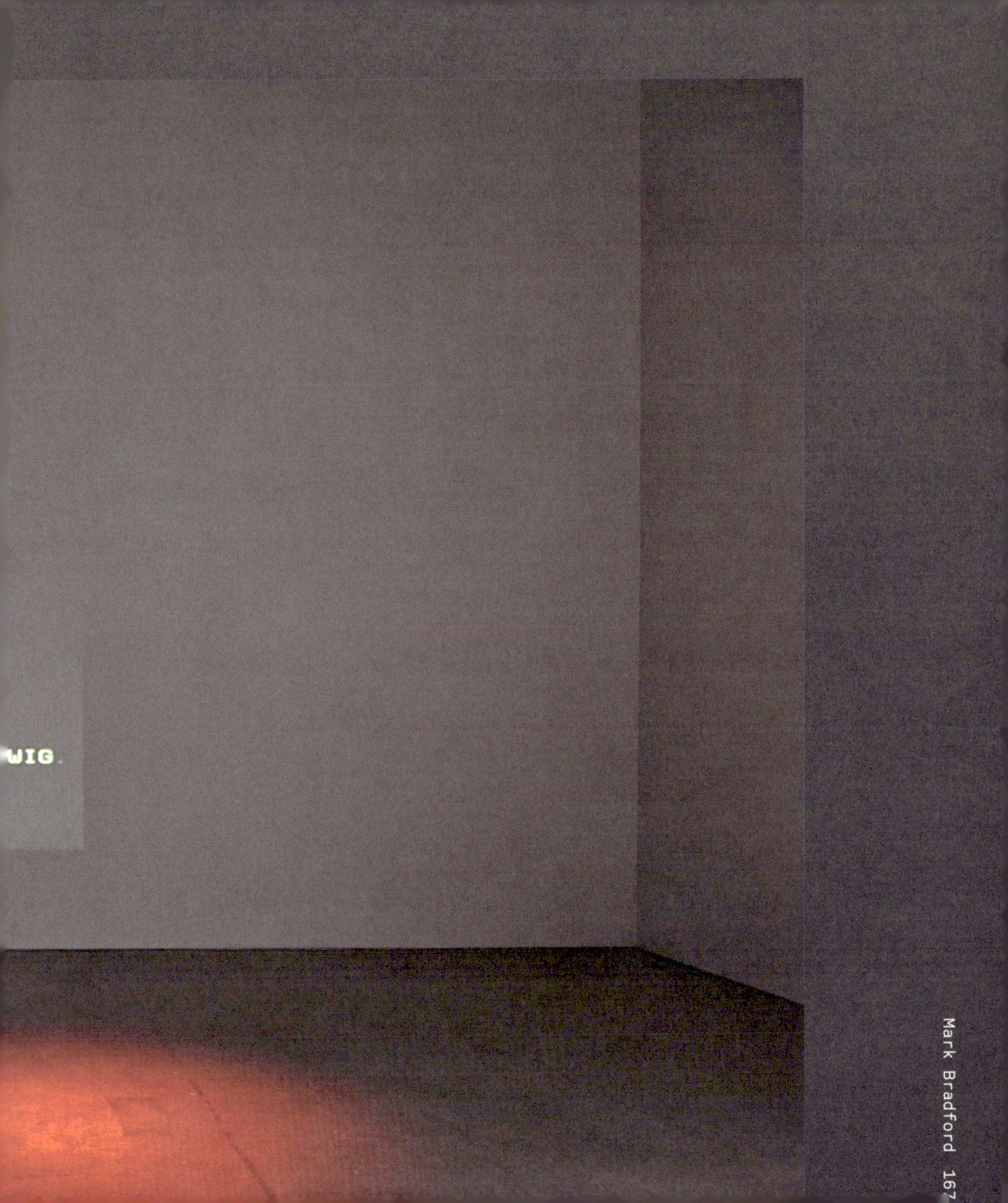
WIG.

Rachel Rose

Everything and More, 2015
High-definition digital video, color, sound
Running time: 11:33 minutes
Dallas Museum of Art, gift of Marguerite Steed Hoffman, 2016.34

Rachel Rose (American, b. 1986) creates immersive video and sound installations using found and self-produced footage. She received a BA in humanities and art from Yale University, New Haven, Connecticut; an MA in art history from the Courtauld Institute of Art, London; and an MFA in visual art from Columbia University, New York. Rose received the illy Present Future Prize at Artissima for her video *A Minute Ago* (2014), a Frieze Artist Award (2015), and the Future Fields Commission in Time-Based Media from the Philadelphia Museum of Art and the Fondazione Sandretto Re Rebaudengo (2017). Solo exhibitions include *Interiors*, Castello di Rivoli, Turin (2015); *Palisades*, Serpentine Sackler Gallery, London (2015); *Everything and More*, Whitney Museum of American Art, New York (2015); Aspen Art Museum (2016); Museu Serralves, Porto (2016); and Kunsthaus Bregenz (2017). Her work was also included in *Viva Arte Viva*, the 57th Venice Biennale (2017). Rose lives and works in New York.

INTERVIEW WITH RACHEL ROSE

by Aily Nash

AILY NASH: You started out as a painter, then you studied art history, and you've transitioned into making moving-image work for installation. How did you land in this current mode of operation?

RACHEL ROSE: I was trying to expand what I thought I could do, or was interested in. In that process, I developed doubt about making art. Robert Irwin says that the key to the tool that you use to make something is whether it has the dimensions to deal with your questions. I was looking for a tool. Idealizing documentary films led me to learn how to research, write, shoot, edit, and design sound. That combination right now has the dimensions to deal with my questions.

AN: What initially led you to make documentaries?

RR: I didn't understand how I could be an artist and also care deeply about the things around us that affect how we live and think. Art felt like a vacuum, so formal. Documentary film, to me, symbolically meant going out into the world, being openly curious, and then trying to make work that produced meaning from that.

AN: You could investigate something?

RR: Yes, going outside of myself and outside of the conditions that I thought made a thing a thing. But when I actually learned how to shoot, edit, put together a project—cold-calling people, traveling to shoot—I found that what I loved most was piecing those materials together. That itself also was meaning. Then I thought: I can't be a documentary filmmaker. I'm too attached to the surface and the materiality of putting a work together and unfolding how that connects to the feeling within the work. So I guess I'm an artist.

AN: Through researching and organizing a film project, you found that you were making meaning in the way you brought together disparate elements—and that's palpable in the experience of the work itself. In *A Minute Ago* you combine various distinct places and occurrences into a single image. Can you speak to your approach of colliding not only images, but also time through this technique?

RR: In *A Minute Ago* the quick shifts in time are brought about by collage. When something suddenly comes in, like a hailstorm or a larger catastrophe, it feels as though that thing's been cut and pasted into your reality. That's akin to the cut-and-paste structure of collage. I tried to infuse every point of reference within the work with collage: from compositing the hailstorm to the outside of the Glass House to suturing the [Philip] Johnson of the past with the house in the present. When I shot in the house, I replicated the camera movements from that original Johnson footage, so it felt like the two times were one. That's another kind of collage in the edit itself. With the sound I brought together pretty disparate times, too. For example, in the opening sequence you hear the sound of Pink Floyd's *Echoes*, [from] a concert they played in an empty amphitheater in Pompeii in 1971. At the end you hear the sound of an audience at a Big Sean concert in 2012, erupting with no performer. Like Johnson being back in the current house, together these two sounds form one space.

AN: We experience all those layers of time through sound and images.

RR: You might not identify the image or sound, but you get a sense that things are shifting and that they are sutured together. And that's integral to the design of the Glass House itself and to the property—it's one giant physical collage. You have a Mies van der Rohe chair next to a Nicolas Poussin painting inside this steel-and-glass structure situated within an artificially pastoral landscape. . . .

AN: I'm curious about your work process. You said that in the initial stages of your earlier videos, there was a collision of a personal or conceptual question that you were investigating, alongside a formal technique or a new image-rendering process that you would work out in tandem. Can you speak about that?

RR: Usually a work starts with just a subtle basic feeling, which translates into a question like, What the fuck—I feel really uneasy about the state of weather now. It's something basic that I feel but don't really have room to pay attention to because of the nature of living. It's in the back of my mind, yet it keeps coming up. And then I try to think, What am I projecting onto this? What am I feeling about it? So in the case of the weather, I'm feeling unease.

AN: By weather you mean global warming? Climate change?

RR: Exactly. I don't describe it that way because I want to address it not politically, not morally, but through its underlying structure and the feeling associated with it. In *A Minute Ago* I approached it from that perspective. But in all of my work it's like that—I'm first marking the general feeling, the general territory I want to work in. Then I try to hone it down more specifically, maybe to some tangible experiences I've had with that thing. I sort of hyperbreak it down for myself. For example, with *A Minute Ago* it was an experience I had in a coffee shop when all of a sudden this crazy storm came in. There was a gust of wind, and then it went away. Everyone in the coffee shop paused, and a few minutes later we just went on with our lives. I kept thinking about that and about glass as this barrier. So I looked into the history of glass and glass manufacturing. Looking around New York City, so many buildings are conceived around glass, and how did that come to be? My research led me to Ohio, and I shot in a glass museum in Toledo. In the end I didn't use that footage in the film. My research tends to be sprawling. It's exploratory, very free-form, but I'm also simply trying to figure out what I'm going to do. The glass question led me to think about its equivalent in technology—compositing, which is basically collaging within the frame. I wanted to learn compositing in postproduction, and then I thought about compositing in-camera, which is how I arrived at the method I used while in the Glass House.

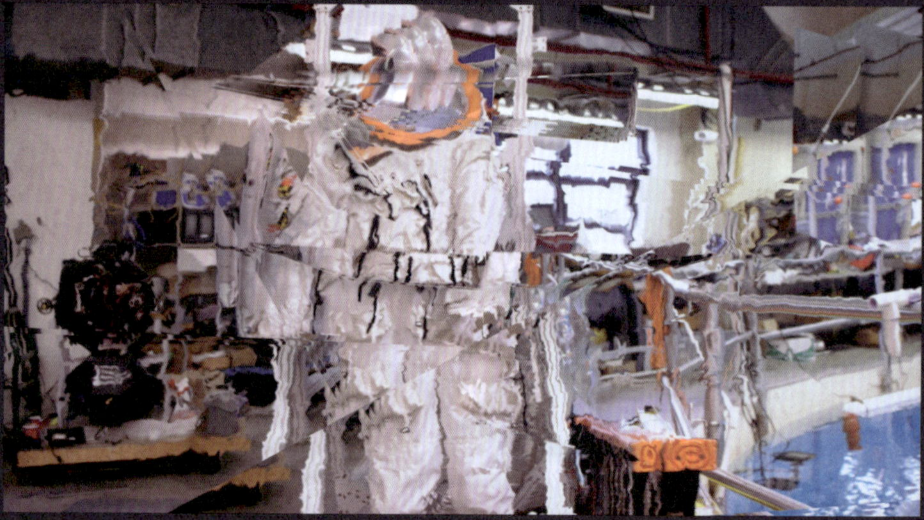

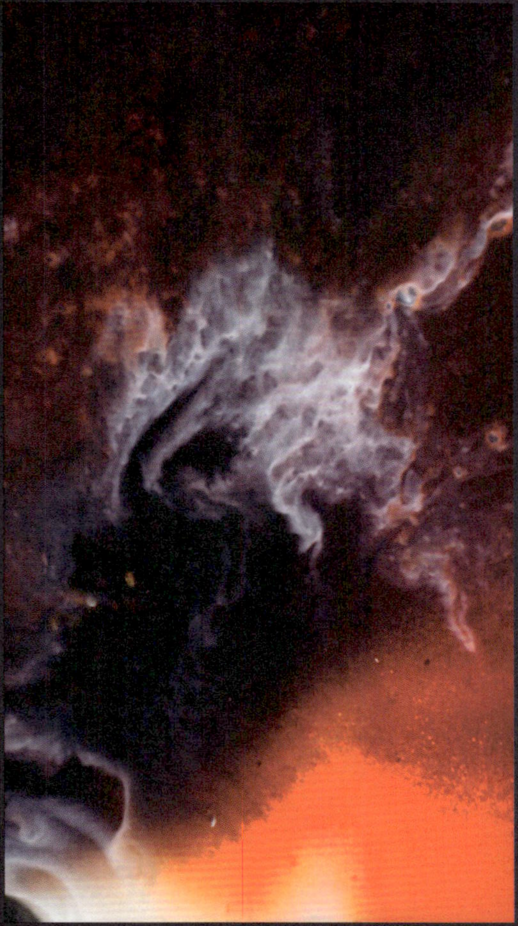

Arthur Jafa

Love Is the Message, The Message Is Death, 2016
High-definition digital video, color and black and white, sound
Running time: 7:30 minutes
Dallas Museum of Art, gift of Marguerite Steed Hoffman and Thomas W. Lentz, 2017.31

Arthur Jafa (American, b. 1960) was born in Tupelo, Mississippi, and is a renowned artist, filmmaker, and cinematographer based in Los Angeles. He studied architecture and film at Howard University from 1979 to 1983. Jafa's body of work, from short films to full-length documentaries, is concerned with black identity and aesthetics in American culture. His work has been widely exhibited and screened at many venues, including the Serpentine Sackler Gallery, London; the Museum of Contemporary Art, Los Angeles; and the Museum of Contemporary African Diasporan Arts, New York. Jafa also participated in the Whitney Biennial (2000) as well as the Hammer Museum's *Made in L.A.* exhibition (2016). Jafa, along with Elissa Blount-Moorhead and Malik Sayeed, directs TNEG, a motion-picture studio focused on creating cinema that "replicates the power, beauty, and alienation of Black Music." Since the 1990s Jafa has worked as a cinematographer on a number of notable films, including Julie Dash's *Daughters of the Dust* (1991), for which he won the Sundance Award for Best Cinematography, and Spike Lee's *Crooklyn* (1994).

ARTHUR JAFA AND THE FUTURE OF BLACK CINEMA

Interview by Antwaun Sargent

ANTWAUN SARGENT: What inspired *Love Is the Message, The Message Is Death?*

ARTHUR JAFA: That's a hard question to answer. It wasn't any sort of direct response to Trump or anything. I'm always making things, and I have an ongoing practice of compiling stuff that strikes me. Over the course of my life, I've trained myself to do the opposite of what's human nature, and that is to recoil from things that disturb. I've taught myself to push toward things that disturb me, not pull away. And I've developed a habit of recording these things because they often disappear. To a certain degree *Love Is the Message* grew out of this practice.

AS: How did you organize the imagery?

AJ: The things sort of organize themselves organically. One of my friends, John Akomfrah, said in a recent interview that fundamentally what he's trying to do is to put things in an affective proximity to one another, and I think that really crystallizes it. When you are talking about a picture, a representational image, or a rendering, it's not "for real." It always functions in this space as a sign or signifier. These things tend to resonate in specific ways, but what happens is, when you place a resonant artifact next to another resonant object, they create a new harmonic. So at a certain point I had a set of images that resonated in response to one another. And like a strand of pearls, I just laid them out. Then I watched it and said, "Oh, this is kind of interesting," and I made adjustments accordingly.

AS: How long did it take you to make *Love*?

AJ: I would say 85 percent of it was done in two hours.

AS: Really?

AJ: Yeah. Then a few days later, I happened to be looking at television and *Saturday Night Live* came on. Kanye [West] came out, and he was performing "Ultralight Beam," and I was like, "Wow, that's a really amazing song." So I downloaded the live performance, and maybe a few days after that, I laid the music down on top of my image strand, and I was like, "Wow—really interesting." There were gaps in the piece where I felt like the images were at best just treading water; they weren't really pushing the piece forward. So I tweaked it and closed the gaps around the fixed landmarks. Like the sister who gets pulled over and tells the cops, "You are terrorizing my kids," that was an anchor in the film that I built around.

AS: The film is tough to watch because it shows how black suffering and creativity are bound together. What was your reaction to *Love* the first time you watched it in full?

AJ: I gave Kahlil [Joseph] a really early cut, prior to putting in his brother, Noah [Davis], who passed away, last year and he was really obsessed with this early cut. He said it was really volatile. When I first put it together, I cried, then I never cried again. Actually. It's disturbing. When I look at it now, I'm sort of dead inside.

AS: What made you cry?

AJ: These are verifications of what black people know to be true about our status in society, positive and negative. I remember when someone told me phones were going to have cameras on them, and I thought that was the dumbest idea I'd ever heard. Why would you want a camera on your phone? But as we see the impact of it, it has allowed for a mass verification of what black people have been saying.

AS: The Walter Scott scene was probably the hardest for me to watch soundtracked to "Ultralight Beam." In that moment West is saying, "We on an ultralight beam," repeatedly as Scott is running away from a cop who shoots him from about fifteen feet away. He crumbles to the ground. The whole thing shook me and my faith. The visual and music in constructing that moment seemed perfectly intentional.

AJ: Well, a lot of it was instinctual, because it's just raw material for me; it's not a group of images set to Kanye's song. But the song is a masterpiece because it does something that's almost impossible to do: It takes a given form, the gospel song, and creates a new synthesis of gospel and R&B, like Ray Charles did to create soul music. Kanye in that song basically made the first formal evolution of gospel music in about a hundred years. Now, Kanye is a genius, people just don't like it because he's so self-determinedly so.

AS: The film is as much about presenting a black history as it is about your vision of a black cinema.

AJ: I have a very simple mantra, and it's this: I want to make black cinema with the power, beauty, and alienation of black music. That's my big goal. The larger preoccupation is, how do we force cinema to respond to the existential, political, and spiritual dimensions of who we are as a people? Music to me is a convenient marker of that. Music is the one space in which we [as black people] know we've totally actualized ourselves, and even though we keep inventing shit, we don't ever have to write another song to confirm the magnificence of what we've already accomplished. So a cinema is like the music—that's what *Love Is the Message* is trying to do.

AS: That's the message? To make cinema match the intensity of black music?

AJ: For so long people have tried to tell me, "That's interesting, that's cool, that's polemical!" And I'm like, "Man, I just have to show these motherfuckers."

AS: I think you showed that with your cinematography that dates back to *Daughters of the Dust* [1991], Spike Lee's *Crooklyn* [1994], and *Eyes Wide Shut* [1999].

AJ: This [film] seems like a big arrival, but it's what I've been working toward since I shot *Daughters of the Dust*. *Daughters* was the first film that I'd ever shot. At this point in my life, I'm not just at war with the fucked-up images of black folks that diminish us and society at large but with the forms that deliver these images as well. When *Daughters* was originally in theaters, I gave a talk at The New School, and this older white woman stood up and said:

"When I see *Daughters* and I see the grandmother, I don't see race. I don't see color. I see my own grandmother." She was actually trying to be progressive, but I immediately said: "Yeah, that's all cool and well, but how come you can't see color *and* see your grandmother? How come those two things are mutually exclusive? How come you have to erase something we cannot erase—our color? How come you have to suspend that for you to be able to have a point of identification?"

The question is, how come we can't be as black as we are and still be universal? How come we have to refuse who we are in order for someone to be able to identify with us? How come the audience can't see themselves in a thing, whether it looks like them or not? It's what black people do because most of what we see [when we watch movies] are white people. It's what women have developed the ability to do because mostly what they see are men. It's what gay people are able to do because mostly what they see is heteronormative stuff. It's a muscle that everybody needs to develop: the ability to see [oneself] in someone else's circumstances without having to paint that person white, make that person straight, or a man. How can you see yourself in the Other? That's what it really comes down to—empathy. I'm trying to make my shit as black as possible and still have you deal with my humanity.

AS: So, what's the problem with contemporary cinematic representations of black folks?

AJ: The problem with black cinema in its current form is, on the one hand, it is the only game in town—meaning, there's just not enough of us making films. On the other hand, the setup, the cinematic apparatus as it's presently constituted, isn't optimized to get at the fact of black sociality, that it exists, and how it functions. Shit on Worldstar Hip Hop is way more interesting than 99.9 percent of the bullshit black filmmakers in Hollywood are doing. To me, not every black filmmaker who is making black films is trying to make *black cinema*.

See, the thing that's great about Aretha Franklin, when you hear her, is not just her individual genius, her singular expressive capacity, but that she's working in a form that's evolved over time in response to our expressive desires, and the pressures of what it means to be black. Part of it is just trying to get people to see these things—the evidence is everywhere.

Arthur Jafa and Antwaun Sargent, "Arthur Jafa and the Future of Black Cinema," first published in *Interview*, January 11, 2017. http://www.interviewmagazine.com/art/arthur-jafa. Courtesy of BMF Holdings, LLC.

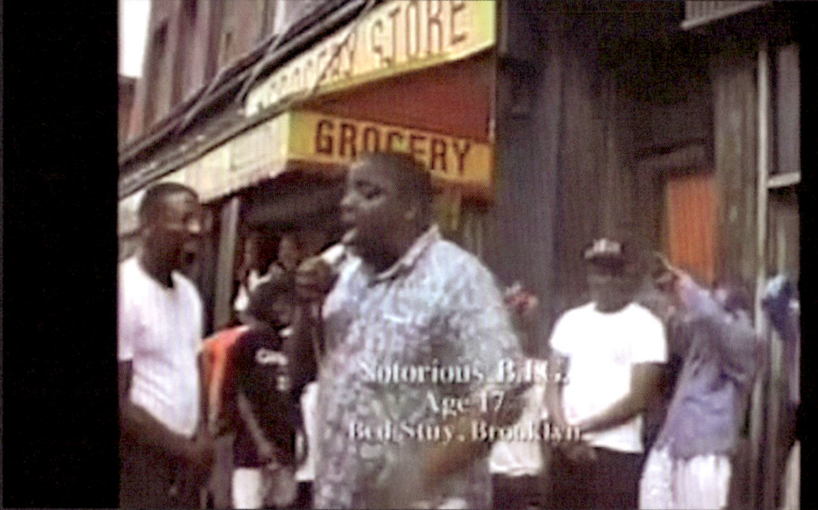
STORE
GROCERY
Notorious B.I.G.
Age 17
Bed Stuy, Brooklyn

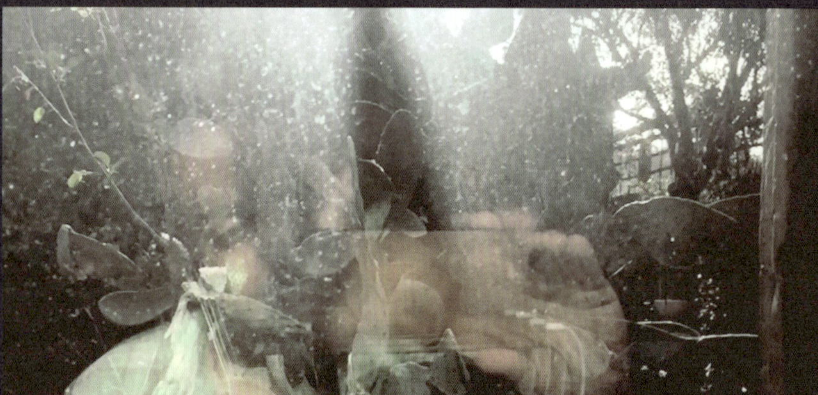

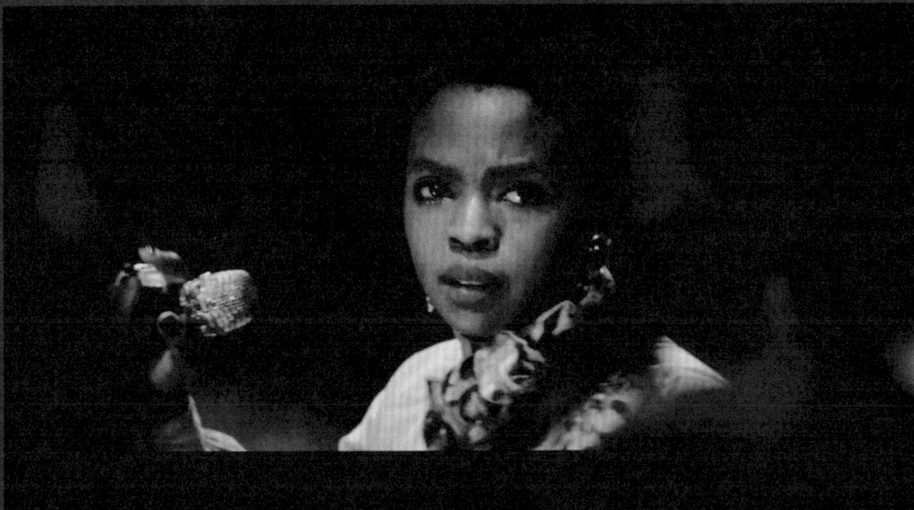

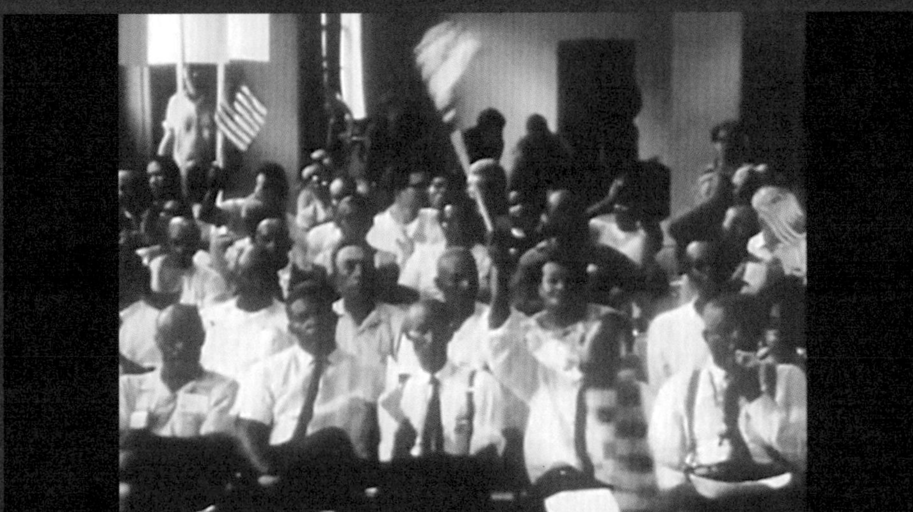

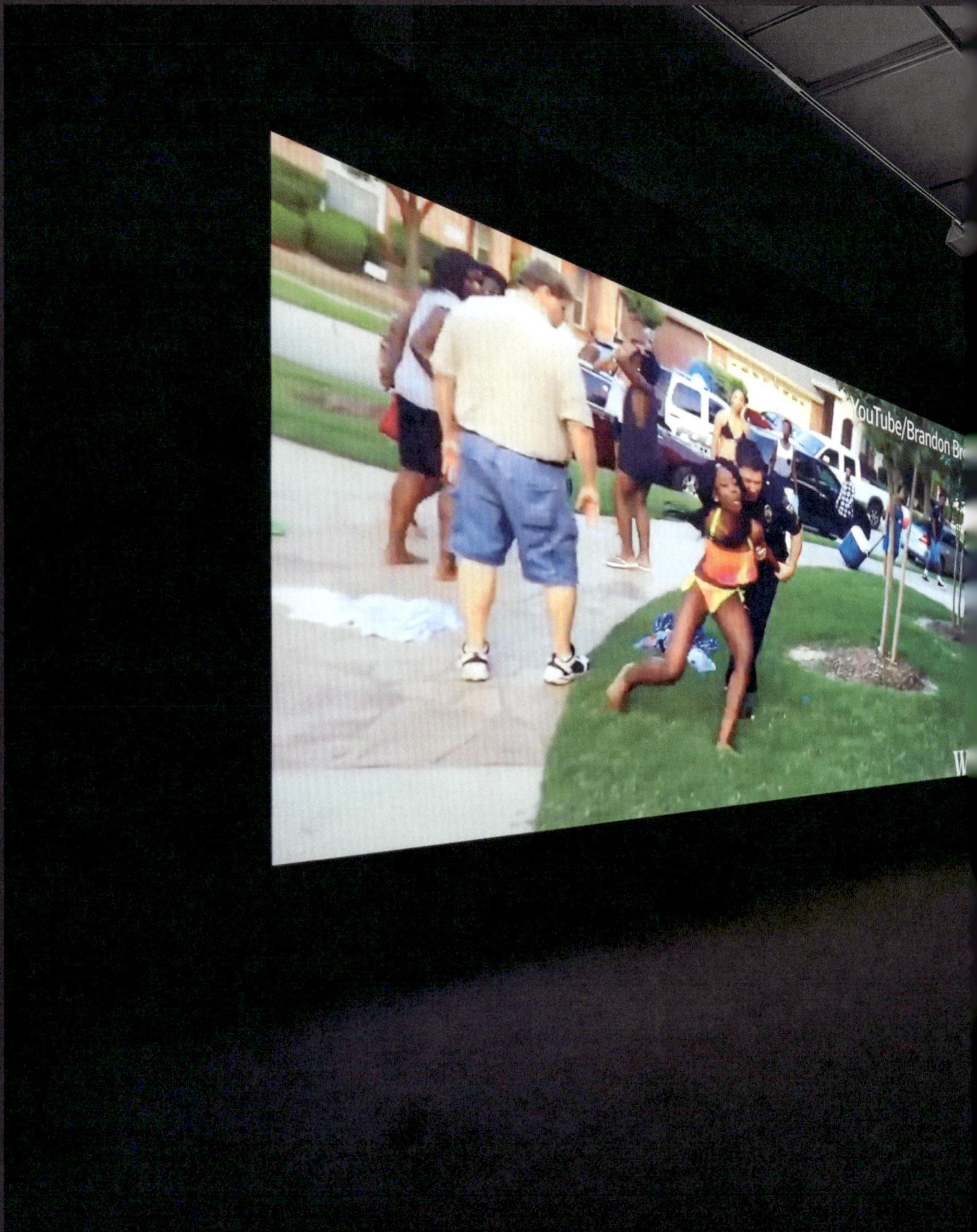

John Gerrard

Western Flag (Spindletop, Texas), 2017
Real-time, three-dimensional simulation, color
Courtesy of Simon Preston Gallery, New York, and
Thomas Dane Gallery, London

John Gerrard (Irish, b. 1974) was born in North Tipperary and lives and works between Dublin and Vienna. In 1997 he received a BFA in sculpture from the Ruskin School of Fine Art and Drawing, Oxford University, followed by an MFA from the School of the Art Institute of Chicago in 2000 and an MSc from Trinity College, Dublin, in 2001. From 2002 to 2004 he held residencies at Ars Electronica Futurelab in Linz, Austria, where he developed his innovative use of three-dimensional modeling and real-time simulation. Gerrard has exhibited worldwide at venues including Ullens Centre for Contemporary Art, Beijing; the San Francisco Museum of Modern Art; Tate Britain, London; and Lincoln Center in association with the Public Art Fund, New York. In 2017 he presented the large-scale outdoor commission *Western Flag (Spindletop, Texas)* at Somerset House, London. The artist's works are in the collections of the Fondation Louis Vuitton, Paris; the Irish Museum of Modern Art, Dublin; the Los Angeles County Museum of Art; the Museum of Modern Art, New York; Tate, London; Pinakothek der Moderne, Munich; Hirshhorn Museum and Sculpture Garden, Washington, DC; and Inhotim Collection, Brumadinho, Brazil.

ONE TAKE: JOHN GERRARD'S *WESTERN FLAG (SPINDLETOP, TEXAS)*

by Ben Eastham

On January 10, 1901, a ragged band of men in a blasted corner of Southeast Texas changed the course of history. Following the hunch of a one-armed geologist—whose past included shooting dead a sheriff who interrupted his attempt to burn down a black Baptist church—prospectors dug an exploratory oil well near the Louisiana border. It was a risky investment. Innumerable wildcat speculators had bankrupted their creditors by drilling into a Texas landscape considered by the most reputable oilmen to be dry. Yet, three hundred meters down, the drill hit a reservoir so vast that its puncture caused a small earthquake. Spitting out the six-long-ton bit, a yellow-black geyser coursed up the borehole and sprang to a height of forty-five meters, spilling a volume of petroleum that exceeded the combined production of every other well in the US on that day.

The Lucas Gusher at Spindletop was the largest oil strike the world had ever seen and the starting gun for a boom that would transform Western society and, ultimately, the earth's entire ecosystem. The immediate availability of seemingly unlimited supplies of cheap petroleum—the price of oil dropped from two dollars to just three cents per barrel in the wake of the discovery—ensured that the internal combustion engine rather than electric batteries powered the automobiles that would soon crisscross an American landscape punctuated by gasoline stations. Spindletop laid the foundation for the economic expansion that shaped the twentieth century as well as the conflicts for resources and environmental catastrophes that look set to define the twenty-first.

Two remarkable photographs capture this moment of crisis. The first, taken on the day the well "came in," shows a narrow jet of oil spurting through the latticed wooden framework that supports the rig's drilling apparatus before, tipped over by the breeze, it cascades down into the surrounding earth. The second shows the same landscape two years later, overlaid by a tightly packed grid of several hundred derricks operated by newly founded companies, including the first incarnations of ExxonMobil, Gulf Oil, and Texaco. Inspired by these images and the industrialized societies they portend, the artist John Gerrard created a computer-generated portrait of Spindletop as it is today: *Western Flag (Spindletop, Texas)* (2017). This virtual reconstruction of the birthplace of modernity has been realized in three media: broadcast on the British television network Channel 4 over twenty-four hours on April 22, 2017; streamed online; and erected in the courtyard of London's Somerset House as a vast LED-screen sculpture.

Gerrard's restaging of what is now a pockmarked, postindustrial wasteland places a tall, slim flagpole at its center. Smoke pours out from seven equally spaced nozzles at its peak, coalescing into a rectangular cloud of thick smoke that billows outward like a ragged flag in a stiff wind. The sterile ground is littered with what appears to be abandoned machinery, while distant rigs scrape the smooth sky like the few remaining teeth of a broken comb. The camera traces a repetitive circuit at head height and walking pace around the flagpole, in the manner of a dog testing the end of its tether, while the simulation follows the same unending rhythms as the location it re-creates: when night falls on Texas, so is the black flag cast into darkness. The scene suggests an aggression—a burning flag planted in the land, its image relayed as a warning to those who might oppose its claim—at the same time as it intimates mourning for a catastrophe.

Western Flag (Spindletop, Texas) is the latest in Gerrard's series of uncannily "realistic" digital portraits of physical locations. The scare quotes surrender to a recurring difficulty when writing about the Irish artist's work, which questions where the boundary between reality and unreality lies. Given that this pin-sharp representation of the Texas landscape is constructed from a comprehensive photographic survey of the site, translated into code, what makes its moving images any less "real" than a digital video of the same location? Simple categorical distinctions are further complicated by the fact that this live simulation "exists" as a piece of software whose instructions are rendered in real time by a computer at the rate of fifty frames per second. Every image is both unique and instantly discarded, meaning that the work is closer in spirit to the live interpretation of a score than the transmission of prerecorded information. The television interventions, for instance, required two computers—one serving as an emergency understudy—to be installed into the Channel 4 mainframe. There they performed the work continuously for twenty-four hours, cutting occasionally into broadcasts. The fidelity to real life, simulated by the passage of day into night, is consistent with the live nature of the work, constituted of infinitesimal moments that disappear without hope of recovery.

Since *Western Flag* is not a record of a place but a live interpretation of it, the work has no enduring form beyond that which survives in the memory of its audience; this is consistent with the artist's intention to provoke critical thought rather than simply memorialize or reproduce. From a Google server facility to a mechanized pig farm in the American Midwest, Gerrard's previous choice of subjects has drawn attention to hidden infrastructures. *Western Flag* extends that preoccupation by giving visible form to the invisible offshoot of industrial production—carbon dioxide—which has contributed to halving the earth's biodiversity since Spindletop and threatens to make large swaths of its surface uninhabitable. The invisible systems and processes upon which our gilded Western lifestyles depend are further evoked by the carbon flag's play upon the double entendre of *power*: energy and force. Alluding to the different means by which our dependence on oil manifests in the real world, *Western Flag* might helpfully be understood as a companion piece to Gerrard's apocalyptic *Dust Storm (Texas)* (2007), based on an archival photograph from the 1930s of a vast particulate cloud engulfing a farmhouse during the Dust Bowl. The work showed the first great ecological catastrophe of the petroleum age, caused by the conversion of vast grassland plains into cropland suitable for industrial farming by gasoline tractors and harvesters; the eerie absence of any higher form of life in *Western Flag* might be taken to hint at the longer-term impacts of humanity's continued dependence upon fossil fuels. No citizen of the United Kingdom or the United States, meanwhile, should need reminding that the expropriation of oil under the flimsy pretext of national security imperatives has motivated catastrophic military interventions.

Yet, for all its polemical punch, this swirling black flag carries an ambiguity and emotional register that—crucially for a work of public art intended to engender its audience's active engagement with live issues, rather than browbeat—distinguishes it from agitprop or investigative journalism. It calls to my mind, for example, the childhood memory of walking with my grandfather across Preston toward the cattle market in which he worked. From a street overlooking the British city, he was apt to point out the few remaining cotton-factory chimney stacks as well as marking the places where dozens of others once stood. Their dwindling number was, for him, a cause for lament, an index of the city's decline from an industrial powerhouse of whose status its citizens were proud. I envisioned the horizon jagged with chimneys, each coughing thick smoke into the sky—an imagined landscape that retains its romantic quality undiminished by its obvious perversity. (My grandmother, who had worked in one of the factories as a teenager, did not suffer from the same nostalgia.)

In art historical terms the scenery of *Western Flag* evokes the landscape that hosts so many examples of land art—perhaps the quintessential expression of the oil age. Speaking on the telephone, Gerrard cites Robert Smithson's *Asphalt Rundown* (1969)—for which the artist unloaded a dump truck of hot asphalt down the steep edge of an open mine in Italy—as possessing a similarly unconscionable allure. Smithson's preoccupations with entropy and the cooling of the universe seem now darkly ironic in the context of global warming being accelerated by the earth-moving machines of which he was so fond. But it is difficult not to envy the freedom of those times even as we condemn their irresponsibility. Something of that wistfulness imbues *Western Flag*, a symbolic conflation of the triumphalist nationalism for which flags are established metonyms and the longed-for return to a mythical past in the highly industrialized, heavily polluting "heartlands" that has catalyzed its resurgence. That the political Right on both sides of the Atlantic has capitalized on the nostalgia of industrial decline, while the Left has been slow to recognize the debilitating effects on communities of the associated loss not only of jobs but of civic identity, suggests that this work can be read as social, as much as environmental, commentary.

For the broadcast on Channel 4, *Western Flag* was cut into short clips that interrupted regular programming without any title card or explanation—like hacks from a hostile power. This stark juxtaposition of the "real" and the "virtual" was also central to the freestanding sculpture's disconcerting effect at Somerset House, which had no frame to separate its postapocalyptic landscape from the elegant neoclassical architecture that served as a backdrop. The work, seen from the gate that protects Somerset House from the Strand, gave the effect of a vast photomontage in the style of John Stezaker: one image rudely superimposed onto another. Staked in a palace at the center of London and beamed directly into our living rooms, *Western Flag* brought the consequences of the petroleum age home.

Ben Eastham, "One Take: John Gerrard's *Western Flag (Spindletop, Texas)*," first published in *Frieze*, no. 188 (June/July/August 2017), 180–182. Courtesy of *Frieze* and Ben Eastham.

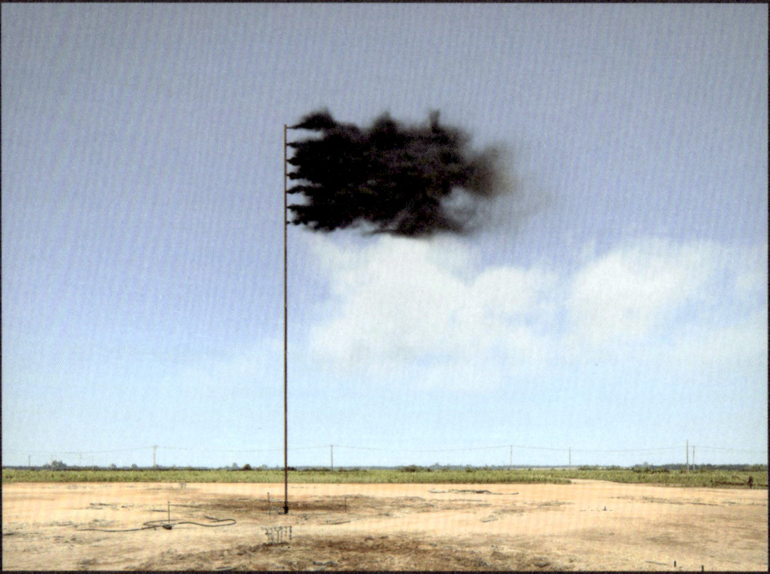

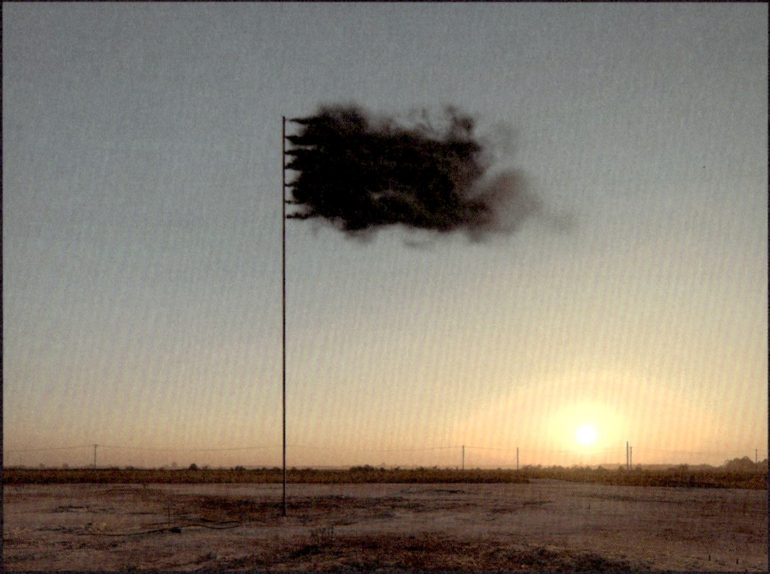

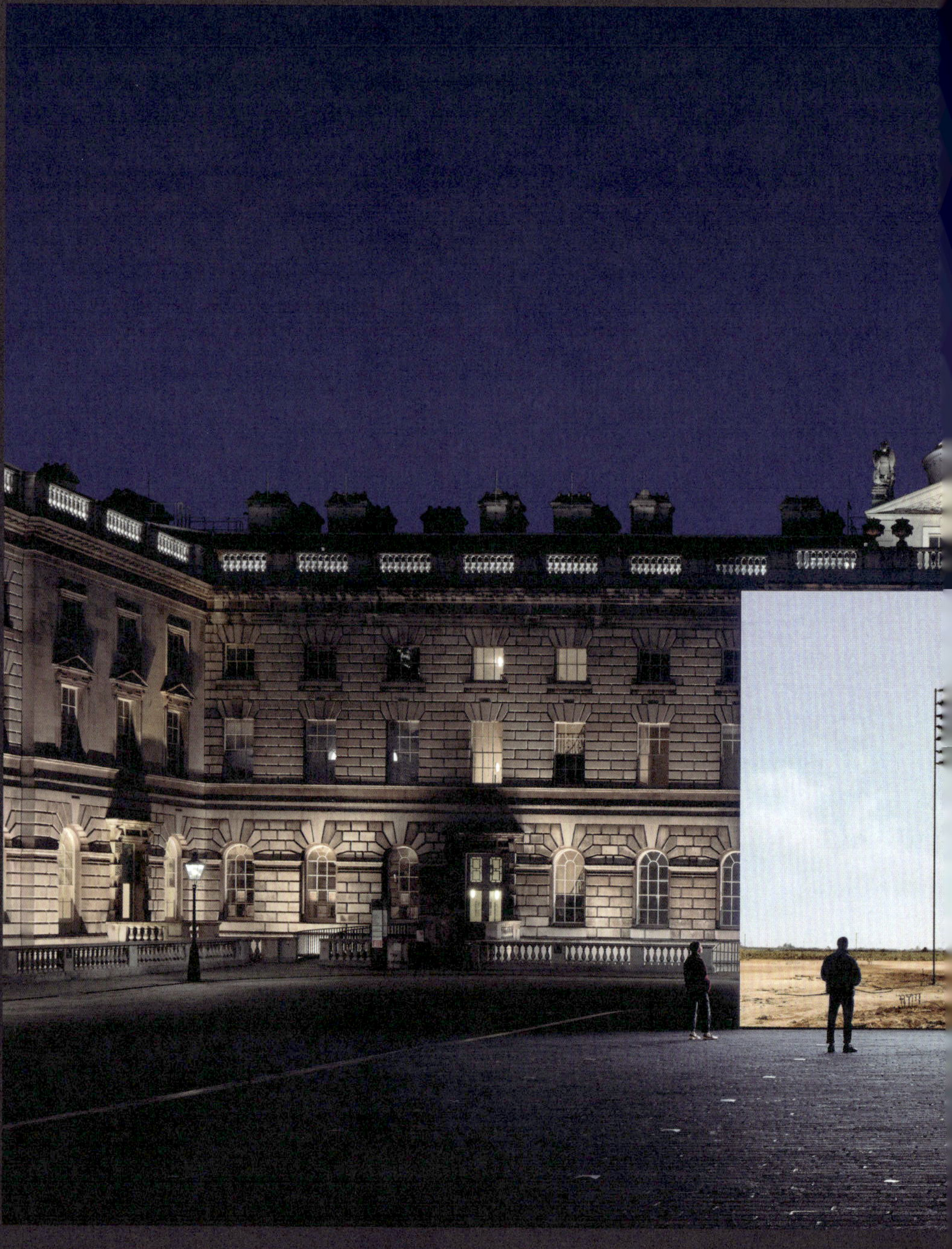

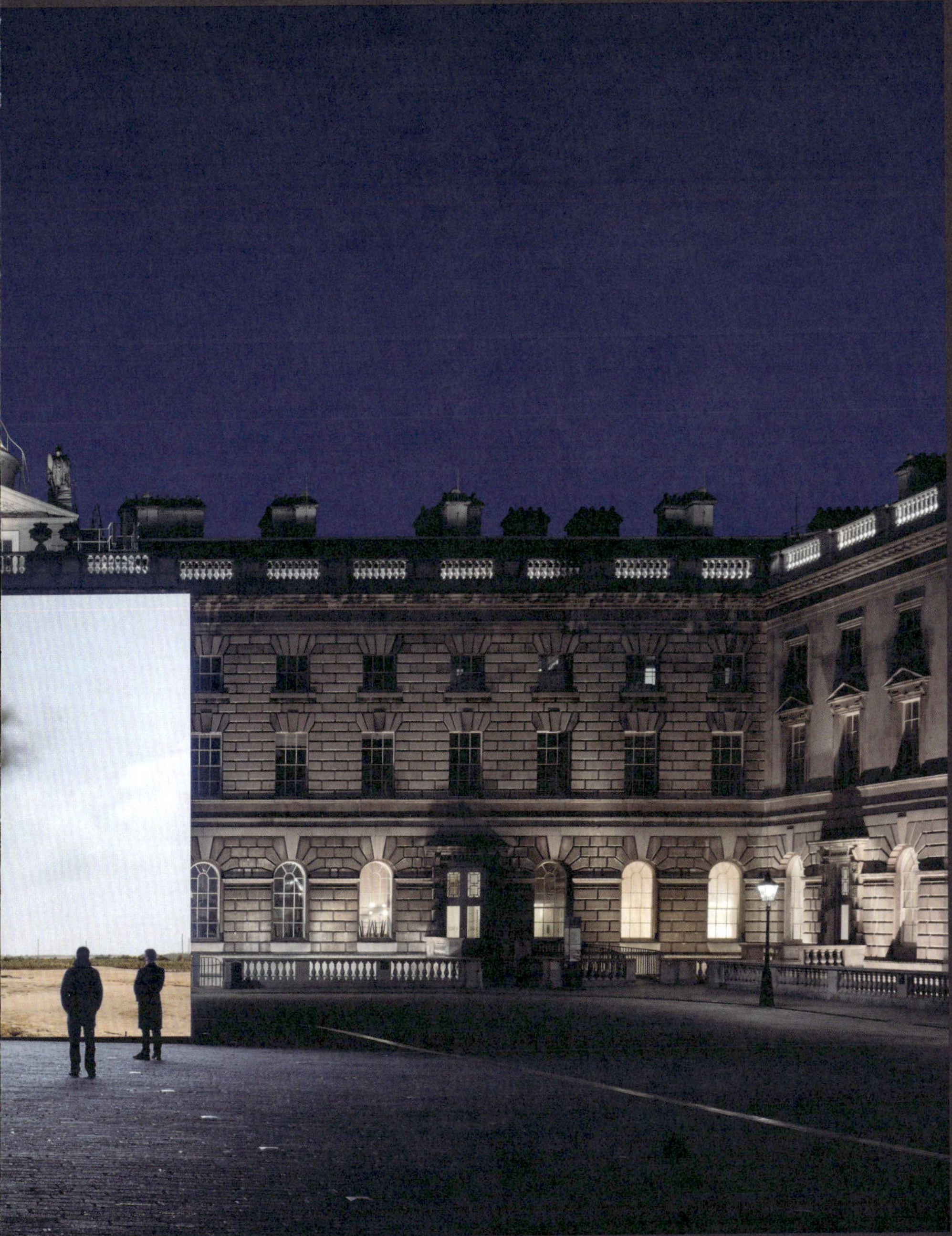

Anne Tallentire

Drift: diagram xvii, 2017
Standard-definition digital video, color, silent; site-specific installation with monitors, media players, and scaffold structure
Running time: looped
Courtesy of the artist and Hollybush Gardens, London

Anne Tallentire (Irish, b. 1950), born in County Armagh, Northern Ireland, is a London-based artist. She studied at the Slade School of Art from 1986 to 1988. Since 1993 she has also worked with artist John Seth under the name work-seth/tallentire. Her videos, collaborative performances, and site-specific installations explore aspects of mobility, time, and labor in daily life. She has participated in numerous group and solo exhibitions, held at venues such as MoMA PS1, New York (as work-seth/tallentire); Camden Arts Centre, London; Technisches Museum Wien, Vienna; and Tate Liverpool. She exhibited *This, and Other Things, 1999–2010*, a major survey of key works, at the Irish Museum of Modern Art, Dublin (2010). She represented Ireland at the 48th Venice Biennale (1999).

DRIFT

by Caoimhín Mac Giolla Léith

While many of [Anne] Tallentire's earlier works invoked a fragile sense of community, her more recent work has tended to focus on the relatively isolated figures that move imperceptibly through our civic spaces, variously attending to society's needs, great and small. This sequence of video works, collectively titled *Drift* (2002–2012), are slow-motion, silent meditations on the unregarded drift and flow of human life and labor. More specifically, these works concentrate on the figure of the lone downtown worker whose generally thankless job it is to maintain the material fabric of the deep-city environment. These we may number among what Michel de Certeau has called the "ordinary practitioners of the city"

> The ordinary practitioners of the city live "down below," below the threshold at which visibility begins. They . . . are walkers . . . whose bodies follow the thicks and thins of urban "text" they write without being able to read it.[1]

While many commentators on the contemporary city have tended to erase or elide important differences between disparate urban cultures, it is indisputable that Tallentire, as a long-term resident of London, one of the most self-evidently multicultural cities in the world, has had ample time to reflect on the ethical dimensions of living in close quarters with a mass of individuals whose multiple affiliations in terms of race, ethnicity, politics, class, religion, gender, sexuality, and so forth, may differ significantly from her own. As Richard Sennett has noted

> A city [is] . . . a place that implicates how one derives one's ethics, how one develops a sense of justice, how one learns to talk with and learn from people who are unlike oneself, which is how a human being becomes human.[2]

As Bö Grünlund pointed out in a synoptic account of Sennett's many writings on urbanism and urbanity, if the city is "the perfect moment for confronting difference," then, for Sennett, "the most important element of exchange in the city is talk."[3] This vital form of exchange, however, is absent from Tallentire's *Drift* works, which are mostly silent. Or at least it takes place outside the frame of these works, principally in the form of her scrupulous insistence on securing from each of her identifiable, filmed subjects their verbal permission to use their image in her artwork. What does remain within the frame is a distilled action or activity offered up to the viewer, often in a tight focus that crops the protagonists partially out of the picture. This strategy highlights their perceived anonymity while underlining the simple, life-affirming nature of labor per se, as opposed to work, whose value is more properly assessed in terms of its products and achievements. (Hannah Arendt's discussion on this classic distinction, as well as her further distinction between these two categories and that of "action," continue to inform Tallentire's reflections on her own practice.)[4]

The intensity of concentration with which Tallentire's anonymous workers pursue their tasks is in stark contrast to their routine and putatively menial nature. A well-equipped window cleaner hanging in a safety harness, with his back to the viewer, works his way methodically across the glass-fronted facade of an office block. An industrial-size sweeping brush plows with improbable grace through the dirty sludge of a water-clogged pond, propelled by workers whose Wellington boots are all we see of them. A bright yellow stop sign is carefully painted on a tarmacadam road by a roadworker who is similarly invisible from the knees up. A shadowy, faceless worker performs some inscrutable task in the sickly green glow of ambient street lighting. A woman is seen at night through the glass curtain-wall of a commercial high-rise, cleaning an upmarket office bedecked with blue-chip contemporary art. A window is slowly lowered into place by construction workers. A man carefully wipes down a revolving door, then walks away. A camera crew sits patiently outside the Old Bailey [Central Criminal Court of England] waiting for something to happen, something to film, something to report.

All the works in the *Drift* series, which number twenty-one to date and range in duration from twenty-three seconds to five and a half minutes (each work in the *Drift* series is identified by the precise time when the first shot of a sequence of video is recorded), were filmed within the Square Mile of London's financial district. This is a busy area of bustling office workers by day that, like many downtown areas the world over, grows quieter at night as a silent army of nighttime tenders and carers, many of whom are migrant laborers, take over the relatively empty streets and deserted office buildings. While these video sequences have been variously shot at many times of the day and night throughout the changing seasons, Tallentire seems particularly attracted to that indeterminate, liminal time when night shades into day. While nothing is staged or choreographed, she has a deft, probably instinctive, ability to focus on a particular activity that appears both complete in itself, with its own inherent logic, and yet is often apparently purposeless. (In this the *Drift* series retains the memory of some of her earlier performances.)

Any or all of these videos may be combined and arranged in various configurations, depending on the exigencies of the specific exhibition context. The particular presentation at Void in Derry [Northern Ireland], for instance, is titled *Drift: diagram vii*, a name that clearly indicates the fluid and provisional nature of any particular constellation of these individual films. (Tallentire readily acknowledges that the *Drift* sequence is both more "epic" in ambition and scale, and less subject to absolute control in its individual elements, than any of her previous works.) In Gallery One, the larger of Void's two spaces and the one people tend to go into first, a selection of looped works were displayed in three corners of the room, projected just below eye level, with one edge of each projection butted up to the corner. They ran continuously, starting with the first three films at dawn at the beginning of each day. Given that the individual works vary in length, as the day proceeded, the time line inevitably ran out of sync, resulting in what gradually appeared to be a random selection rather than the carefully orchestrated ensemble suggested at the outset. In Gallery Two three larger screens were placed simultaneously showing three DVDs (*Drift 04.05*, *Drift 05.00,* and *Drift 05.14*). In view of the architecture of the two spaces, with their intermittently obscured sight lines, and the decision to project images of varying scale and orientation vis-à-vis the viewer, it was impossible to see all the videos simultaneously. Instead, it was necessary for the viewers to move around the space, thereby increasing their awareness of their own physical presence as well as the presence of others and amplifying the sense of constant flux. Subtle references to the history of painting and sculpture seeped into the installation, given the pictorial quality of the works—the saturated colors produced by the twilit interior contrasted with the nature and context of the images being displayed—as well as the decision to place the projectors on small white plinths reminiscent of the "primary structures" of early minimalism. The potentially frustrating impossibility of a panoptic view of this rich tapestry of silent, urban activity is especially resonant when day-to-day inner-city living is being subjected to ever more intrusive surveillance. It is becoming increasingly difficult for any individual, community, or subculture to remain below society's threshold of visibility. Yet the power a given individual or community may exert over the particular ways in which they are rendered visible varies enormously. Questions of visibility and invisibility, of representation and self-representation, remain at the heart of Tallentire's art. Such questions are crucial in a culture ever more willing to condone the invasion of privacy in the name of the public good and the curtailment of basic human rights for the benefit of national and international security.

Summarizing one of the more influential theorizations of urbanization in recent years, David Harvey's 1978 essay "The Urban Process Under Capitalism," Edward Soja has noted that

> The city, the built environment, is embedded in the restless geographical landscape of capital, and specified as part of a complex and contradiction-filled societal spatialization that simultaneously enhances and inhibits, provides new room and imprisons, offers solutions but soon beckons to be destroyed.[5]

These enduring ambiguities are the stuff of Tallentire's art, which poignantly acknowledges certain aspects of the ongoing impoverishment and constriction of public space. Yet it does so, paradoxically, within the context of a highly personal practice that continues to grow in richness and broaden in scope.

This text has been excerpted from "Drift," an exhibition brochure first published by Hollybush Gardens, October 2005. Courtesy of Hollybush Gardens.

Notes

1 [footnote 2 in source] Michel de Certeau, *The Practice of Everyday Life,* trans. Stephen Randall (Los Angeles; London; Berkeley: University of California Press, 1984), 93.

2 [footnote 3 in source] Richard Sennett, "The Civitas of Seeing," *Places,* vol. 5, no. 4 (April 1989). Quoted in Bö Grönlund, "The Civitas of Seeing and the Design of Cities," https://placesjournal.org/article/the-civitas-of-seeing/.

3 [footnote 4 in source] Ibid.

4 [footnote 5 in source] Hannah Arendt, *The Human Condition* (Chicago: The University of Chicago Press, 1958).

5 [footnote 6 in source] Edward Soja, *Postmodern Geographies: The Reassertion of Space in Critical Social Theory* (London; New York: Verso, 1989), 102.

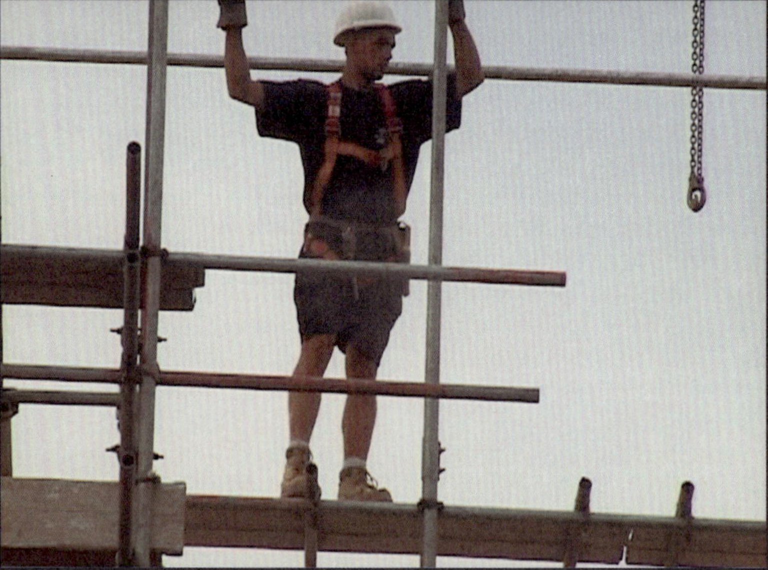

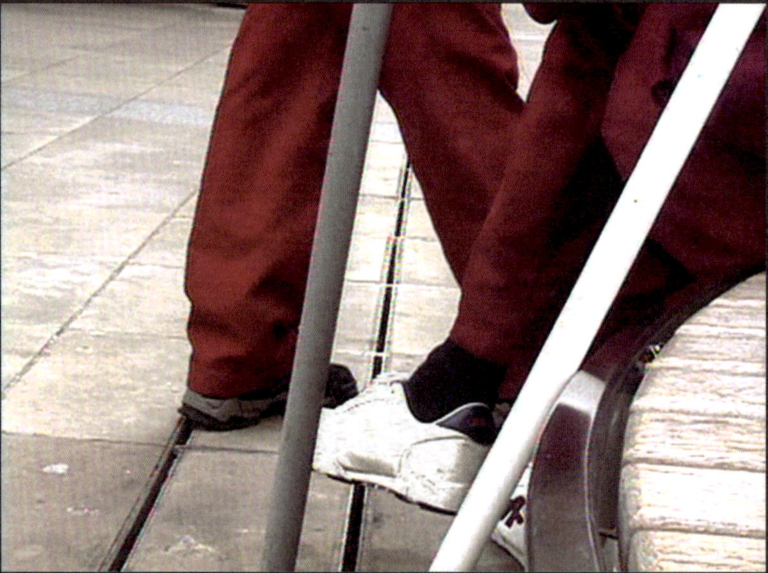

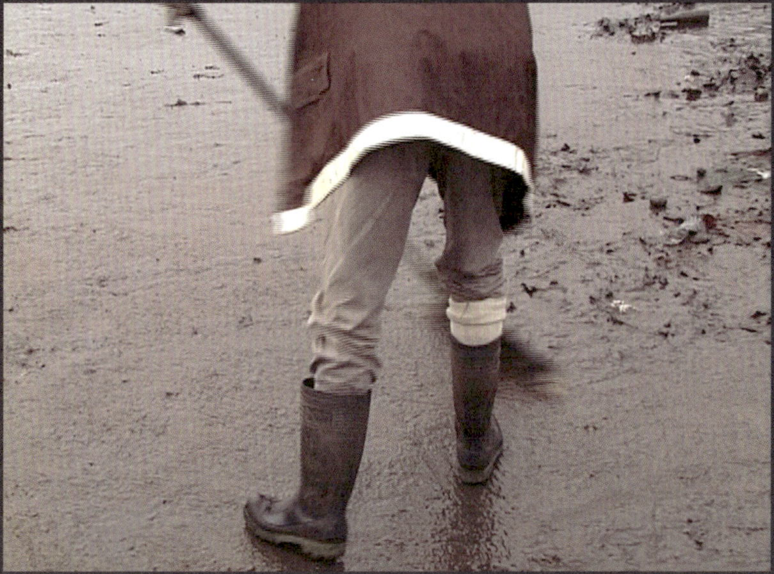

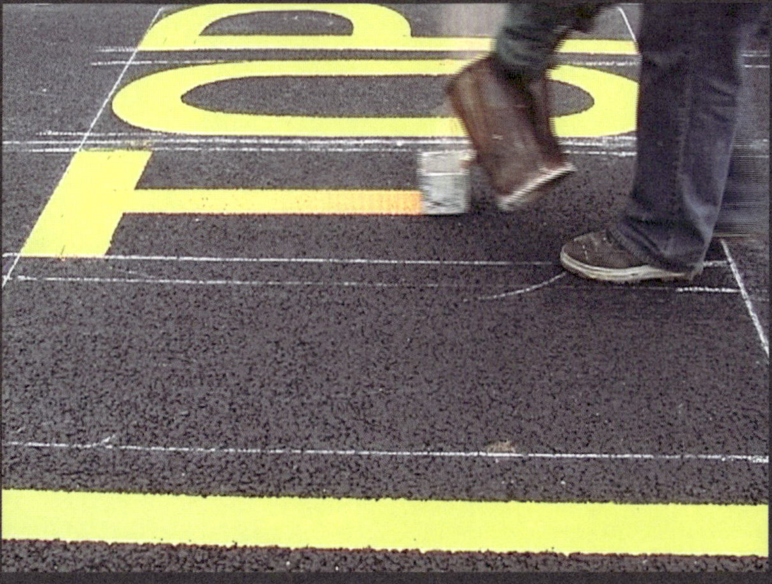

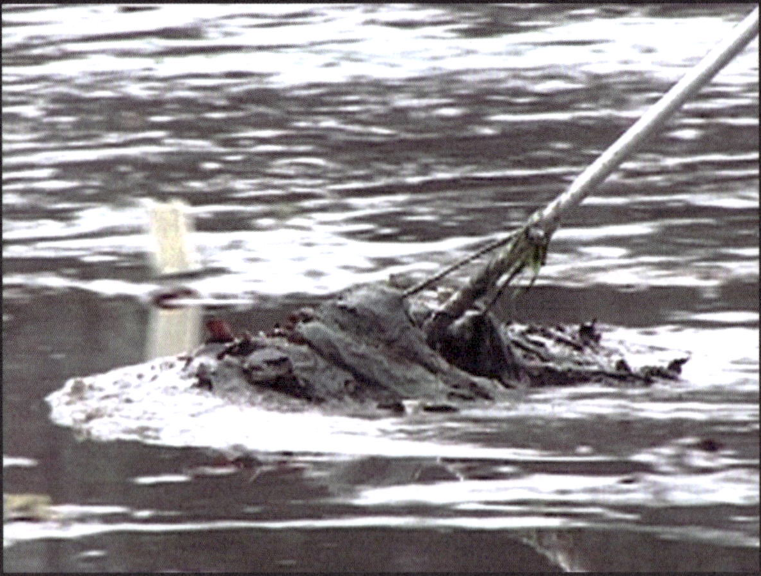

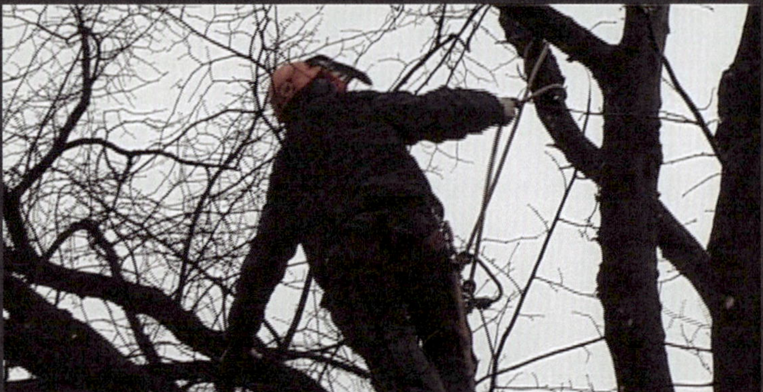

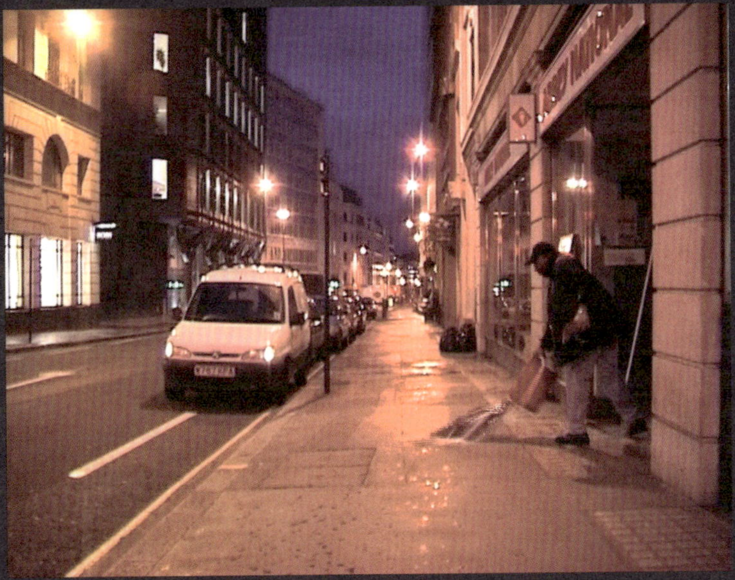

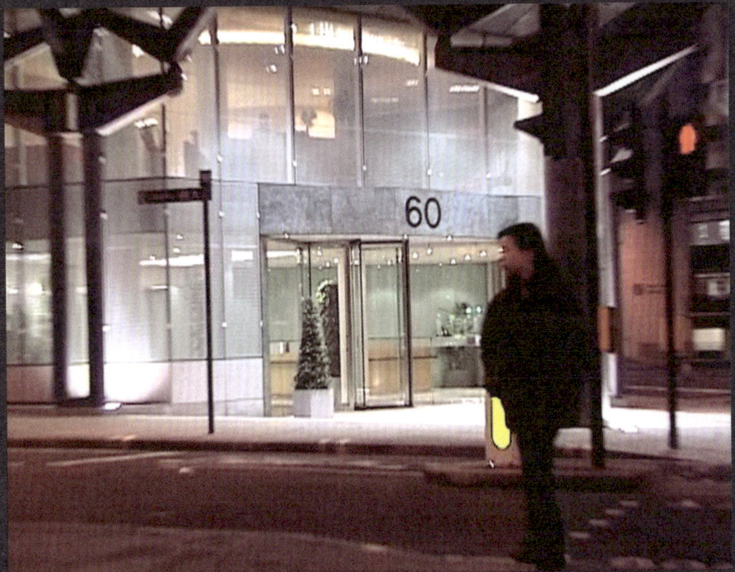
60

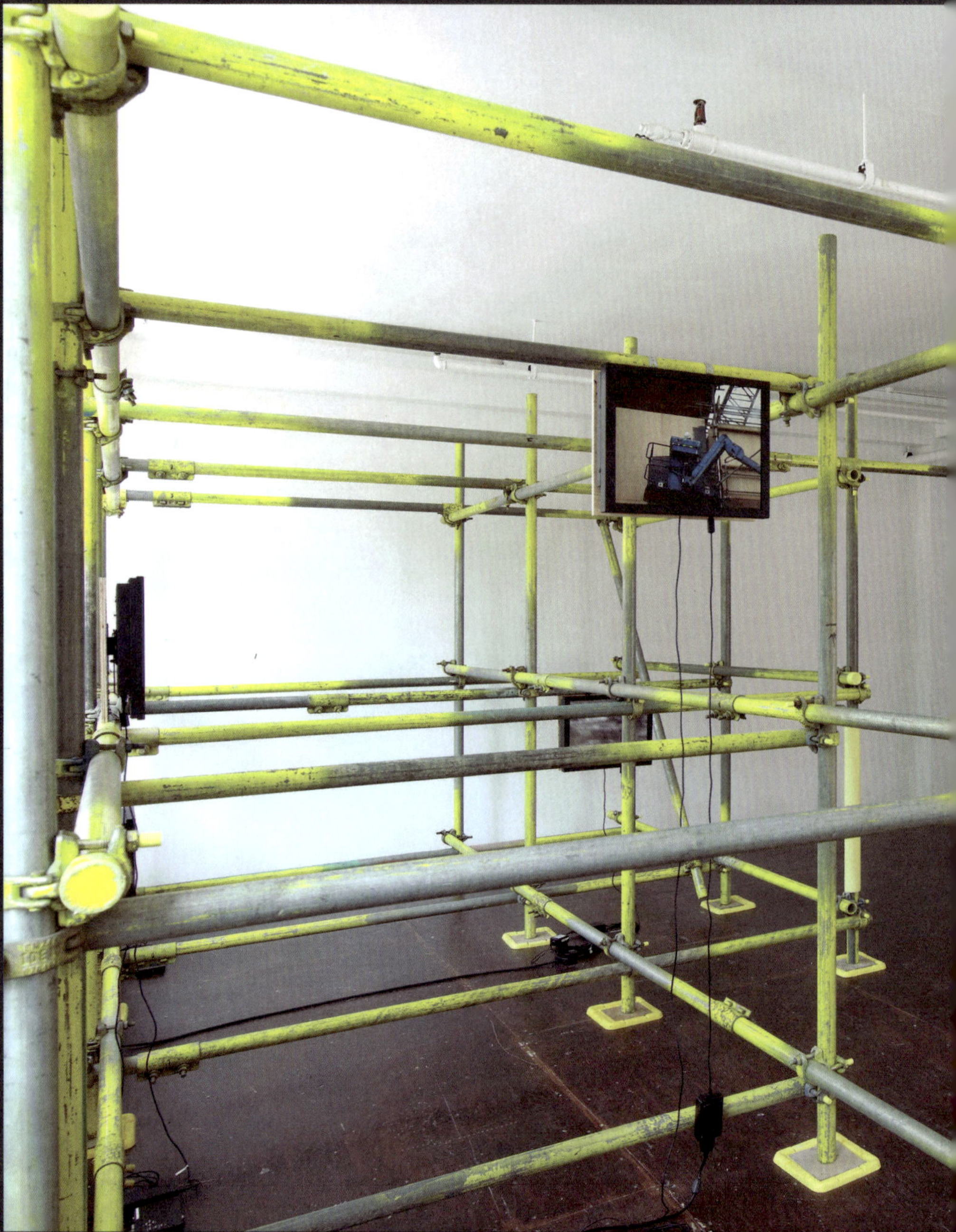

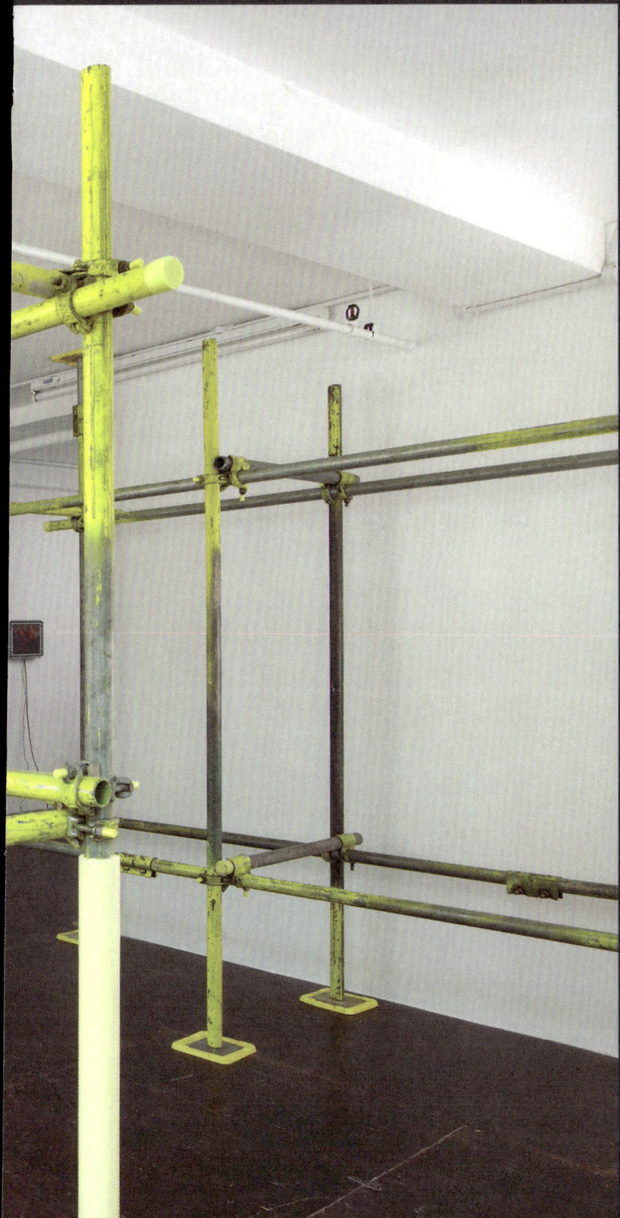

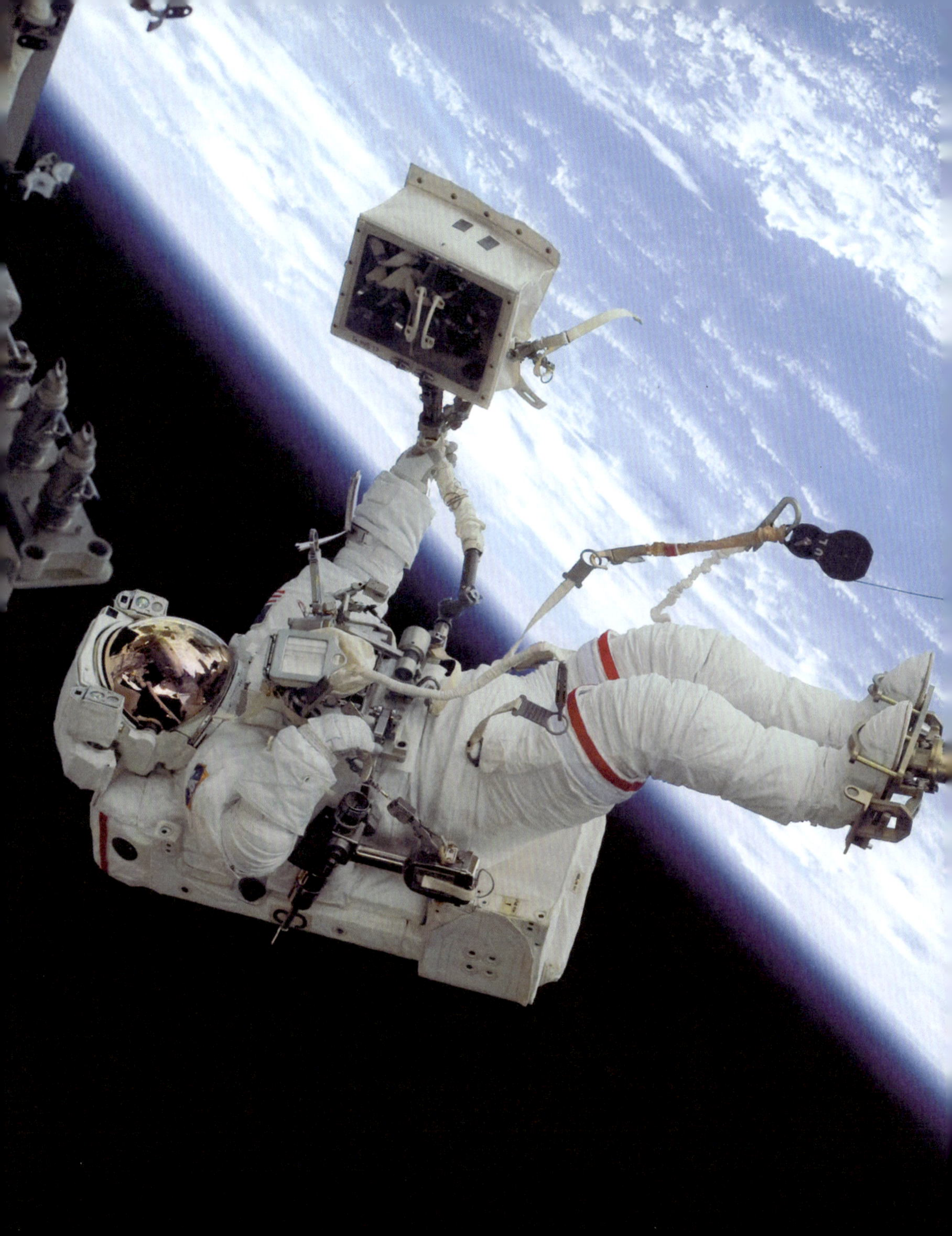

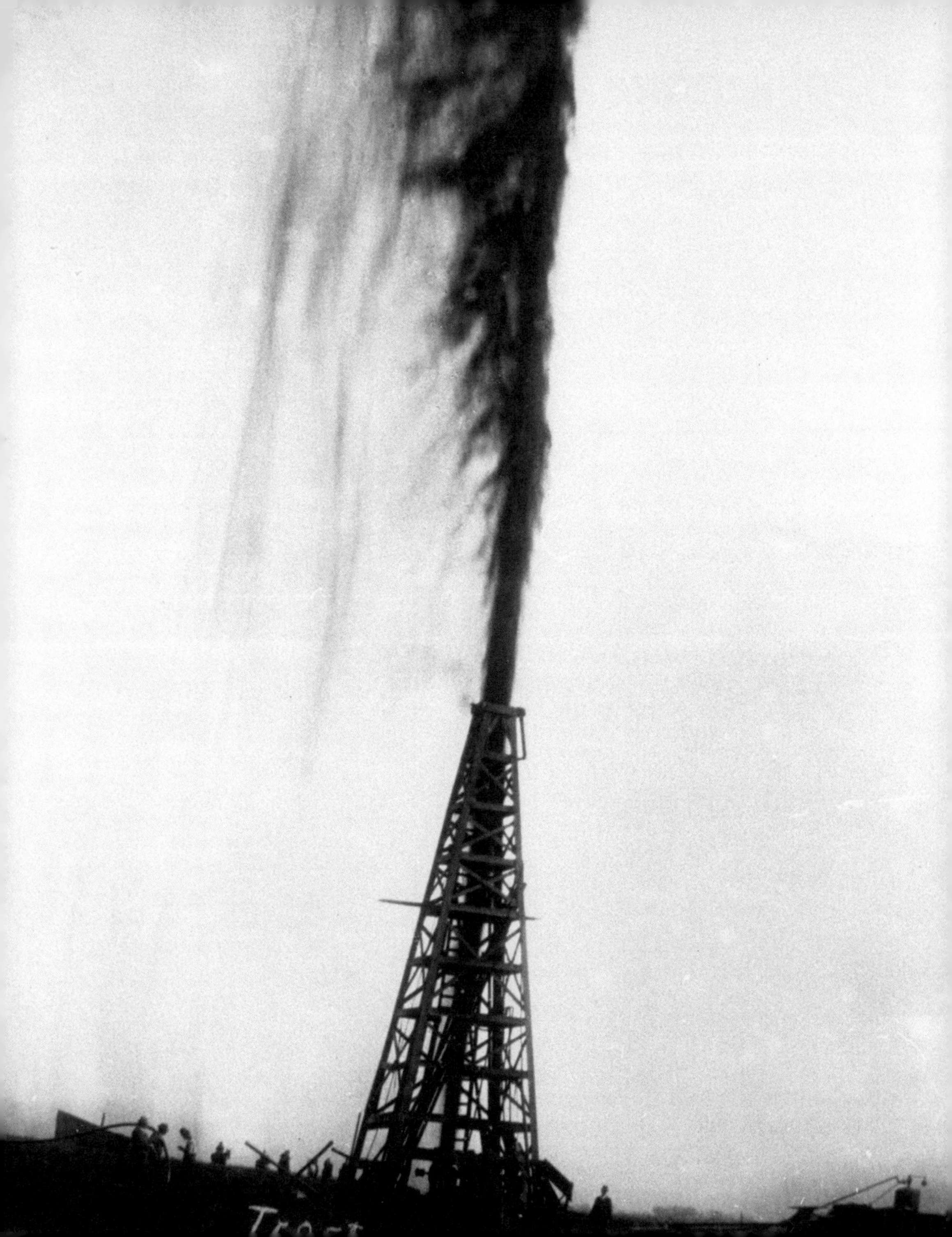

BIBLIOGRAPHY

Birnbaum, Dara, and Hans Ulrich Obrist, "Conversation: Hans Ulrich Obrist and Dara Birnbaum." In *Dara Birnbaum: The Dark Matter of Media Light*, edited by Karen Kelly, Barbara Schröder, and Giel Vandecaveye. Ghent; Stedelijk Museum voor Actuele Kunst; Porto: Museu de Arte Contemporânea de Serralves; Munich: Prestel DelMonico Books, 2011: 15–24.

Bradford, Mark, and Anita Hill. "Conversation: Mark Bradford and Anita Hill." Hammer Museum, Los Angeles, August 2, 2015. Transcribed by Eric Zeidler and Kelly Filreis. hammer.ucla.edu/programs-events/2015/08/mark-bradford-anita-hill/.

Collins, Phil, and Suzanne Weaver. "Don't Blow Your Own Horn." In *Phil Collins: the world won't listen*, edited by Suzanne Weaver. Dallas: Dallas Museum of Art, 2008: 85–98.

Conner, Bruce. "Bruce Conner." *Film Comment,* vol. 5, no. 4 (Winter 1969): 16–25.

Eastham, Ben. "One Take: John Gerrard's *Western Flag (Spindletop, Texas)*," *Frieze,* no. 188 (June/July/August 2017): 180–182.

Fast, Omer. "Artist Talk: Omer Fast." Dallas Museum of Art. July 19, 2012. Transcribed by Kelly Filreis.

Fisher, Jean. "The Place of the Spectator in the Work of James Coleman," In *James Coleman*, edited by George Baker. Cambridge, MA; London: MIT Press, 2003: 19–35.

Fisher, Morgan. "Documentary Footage." In *Morgan Fisher: Writings*, edited by Sabine Folie and Susanne Titz. Cologne; London: Walther König, 2012: 18–20.

Fusco, Coco, Guillermo Gómez-Peña, and Anna Johnson. "Guillermo Gómez Peña and Coco Fusco." *BOMB*, no. 42 (Winter 1993): 36–39.

Groos, Ulrike. "Rosemarie Trockel," *Drehmomente,* St. Gallen: Sammlung Hauser und Wirth Lokremise (2000): n.p.

Gund, Catherine. ACT UP Oral History Project. Interview by Sarah Schulman, April 20, 2007. http://www.actuporalhistory.org/interviews/images/gund.pdf.

Jafa, Arthur, and Antwaun Sargent. "Arthur Jafa and the Future of Black Cinema." *Interview* magazine (January 2017). http://www.interviewmagazine.com/art/arthur-jafa.

Léith, Caoimhín Mac Giolla. "Drift." London: Hollybush Gardens, 2005: n.p.

Leonard, Zoe. ACT UP Oral History Project. Interview by Sarah Schulman, January 13, 2010. http://www.actuporalhistory.org/interviews/images/leonard.pdf.

McQueen, Steve, and Adrian Searle. "A Conversation with Steve McQueen." In *Steve McQueen: Works, 1993–2012.* Heidelberg; Münchenstein: Kehrer Verlag; Laurenz Foundation, Schaulager Basel, 2013: 28–34.

Mellencamp, Patricia. "Ant Farm Redux: Pyrotechnics and Emergence." *Journal of Film and Video* 57, no. 1/2 (Spring/Summer 2005): 40–56.

Neshat, Shirin, and Gerald Matt. "In Conversation with Shirin Neshat." In *Shirin Neshat*. Vienna; London: Kunsthalle Wien; Serpentine Galleries, 2000: 10–29.

Parmar, Pratibha. "That Moment of Emergence." In *Queer Looks*, edited by Martha Gever, Pratibha Parmar, and John Greyson. New York; London: Routledge, 1993: 3–11.

Rivers, Ben. "Ben Rivers: Statement." In *Tacita Dean: Film*, edited by Nicholas Cullinan. London: Tate Publishing, 2011: 114.

Rose, Rachel, and Aily Nash. "Rachel Rose." *BOMB*, no. 133 (September 2015). http://bombmagazine.org/article/8919825/rachel-rose.

Sala, Anri, Massimiliano Gioni, and Michele Robecchi. "Anri Sala: Unfinished Histories." *Flash Art*, no. 219 (September 2001): 104–107.

Strand, Chick. "Woman as Ethnographic Filmmaker." *Journal of the University Film Association* 26, no. 1/2 (Spring 1974): 16.

Straub, Jean-Marie, Danièle Huillet, and Claude-Jean Philippe. "Cinema Must Set Fire to Life." Transcribed, translated, and edited by Sally Shafto, 2017.

Wylie, Charles, and Erin K. Murphy. "Requisite Distance." In *Willie Doherty: Requisite Distance: Ghost Story and Landscape*. Dallas: Dallas Museum of Art, 2009: 33–37.

STILL AND INSTALLATION PHOTOGRAPHY CREDITS

Front cover: Detail of a still photograph from *Untitled*, 2011–2015, by James Coleman; © James Coleman. Courtesy of Marian Goodman Gallery, New York

Pages 31–33: All stills from REPORT © The Conner Family Trust. Courtesy of the Conner Family Trust and Kohn Gallery, Los Angeles

Page 39: Both stills from *Documentary Footage* © Morgan Fisher. Courtesy of the artist and Bortolami, New York

Page 43, top: Ant Farm: Artist Dummies (Doug Michels and Curtis Schreier) on Phantom Dream Car with Secret Service agents (Homer Flynn and Hardy Fox) during the playing of the national anthem at *Media Burn*, July 4, 1975; performance, Cow Palace, San Francisco. © Ant Farm (Chip Lord, Doug Michels, Curtis Schreier with Tom Weinberg); photo © 1975 Chip Lord. Courtesy of Berkeley Art Museum and Pacific Film Archive

Page 43, bottom: Ant Farm: The Artist-President (Doug Hall) giving a speech at *Media Burn*, July 4, 1975; performance, Cow Palace, San Francisco. © Ant Farm (Chip Lord, Doug Michels, Curtis Schreier with Tom Weinberg); photo © 1975 Chip Lord. Courtesy of Berkeley Art Museum and Pacific Film Archive

Page 44, top: Ant Farm: *Media Burn*, July 4, 1975; performance, Cow Palace, San Francisco. © Ant Farm (Chip Lord, Doug Michels, Curtis Schreier with Tom Weinberg); photo © 1975 Chip Lord. Courtesy of Berkeley Art Museum and Pacific Film Archive

Page 44, bottom: Ant Farm: *Media Burn*, July 4, 1975; performance, Cow Palace, San Francisco. © Ant Farm (Chip Lord, Doug Michels, Curtis Schreier with Tom Weinberg); photo © 1975 Ant Farm. Courtesy of Berkeley Art Museum and Pacific Film Archive

Page 45, top: Ant Farm: *Media Burn*, July 4, 1975; performance, Cow Palace, San Francisco. © Ant Farm (Chip Lord, Doug Michels, Curtis Schreier with Tom Weinberg); photo © 1975 John F. Turner. Courtesy of Berkeley Art Museum and Pacific Film Archive

Page 45, bottom: Ant Farm: *Media Burn*, July 4, 1975; performance, Cow Palace, San Francisco. © Ant Farm (Chip Lord, Doug Michels, Curtis Schreier with Tom Weinberg); photo © 1975 Philip McKanna. Courtesy of Berkeley Art Museum and Pacific Film Archive

Pages 50–51: All stills from *Cosas de mi vida* courtesy of Canyon Cinema Foundation

Pages 56–57: All stills from *En rachâchant* courtesy of Miguel Abreu Gallery

Pages 61–63: All stills from *No me olvides* © Tatiana Gaviola

Pages 70–71: Both stills from *Memory Pictures* © Pratibha Parmar; photos by Sunil Gupta. Courtesy of the artist and Kali Films

Pages 75–79: All still and installation photography from *Tiananmen Square: Break-In Transmission* © Dara Birnbaum

Pages 86–87: All still photography from *Keep Your Laws off My Body* © Catherine Gund and Zoe Leonard. Courtesy of the artists, Aubin Pictures, and Hauser & Wirth, New York

Pages 88–89: Installation view from *Keep Your Laws off My Body* © Catherine Gund and Zoe Leonard. Courtesy of the Portland Art Museum Library and Archives, Portland, Oregon

Pages 94–95: All still and installation photography from *The Couple in the Cage: A Guatinaui Odyssey* © 2017 Coco Fusco/Artists Rights Society (ARS), New York

Pages 102–103: All stills from *Zum Beispiel Balthasar, 6 Jahre* © 2017 Artists Rights Society (ARS), New York/VG Bild-Kunst, Bonn

Pages 106–107: Both stills from *Intervista* © 2017 Artists Rights Society (ARS), New York/ VG Bild-Kunst, Bonn

Pages 115–117: All stills from *Soliloquy* © Shirin Neshat; photography by Larry Barns. Courtesy of the artist and Gladstone Gallery, New York and Brussels

Pages 120–121: Both stills from *This Is My Land* © Ben Rivers. Courtesy of the artist and Kate MacGarry, London

Pages 125–129: All still and installation photography from *the world won't listen* © Shady Lane Productions, Berlin

Pages 134–135: All stills from *Ghost Story* © Willie Doherty

Pages 140–141: All stills from *Gravesend* © Steve McQueen

Pages 145–147: All stills from *5,000 Feet Is the Best* © Omer Fast

Pages 157–158: All still and installation photography from *Untitled* © James Coleman. Courtesy of Marian Goodman Gallery, New York

Page 165: Still from *Spiderman* © Mark Bradford. Courtesy of the artist and Hauser & Wirth, New York

Pages 166–167: Installation view from *Spiderman* © Mark Bradford; photo by Kevin Todora. Courtesy of The Rachofsky Collection

Pages 172–173: Both stills from *Everything and More* © Rachel Rose. Courtesy of Pilar Corrias Gallery

Pages 178–181: All still and installation photography from *Love Is the Message, The Message Is Death* courtesy of Arthur Jafa and Gavin Brown's enterprise, New York/Rome

Pages 186–187: All stills from *Western Flag (Spindletop, Texas)* © John Gerrard. Courtesy of the artist and Simon Preston Gallery, New York, and Thomas Dane Gallery, London

Pages 188–189: Installation view, *Western Flag (Spindletop, Texas)*, April 21–April, 27, 2017, Somerset House, London; photo by Will Price. Courtesy of the artist and Simon Preston Gallery, New York, and Thomas Dane Gallery, London

Pages 194–199: All still and installation photography from *Drift: diagram xiii* © Anne Tallentire. Courtesy of Anne Tallentire and Hollybush Gardens, London

ARCHIVAL PHOTOGRAPHY CAPTIONS AND CREDITS

Page 26: Commuters reading of John F. Kennedy's assassination, November 22, 1963. Photo by Carl Mydans/The LIFE Picture Collection/Getty Images

Page 27: Black Lives Matter demonstration encouraging a boycott of Black Friday consumerism, November 28, 2014. Photo by The All-Nite Images. Courtesy of Wikimedia Commons

Page 64: Woman walks past protest posters for disappeared forty-three students, Chiapas, Mexico, 2014. Photo by Adam Jones. Courtesy of Wikimedia Commons

Page 65: Protesters hold signs at a protest organized by AIDS activist group ACT UP (AIDS Coalition to Unleash Power) at the headquarters of the Food and Drug Administration (FDA) in Rockville, Maryland, October 11, 1988. The action, called SEIZE CONTROL OF THE FDA by the group, shut down the FDA for the day. Catherine McGann/Getty Images

Page 108: Marchers hold portraits of Communist leaders aloft at a military parade in Albania, 1974. © Hulton-Deutsch Collection/CORBIS/Corbis via Getty Images

Page 109: M8 Greyhounds at a demonstration at the Zócalo in Mexico City, 1968. Uploaded by user Cel·lí. Courtesy of Wikimedia Commons

Page 148: Burning Capri Cinema during the Iranian revolution in Tehran, November 5, 1978. Uploaded by user Chyah. Courtesy of Wikimedia Commons

Page 149: The NAMES Project AIDS Memorial Quilt on display at the National Mall in Washington, DC, October 13, 1996. Photo by Elvert Barnes. Courtesy of Flickr Commons

Page 200: Astronaut David A. Wolf, STS-112 mission specialist, with a portable tool box on a tether during the second of three extravehicular activities of the mission, 2002. Courtesy of the National Archives

Page 201: The Lucas Gusher, Spindletop, Texas, 1901. Courtesy of the Texas Energy Museum, Beaumont, Texas

ABOUT THE AUTHORS

Anna Katherine Brodbeck is the Nancy and Tim Hanley Assistant Curator of Contemporary Art at the Dallas Museum of Art.

Gavin Delahunty is the Hoffman Family Senior Curator of Contemporary Art at the Dallas Museum of Art.

Ben Eastham is a London-based cofounder and editor of *The White Review.*

Jean Fisher was a London-based art critic and writer.

Massimiliano Gioni is a curator and the artistic director at the New Museum, New York.

Guillermo Gómez-Peña is a San Francisco–based artist, performer, and the artistic director of La Pocha Nostra.

Ulrike Groos is an art historian and the Director of Kunstmuseum Stuttgart.

Anita Hill is an attorney and professor of social policy and law at Brandeis University.

Anna Johnson is a New York–based writer.

Caoimhín Mac Giolla Léith is an art critic and associate professor at University College Dublin.

Gerald Matt is a curator, writer, and the Director of Art Institute Vienna.

Patricia Mellencamp is a distinguished professor emerita at the University of Wisconsin—Milwaukee.

Aily Nash is an independent curator based in Brooklyn and Hudson, New York.

Hans Ulrich Obrist is a curator and the artistic director of the Serpentine Galleries, London.

Michele Robecchi is a London-based critic, curator, and editor for contemporary art at Phaidon Press.

Antwaun Sargent is a writer and art critic based in Brooklyn, New York.

Sarah Schulman is a historian, novelist, activist, and distinguished professor at the College of Staten Island.

Adrian Searle is a London-based art critic for the *Guardian*.

Sally Shafto is a scholar of French and Francophone film and research associate at Williams College.

Suzanne Weaver is the Brown Foundation Curator of Modern and Contemporary Art at the San Antonio Museum of Art. She was the Nancy and Tim Hanley Associate Curator of Contemporary Art at the Dallas Museum of Art from 1995 to 2008.

Charles Wylie is the Curator of Photography and New Media at the Santa Barbara Museum of Art. He was the Lupe Murchison Curator of Contemporary Art at the Dallas Museum of Art from 1996 to 2011.

Truth: 24 frames per second is organized by the Dallas Museum of Art. Generous support provided by Marguerite Steed Hoffman and Thomas W. Lentz; TWO x TWO for AIDS and Art Fund; Marian Goodman Gallery, New York; and Culture Ireland. Air transportation provided by American Airlines.

The Dallas Museum of Art is supported, in part, by the generosity of DMA Members and donors, the citizens of Dallas through the City of Dallas Office of Cultural Affairs, and the Texas Commission on the Arts.

The catalogue has been published in conjunction with the exhibition *Truth: 24 frames per second*, on view at the Dallas Museum of Art from October 22, 2017, to January 28, 2018.

Published by the Dallas Museum of Art
www.DMA.org

Distributed by Yale University Press,
New Haven and London
www.yalebooks.com/art

Produced by Miko McGinty, Inc.
www.mikomcginty.com

Edited by Catherine Comeau
Designed by Miko McGinty, Rebecca Sylvers, and Claire Bidwell
Typeset in GT Cinetype and Fakt
Printed and bound in Italy by Conti Tipocolor

Library of Congress
Cataloging-in-Publication Data
Names: Dallas Museum of Art, author, host institution. | Delahunty, Gavin, editor. | Filreis, Kelly, editor.
Title: Truth : 24 frames per second / edited by Gavin Delahunty with Kelly Filreis.
Description: Dallas : Dallas Museum of Art, 2017. | "The catalogue has been published in conjunction with the exhibition, Truth: 24 frames per second, on view at the Dallas Museum of Art from October 22, 2017, to January 28, 2018." | Includes bibliographical references.
Identifiers: LCCN 2017034656 | ISBN 9780300233056 (alk. paper)
Subjects: LCSH: Video art—Texas—Dallas—Exhibitions. | Experimental films—Texas—Dallas—Exhibitions. | Dallas Museum of Art—Exhibitions.
Classification: LCC N6494.V53 D35 2017 | DDC 777.09764/2812074—dc23 LC record available at https://lccn.loc.gov/2017034656

TWO x TWO for AIDS and Art Dallas 2017

Culture Ireland
Cultúr Éireann